Popular Politics and Society in Late Victorian Britain

The Origins of the Labour Party
The Challenge of Socialism
America and the British Left
Labour and Politics, 1900–1906
(with Frank Bealey)
The British Communist Party
Modern Britain, 1885–1955
American Labor
A Short History of the Labour Party
A History of British Trade Unionism
Social Geography of British Elections, 1885–1910
Britain and the Second World War
Winston Churchill

Popular Politics and Society in Late Victorian Britain

Essays by

Henry Pelling

Fellow of St John's College, Cambridge

Second Edition

First edition 1968
Second edition 1979

Published by
THE MACMILLAN PRESS LIMITED
London and Basingstoke
Associated companies in Delhi
Dublin Hong Kong Johannesburg Lagos
Melbourne New York Singapore Tokyo

Typeset and printed in Great Britain by
LOWE AND BRYDONE PRINTERS LIMITED
Thetford Norfolk

British Library Cataloguing in Publication Data

Pelling, Henry
   Popular politics and society in late Victorian Britain
   – 2nd ed.
   1. Great Britain – Social conditions – 19th century   2.   Great Britain – Social conditions – 20th
   century
   I.   Title
   309.1′41′081   HN385

   ISBN 0–333–26658–7
   ISBN 0–333–26659–6 Pbk

Contents

Introduction to the Second Edition

SINCE this work was first published over ten years ago, fresh evidence has become available about political attitudes and social conditions in the late Victorian era, though not such as to disturb the general conclusions of these essays. There has also been lively controversy about particular issues, notably the nature and standpoint of the labour aristocracy, and the timing of the decline of the Liberal Party.

So far as the raw material of reminiscence is concerned, apart from two perceptive works by Robert Roberts, *The Classic Slum* (Manchester, 1971) and *A Ragged Schooling* (Manchester, 1976), the main contribution has been in the form of oral history. Paul Thompson and Thea Vigne of Essex University have recorded the memories of many surviving Edwardians, and thereby rendered an important service to students of the period. Their tapes have been drawn upon, not only in Paul Thompson's own volume of social history, *The Edwardians* (1975) but also in Standish Meacham's *A Life Apart* (1977), which is specifically a study of working-class life in the period 1890 to 1914. Professor Meacham's account does not allow for regional variations within Britain, and does not discuss the tensions that arose from Irish and Jewish immigration; but it provides a vivid picture of many aspects of popular behaviour in the period. He quotes a comment by Gareth Stedman Jones that the tone was 'not one of political combativity but of an enclosed and defensive conservatism.'[1] But he also speaks of 'the sense of impending clash' in the last years before the war broke out in 1914.[2] However, there is also fresh work to suggest that the 'labour unrest' was settling down before 1914, and that the peak of enthusiasm for syndicalism, such as it was, had come and gone. G. A. Phillips, who has examined the 'Triple Alliance'

---

[1] Meacham, p. 200; G. Stedman Jones, 'Working-Class Culture and Working-Class Politics', *Journal of Social History*, vii (1974), 462.

[2] Meacham, p. 219.

(for which, see below, p. 159) has concluded that:

In no sense did the launching of the Triple Alliance in 1914 anticipate or entail an imminent 'General Strike' . . . The 'General Strike of 1914' is, it seems, a mirage of historians treading the infertile deserts of British labour history in search of a *révolution manquée*.[1]

An almost simultaneous study of the Alliance by Professor P. S. Bagwell came to the same conclusion: its framers, he finds,

were more concerned to maintain freedom of action for each union than they were to establish an instrument for the conquest of industrial power.[2]

S. D. Chapman's volume of essays on *The History of Working-Class Housing*[3] tends to confirm the view that municipal intervention in the clearance of slums was heartily unpopular. A. S. Wohl, who contributes an essay about London, quotes the Medical Officer of Health for St Marylebone arguing that for the poor

sanitary improvement is a very car of juggernaut, pretty to look at, but which crushes them. Not a house is rebuilt, not an area cleared, but their possibilities of existence are diminished, their livings made dearer and harder.[4]

Chapter 5 of the present work, dealing with Imperialism, receives striking support from a careful study by Professor Richard Price, *An Imperial War and the British Working Class* (1972). This book also incorporates the evidence to be drawn from the examination of working men's clubs at the time of the South African War. Professor Price's conclusion is that:

The lack of jingoism in the working-class institutions, the lack of a working-class jingoistic reaction to the Khaki Election, peace meetings and volunteering, should be explained not in terms of opposition to the war, but in terms of indifference.[5]

---

[1] G. A. Phillips, 'The Triple Industrial Alliance in 1914', *Economic History Review*, xxiv (1971), 66f.

[2] P. S. Bagwell, 'The Triple Industrial Alliance, 1913–22', in A. Briggs and J. Saville (eds), *Essays in Labour History, 1886–1923* (1971), p. 102.

[3] Newton Abbot, 1971.

[4] Op. cit., p. 20.

[5] Price, p. 238.

Indifference was also a feature of attitudes to religion, as I have argued in Chapter 2. Dr Hugh McLeod, who has published a valuable work on London entitled *Class and Religion in the late Victorian City* (1974), notes

. . . indifference to questions of abstract principle, a low valuation of education, and non-participation in organisations.[1]

More controversy has surrounded the problem of 'dating' the relative decline of the Liberal Party, which is discussed in Chapter 6 below. P. F. Clarke's careful study of *Lancashire and the New Liberalism* (Cambridge, 1971) has drawn attention to the vigour of Liberal thought in the years preceding the First World War. He concludes that

By 1910, the change to class politics was substantially complete. That from Liberalism to Labour had not really begun . . . It looked as though both Labour and Liberalism would be subsumed in progressivism.[2]

Since Dr Clarke's book was published, there has been increased interest in 'progressivism' and in the 'new liberalism' – which seems to be much the same thing. But as Michael Freeden points out in his recent monograph, *The New Liberalism* (Oxford, 1978), the difference between the Liberal and Labour Parties had little to do with political thought. He quotes the comment of Brougham Villiers that

The division is upon the independence of Labour, not upon any economic or political doctrine in any ordinary sense at all.[3]

Dr Clarke gives the impression of believing that the joint Liberal and Labour success in Lancashire in 1906 and in 1910 was due to a policy of social reform. In an article on 'Electoral Sociology of Modern Britain' he goes so far as to maintain that Lancashire was 'the clearest test case for a transition from religion to welfare as

[1] McLeod, p. 43.
[2] P. F. Clarke, p. 406. For effective but belated criticism see J. White, 'A Panegyric on Victorian Progressivism', *Journal of British Studies*, xvi (1977), 143ff.
[3] Villiers, *Modern Democracy* (1912), pp. 147f., quoted Freeden, p. 149.

the core of electoral politics'.[1] But the victory of Liberalism in Lancashire in 1906, and its refusal to return to its older Tory allegiance in 1910, seem to have been due to the Tariff Reform issue more than anything else. The Liberal Party's social reforms were not popular in the country, but they were not directly at issue at the time of the General Elections.[2] Martin Petter, in a brief but succinct study of 'The Progressive Alliance', points out that, so far from 'ideas' being the issue between the two parties,

What even the closest friends of Labour in the Liberal Party often failed to recognise was that the demand for greater representation was itself the greatest single issue for the Labour Party during any election.[3]

It was, in short, in Burkian phraseology, a demand for 'men, not measures'.

In a volume of essays published in 1974 Roy Douglas argues, on the basis of the by-elections of 1911–14, that the Labour Party was 'in decline'. But by-elections are a misleading guide and Mr Douglas ignores the significance of trade-union growth and increased trade-union affiliation to the Labour Party. One may also set against Mr Douglas the findings of Chris Cook in his essay on the growth of Labour municipal activity in the same period.[4] For the first time we also now have a detailed account of Labour Party development as recorded in the party's official documents. R. McKibbin's *The Evolution of the Labour Party, 1910–1924* (Oxford, 1974) sides with those who believe that the First World War could not have been principally responsible for the transformation of British party politics. As he says:

Even if it is true that divisions lost the Liberal Party popular support, it is hard to see why the Labour Party, which was even more divided, should have been the beneficiary.[5]

---

[1] *History*, lvii (1972), p. 51.

[2] On the unpopularity of social reform, see Clarke,'The Electoral Position of the Liberal and Labour Parties, 1910–1914', *English Historical Review*, xc (1975), 833.

[3] *History*, lviii (1973), 58.

[4] R. Douglas, 'Labour in Decline, 1910–14', in K. D. Brown (ed.), *Essays in Anti-Labour History* (1974); C. Cook, 'Labour and the Downfall of the Liberal Party, 1906–14', in A. Sked and C. Cook (eds), *Crisis and Controversy* (1976).

[5] Op. cit., p. 237.

His conclusion is that:

The eclipse of the Liberal Party . . . was not due to 'the war', or to a wrong-headed pursuit of *laissez-faire*, or the split between Asquith and Lloyd George, or the conversion of the workers to Socialism, but to a slow change in the way political affiliations were decided. As political allegiance became more and more determined by class self-awareness, the Liberal Party found it could make no claims on the loyalties of any class. The widening of the suffrage hastened this change.[1]

Later, in an article written jointly with two colleagues, Dr McKibbin has elaborated his argument about the importance of the extension of the suffrage in 1918.[2] Dr Clarke has argued in rebuttal that 'before 1914 the Labour Party was the party of trade unionists; and these were the one section of the working class who were overwhelmingly likely to be already enfranchised'.[3] For some reason, no reference was made on either side of this controversy to the transfer of Irish voters to the Labour Party after the demise of the old Liberal-Nationalist alliance. The point is referred to below, on page 119.

The equally vigorous debate about the labour aristocracy in the nineteenth century has mostly been a conflict among Marxist historians: one feels almost embarrassed to butt in. Unfortunately, though, a number of reviewers of the first edition of the present volume obtained the impression that I was simply denying the presence of a labour aristocracy in Britain. For instance, Professor Hobsbawm wrote that my essay

attempts to maintain two theses which, though each is tenable, are not readily combined, namely, (a) that there was no labour aristocracy, and (b) that it was more radical than the rest of the working class.[4]

Other reviewers took the same standpoint,[5] and so I must make

[1] *Ibid.*, p. 244.
[2] H. C. G. Matthew, R. I. McKibbin and J. A. Kay, 'The Franchise Factor in the Rise of the Labour Party', *English Historical Review*, xci (1976), 723ff.
[3] *Bulletin* of the Society for the Study of Labour History, no. 18 (1969), 52.
[4] *English Historical Review*, xcii (1977), 582.
[5] E.g. Royden Harrison in *Victorian Studies*, xiii (1970), 364.

it clear that it was my intention merely to point out that there
are grave difficulties in delimiting the boundaries of the labour
aristocracy, and that, although it existed in some trades, there
were other trades, such as cotton or coal-mining, where it can
hardly be traced at all. R. Q. Gray has written an interesting
account of the labour aristocracy of Edinburgh, where of course
the printers formed an elite; and G. Crossick, in an article, has
done something similar for the shipyard workers and others of
'Kentish London'.[1] Neither of them, however, has found the
labour aristocrats to be simply accepting bourgeois values. Professor T. R. Tholfsen in another contribution to the debate maintains that:

Clashes between trade unions and employers were an important
factor in maintaining the radicalism and class consciousness of
the labour aristocracy and containing divisive forces that tended
to separate it from other working men.[2]

The most eccentric contribution to the debate has come from
John Foster, who in his *Class Struggle and the Industrial Revolution*
(1974) – a book of novel interest in other respects – adheres to
Lenin's view that the labour aristocracy was a product of the
'super-profits' of imperialism. For him the labour aristocracy is
not to be identified with the old skilled artisan, but only appeared
at mid-century, with the 'massive switch to capital export'.[3]
Furthermore, the skilled worker was now 'firmly identified with
management' and thus involved in the process of assisting the
speed-up of industry. Dr Foster implies that the miners' check-
weighmen, elected to prevent unfair assessment of their stint,
had 'very good reasons not to fall out with the employers'.[4] Yet
Arthur Horner, the Communist leader of the South Wales miners,
wrote in his memoirs that the job of checkweighman was given
by the miners to those of their colleagues who had already been

[1] R. Q. Gray, *The Labour Aristocracy in Victorian Edinburgh* (Oxford, 1976);
G. Crossick, 'The Labour Aristocracy and its Values: a Study of Mid-Victorian
Kentish London', *Victorian Studies*, xix (1976), 303.
[2] T. R. Tholfsen, *Working-Class Radicalism in Mid-Victorian England*
(1976), p. 277.
[3] J. Foster, *Class Struggle and the Industrial Revolution* (1974), p. 204.
[4] Ibid., p. 237.

victimised by the employers.[1] It is not surprising that even the reviewer in the *New Left Review*, Dr Stedman Jones, called Dr Foster's book 'difficult' and concluded:

Clearly there is, as yet, no definitive material theory of the labour aristocracy, and it is questionable whether there could ever be one.[2]

Perhaps the last word – for the time being – should go to H. F. Moorhouse, writing in *Social History:*

The theory of the labour aristocracy [is] unclear, confused and contradictory . . . Like much modern Marxism the theory . . . is too rational, too partial, too naively materialistic, and in a sense, far too optimistic.[3]

S. F. Macintyre has lately reminded us of some of the problems faced by British Labour and Marxist analysts after the First World War.[4] Naturally, leaders of the Labour Party itself were never attracted by the Leninist view of the corruption of the labour aristocracy: they believed that Socialist ideas would eventually appeal to the majority of the working class as a result of 'education'. The unwillingness of many workers to be so 'educated', and the exasperation of the 'educators', whether Marxist or non-Marxist, is summed up, as Dr Macintyre shows, by the Socialist cartoon character 'Henry Dubb'. To explain the persistence of 'Henry Dubb' in the era of mass education.it is perhaps better to employ the ideas of the recently-translated Italian Marxist Antonio Gramsci, who examined the concept of 'hegemony' as a cause of his country's conservative tendencies, rather than those of Lenin, who, even though he translated the Webbs' *History of Trade Unionism* into Russian, had little time for a careful study of the British political scene.[5]

[1] A. Horner, *Incorrigible Rebel* (1960), pp. 34–6.

[2] *New Left Review*, no. 90 (1975), pp. 37, 61.

[3] *Social History*, iii (1978), 82.

[4] S. F. Macintyre, 'British Labour, Marxism and Working Class Apathy in the 1920s', *Historical Journal*, xx (1977), 479ff.

[5] For Gramsci, see J. Femia, 'Hegemony and Consciousness in the Thought of A. Gramsci', *Political Studies*, xxiii (1975), pp. 29ff.; for a summary of Lenin's views of British labour, see E. J. Hobsbawm, 'Lenin and the Aristocracy of Labour', *Marxism Today*, xiv (1970), 207ff.

Preface

Most of these essays originated as special lectures prepared for particular audiences. But all have been revised within the last few months and reflect, I believe, a somewhat different approach to the problems of the period than will be found in earlier works, including my own.

I am grateful to the editor of *Le Mouvement Social* for permission to republish Chapter 1, which was first delivered, in a rather different form, to an Anglo-French conference on Social History in April 1966. I am grateful to the editors of the *Bulletin* of the Society for the Study of Labour History for permission to republish Chapter 7, which originally appeared as a book review, and which has now been slightly expanded. Mr G. Andrew Jones of Corpus Christi College kindly helped me with the proof-reading.

H. M. P.

St John's College,
Cambridge

ABBREVIATIONS IN NOTES

H.C.Deb.	*House of Commons Debates*
P.P.	*Parliamentary Papers*
V.R.	Visitation Returns

1 The Working Class and the Origins of the Welfare State

On 6 September 1903 the secret *entente* between the Chief Whip of the Liberal Party and the secretary of the recently-founded Labour Representation Committee was concluded at the Leicester Isolation Hospital, where Ramsay MacDonald had been admitted for a slight illness during the session of the Trades Union Congress at Leicester, which he was attending.[1] There could have been no more symbolical place for a meeting of the representatives of the two political parties which, between them, were so largely to secure the votes of the working men in the succeeding decade.

The people of Leicester, a predominantly working-class town engaged in boot and shoe and hosiery manufacture, like those of many other working-class districts such as the East End of London, Northampton, and Oldham, were strongly opposed to compulsory vaccination – a service which has been described as 'the first continuous public health activity undertaken by the state'.[2] The merits of compulsory vaccination were hotly debated, and working men resented the fact that the wealthy could easily avoid it by paying a fine, which to a poor man was a serious penalty. The Leicester Town Council did what it could to encourage avoidance of the law, and to salve its conscience ensured that the arrangements for isolating infected persons should be as good as possible – hence the special merits of the Leicester Isolation Hospital.[3] But by the time MacDonald was admitted as a patient the battle was over. In 1898 a Conservative government accepted that pure compulsion, even to accomplish what the best medical advice regarded as a great benefit both to the individual and to the

[1] F. Bealey and H. Pelling, *Labour and Politics, 1900–6* (1958), p. 157.

[2] R. J. Lambert, 'A Victorian National Health Service: State Vaccination, 1855–71', *Historical Journal*, v (1962), p. 1. Cf. R. M. MacLeod, 'Law, Medicine and Public Opinion: The Resistance to Public Health Legislation, 1870–1907', *Public Law* (1967).

[3] On Leicester Isolation Hospital, see Sir Charles Dalrymple's comment in *H.C.Deb.*, ser. 4, lvii, 770 (9 May 1898).

community, would have to be abandoned. Arthur Balfour there-fore sponsored a bill to allow conscientious objection, saying: 'It is possible that we are not a drivable nation. I do not say it is a merit, I do not say it is a demerit, but I say it is a psychological fact.'[1]

I propose to argue that the extension of the power of the state at the beginning of this century, which is generally regarded as having laid the foundations of the welfare state, was by no means welcomed by members of the working class, was indeed undertaken over the critical hostility of many of them, perhaps of most of them. And I shall maintain, in the first instance, that this hostility derived from working-class attitudes of suspicion or dislike towards existing institutions which were the expression of national social policy.

Let us take, first, the Poor Law. It is well known that the new Poor Law of 1834, which proposed to deny outdoor assistance to able-bodied persons in distress, was one of the main causes of the widespread popular support for the Chartist movement. What is less well known is that in practice a great deal of outdoor assis-tance was in fact given; until round about 1870 there occurred what is sometimes called the Poor Law Reaction, which resulted in substantial reductions in the proportion of outdoor relief.[2] All the more importance attached, naturally, to the character of the workhouses; and it is true that in the later nineteenth century the introduction of some degree of classification of the inmates of workhouses led to an improvement in their condition, although this was largely confined to the major cities.[3] But the clearest

[1] *H.C.Deb.*, ser. 4, lxiii, 596 (30 Jul 1898).

[2] W. Chance, *Better Administration of the Poor Law* (1895), pp. 5 ff.; Royal Commission on the Poor Law, *P.P.* 1909, xxxvii, 165 f.; M. E. Rose, 'The Allowance System under the New Poor Law', *Economic History Review*, n.s., xix (1966), p. 615. Cf. also C. Woodard, 'The Charity Organisation Society and the Rise of the Welfare State' (Ph.D. thesis, Cambridge, 1961).

[3] The Minority Report of the Poor Law Commission [published separately by S. and B. Webb as *The Break-up of the Poor Law* (1909)] is largely concerned with the extent and limitations of 'classification'. Cf. B. Abel Smith, *The Hospitals, 1800–1948* (1964), pp. 77–82.

possible evidence exists of the continuing widespread popular dislike, indeed fear, of the workhouse. The Royal Commission on the Poor Law (1905-9) invited the Diocesan Bishops of the Church of England to collect, through their parochial clergy, evidence of popular feeling about both indoor and outdoor relief. The conclusions about indoor relief were quite clear: 'in almost every respect there is said to be great reluctance on the part of the poor to enter the union'.[1] The two most important causes were thought to be the break-up of the home that was involved, and the loss of liberty. Even outdoor relief was widely objected to on the grounds of the loss of self-respect and the social stigma incurred by recipients.

The dislike of the Poor Law is well known and not very surprising. But it is something which we must bear in mind in considering the attitude of working men to an extension of the powers of the state. It might be thought that they would look more favourably upon attempts to improve the quality of their housing. In the later nineteenth century increasing attention was paid to the housing problem, and in 1875 permissive powers were given to borough councils to remove slums and to provide alternative accommodation for slum-dwellers. Although a good many slums were in fact pulled down as a result, alternative accommodation was very rarely provided, and the plight of the slum-dweller was almost invariably worse than before.[2] In Birmingham, Chamberlain replaced a crowded district of homes with a new central thoroughfare of municipal offices and shops – a form of municipal Stalinism, one might say, rather than municipal Socialism. 'The reconstruction and rehousing of the poor', he said, 'can be safely left to private enterprise.'[3] Elsewhere, and most notably in London, where new living accommodation was provided by the municipality, the rent was too high for many to pay. When very poor people were put in improved accommodation which was subsidised by a charity, as happened in the Peabody Buildings, they still found it difficult to accept its standards. For one thing, they received well-ventilated rooms, which were

[1] *P.P.* 1909, xlii, 323.

[2] On this subject see esp. W. V. Hole, 'Housing of the Working Class in Britain, 1850-1914' (Ph.D. thesis, London, 1965).

[3] Royal Commission on the Housing of the Working Classes, *P.P.* 1884-5, xxx, 533.

expensive to keep warm, instead of the poky quarters which they
had had before. The Peabody custodians soon had reason to
complain that 'all the ventilators were carefully stopped up'.[1] For
another thing they were at once faced by all sorts of rules and
regulations.[2] In Glasgow, where large clearances were made, the
Trustees of the Improvement Trust were so unpopular that 'they
were afraid to go into the clearance areas unless accompanied'.[3]

So far as state education is concerned, there is a good deal of
evidence of popular indifference or dislike when it was introduced
in 1870 and made fully compulsory in 1880. The financial burden
on the family, involving loss of earnings by the children and also
the payment of school fees, was commonly held to be 'unjust and
hard upon the parents'.[4] A Royal Commission reported in 1888
that 'The indifference of parents to education for its own sake
must, we fear, be reckoned as an obstacle which has perhaps been
aggravated by compulsion, and has presumably not yet reached
its worst.'[5] The position was somewhat improved when the payment
of fees was abolished in 1891; but much of the old indifference
remained.[6] Early in the new century a district nurse noticed that
'The desire of the Anglo-Saxon parent that his children shall
receive a literary education is indeed pale and shadowy when
contrasted with that of the poorest and least desired alien'.[7]

In the textile industries the abolition of the half-time system
was long resisted by the workers themselves, and as late as 1909 a
plebiscite of the members of the Cotton Operatives' Amalgamation resulted in 151,000 votes, out of a total of 185,000, being

[1] Ibid., p. 224.

[2] For popular reaction to the appearance and regulations of the
Peabody Buildings see T. Archer, *Terrible Sights of London* (1870), pp.
443–4.

[3] C. M. Allan, 'The Genesis of British Urban Redevelopment',
Economic History Review, xviii (1965), p. 610.

[4] See, e.g., W. Plomer (ed.), *Kilvert's Diary, 1870–1879* (1944), p.
279; G. R. Sims, *How the Poor Live* (1883), p. 19.

[5] Royal Commission on the Elementary Education Acts, Final Report,
P.P. 1888, xxxv, 131.

[6] F. Rogers, *Labour, Life and Literature* (1913), p. 52; *Journals of George
Sturt*, ed. E. D. Mackerness (Cambridge, 1967), i, 318 and 394 (7 Oct
1900 and 8 May 1902).

[7] M. Loane, *The Next Street But One* (1907), p. 32. By 'alien' she meant
Jewish immigrant.

cast against a proposal to raise the age-limit of full-time schooling to thirteen years.[1] This was apparently not a matter of families being dependent upon the children's earnings. A government committee reported: 'We have been supplied with returns which show conclusively that the great bulk of half-timers come from families that are earning good wages.'[2] Like the proposal for a compulsory eight-hour day for industrial workers, the extension of education never received that consistent support from the working class which would enable us to say that pressure from below was a factor in its enactment.

There was nothing 'bourgeois' about this popular distrust of state intervention. On the contrary, it can readily be associated with the view of the state taken by the Marxists, that it was an organisation run by and for the benefit of the wealthy. This emerges especially in the almost universal hostility of working men to the legal system of the country. One hesitates to speak of attitudes common to all working men, for the working class, if one can regard it as a unity in any sense at all, was composed of a complex variety of local and occupational sub-groups. But the enormous costs of the legal process and the almost unsurmountable barriers against the entry of people of humble origin into the legal profession, into the magistracy or even into jury service, helped to maintain a general consensus that the law was designed to benefit the rich at the expense of the poor.[3]

A consequence of this was the constant aversion of the trade-union leadership from contact with the law, and the widespread scepticism about the value of any system of compulsory arbitration in trade disputes. If there is a certain antithesis between this attitude and that of the Socialists, nevertheless the former was based upon as profound a distrust of the existing social system as animated any of the advocates of radical change. The difference is, perhaps, that the great bulk of trade-union leaders did not believe that radical change could come about by revolutionary means. Particular unions, for instance the Miners Federation and the Railway Servants, looked to Parliament for certain improvements in conditions in their own trades, especially safety regulations. They

[1] T.U.C. *Report, 1909*, pp. 190 f.
[2] Committee on Partial Exemption from School Attendance, *P.P.* 1909, xvii, 746.
[3] See Ch. 4 for an expansion of this view.

did not think, though, that Parliament could bring what a famous syndicalist pamphlet demanded in 1912 – 'real democracy in real life'.[1]

We may turn now to look at such evidence as can be mustered about the attitude of the working-class voter in the period between 1885, when the Third Reform Act was passed, and 1914. We know that in this period only about 60% of those male citizens who were old enough to vote did in fact have the qualification.[2] But this was a much higher proportion than before, and furthermore, much of the old corruption of British elections was swept away by the Corrupt Practices Act of 1883, so for the first time we can study the election returns with the hope of finding a genuine reflection of popular feeling.

If in this period we examine the issues that apparently moved the working-class voter, we do not find that social reform bulked very large among them.[3] Certain middle-class leaders emphasised social reform questions, but one cannot say that this had a notable impact on the electors. In 1885 Joseph Chamberlain took up Jesse Collings's call for 'three acres and a cow' for the agricultural labourer. Labouchere, seeing in the rural election results a significant swing to the Liberals, assumed that this was due to Collings's slogan, and wrote to Chamberlain to say, 'Next time we must have an urban cow'.[4] But the swing was simply due to the fact that the agricultural labourers were voting for the first time. During the election it was in fact the Conservatives who drew attention to the 'three acres and a cow' slogan, which they regarded as ridiculous. Joseph Arch, the agricultural labourers' leader, although himself a Liberal, thought of it as 'a vain

[1] Unofficial Reform Committee of the South Wales Miners Federation, *The Miners' Next Step* (Tonypandy, 1912), p. 30. The authors of this pamphlet thought that the shareholders in mining companies would demand nationalisation to suit their own interests.

[2] N. Blewett, 'The Franchise in the United Kingdom, 1885–1918', *Past and Present*, no. 32 (1965), p. 31.

[3] Much of the evidence on which this and the ensuing paragraphs is based will be found in my *Social Geography of British Elections, 1885–1910* (1967).

[4] J. L. Garvin, *Life of Joseph Chamberlain* (1932) ii, 124.

promise'.[1] The experience of later years was to show that 'in the majority of cases an agricultural labourer in regular work has neither the time nor the capital to cultivate a smallholding'.[2] Many local newspapers in rural areas pointed out that what made the labourers vote Liberal, in so far as there was one single issue rather than an accumulated resentment against the Conservative Establishment, was the fear of higher prices if tariffs were reintroduced, as was in fact proposed by many Conservatives in this election.[3] In the towns, on the other hand, this proposal may have accounted for a slight swing to Conservatism, although it is difficult to be sure, as the Irish electors, who were largely concentrated in the towns, swung heavily to the Conservative side on instructions from the Irish Nationalist leader Parnell. It is possible, however, that 'Fair Trade' had a positive attraction to many urban workers who were unemployed in the existing trade depression.

It is generally agreed that the 1886 election was fought primarily on the Irish question. The abstention of a large part of the rural vote is sometimes explained by the confusion of the agricultural labourers at a time when Chamberlain and Collings were advocating support of Unionist candidates. The labourers were probably confused about many things; whether they were interested at all in Chamberlain and Collings, who, after all, were urban politicians, is more doubtful. In fact, abstentions appear to have been very numerous in the county constituencies not only at this election but also at those of 1892 and 1895; and the obvious explanation made by newspaper commentators at the time was that these elections took place during the season of the

---

[1] Frances, Countess of Warwick (ed.), *Joseph Arch* (1898), p. 362. On the limited nature of the demand for allotments see J. P. T. Dunbabin, 'Labourers and Farmers in the Late Nineteenth Century: Some Changes', *Bulletin of the Society for the Study of Labour History*, no. 11 (1965), p. 8.

[2] Board of Agriculture, Report on Smallholdings, *P.P.* 1914, xi, 438.

[3] E.g., *Bury and Norwich Post*, 1 Dec 1885; *Lancaster Guardian*, 12 Dec 1885. Sir E. Lechmere, Conservative candidate for West Worcestershire, found that the Big Loaf and the Church Question were 'the questions uppermost in the minds of labourers just now'. Letter to E. A. Davis, 7 Nov 1885: Worcestershire Record Office, Worcester, B.A. 2309.8.

harvest, when labourers commonly could not afford to absent themselves from work in order to go to the poll. In many cases, too, the labourers appear to have come to the conclusion that voting Liberal was fraught with dangers of victimisation by a generally Unionist class of farmers and landlords. They had not unreasonable doubts about the secrecy of the ballot; and the farmers and landlords were much more uniformly on one side of the political fence in 1886 and thereafter than they had been in 1885.

Not even those who regard social reform as an important electoral issue would maintain that the 1892, 1895 or 1900 elections turned on this. In 1892 the Liberals secured a limited success which was largely a matter of making up some of the ground lost in 1886. The so-called 'Newcastle Programme' of the National Liberal Federation, which was not accepted as binding on him by the party's leader, W. E. Gladstone, contained few positive proposals of a social reform character, except for Employers' Liability for Accidents and proposals to create parish councils and to take new powers to acquire land for allotments. These hardly compared favourably with the achievements of the Salisbury government, which had just introduced Free Education, a Factory Act limiting the hours of labour for women and children, and a Small Holdings Act, the limited effect of which was not yet apparent.

In 1895 the Liberals suffered a serious reverse which must be attributed partly to the unpopularity of their proposals for Local Option (on liquor licences), partly to the depression in trade, though it is noteworthy that at the great railway centre of Crewe the Liberal defeat was directly attributable to the railwaymen's dislike of Asquith's Employers' Liability Bill. This measure sought to eliminate contracting-out and so threatened the London and North-Western Railway Company's scheme to which many of the Crewe electors belonged.[1] It is possible that the retirement of Gladstone also adversely affected the Liberal vote, for Gladstone in spite of his opposition to 'construction' – i.e., the extended use of state power for social purposes – was

[1] On this see W. C. Mallalieu, 'Joseph Chamberlain and Workmen's Compensation', *Journal of Economic History*, x (1950), pp. 49 ff.; P. S. Bagwell, *The Railwaymen* (1963), p. 120; and on the Crewe election, *Stockport Advertiser*, 5 Apr and 26 Jul 1895.

by far the most popular political leader among the working-class population. In 1900 the election was fought during the South African War, and the issue had an important bearing on the outcome. In spite of this the Liberals made certain gains, notably in the counties, where an important issue appears to have been concern about ritualistic tendencies in the Church of England. On the other hand, there were losses in East London where an agitation against Jewish immigration proved to be a useful vote-winner for the Conservatives. In general, too, the Irish vote in the towns appears to have been less consistently Liberal than in 1895.

Some authorities refer to the 1906 election as a victory for social reform, and point to the emergence of the Labour Party as a proof of this. I shall deal with the Labour Party later; so far as the main conflict between the two major parties was concerned, it is clear that the principal issues were: Tariff Reform; Chinese Labour; and the 1902 Education Act. It is true that Joseph Chamberlain argued that Tariff Reform would bring social benefits to the working man – in particular, more regular employment; nevertheless, Tariff Reform was on balance unpopular with the working class as a whole both at this election and so far as one can tell at every subsequent election before it was introduced (in 1932). The attitude of the electorate was also negative in the education question, although the interest of working men in the matter was less emphatic, because fewer of them were inclined to hold strong views on religious questions. Chinese Labour, which for the middle class was a matter of humanitarian sympathy with the indentured coolies in the Transvaal mines, was for the working man the apparent closure of an avenue of emigration, for which the South African War had largely been fought. The attitude of the Liberals to any increase in state expenditure was declared unequivocally by the new Prime Minister, Sir Henry Campbell-Bannerman, in March 1906: 'The policy upon which the Government has taken office and upon which they have been supported by their friends is the policy of retrenchment.'[1]

But it is, of course, true that this same government did in the end acquire, and deservedly acquire, a great reputation as a government of social reform. This hardly seemed possible in the period before Asquith replaced Campbell-Bannerman as Prime Minister.

[1] *H.C.Deb.*, ser. 4, cliii, 554 (7 Mar 1906).

Until 1908 only one noteworthy measure of social reform was enacted: the Education (Provision of Meals) Act, 1906, which allowed local authorities, if they saw fit, to provide meals for schoolchildren. The case for this reform had been made out by the official Physical Deterioration Report of 1904, which showed that a large proportion of the volunteers for military service during the South African War had had to be turned down on grounds of physical unfitness.[1] It is true that the Socialists had also been pressing for action on this matter for some years; their political pressure, however, was hardly sufficient to pass the Act by itself.

In 1907 Asquith, as Chancellor of the Exchequer, indicated that he intended to proceed with proposals for a non-contributory Old Age Pension, and he actually introduced his scheme shortly after he had become Prime Minister in 1908. The Liberal Party, as Asquith pointed out, was in no sense collectively pledged to Old Age Pensions as a result of the 1906 election. Nevertheless, the idea of pensions for the aged had been in discussion by the leaders of both parties since the early 1890s, when Joseph Chamberlain first proposed a contributory scheme. It is sometimes said that the pressure-group which finally secured the measure was the National Committee of Organised Labour on Old Age Pensions – although that body advocated pensions at 65, and the government's scheme only provided them for people over 70. The National Committee, however, was in no sense a spontaneous organisation of working men. Its real founder was Charles Booth, the social investigator, who with the Cadburys financed the work of the Committee and provided the driving power.[2] Frederick Rogers, the organising secretary, has described the difficulty that he had in persuading working men of the merits of the scheme. The Committee founded in 1899 made headway for a few years, but 'In March 1904, it seemed hardly possible for the Pensions movement to survive. . . . The trade union subscriptions grew more and more uncertain.'[3] It proved impossible to get the 'Lib-

[1] See B. B. Gilbert, 'Health and Politics: the British Physical Deterioration Report of 1904', *Bulletin of the History of Medicine*, xxxix (1965).

[2] F. H. Stead, *How Old Age Pensions Began to Be* (1909), p. 66; A. G. Gardiner, *Life of George Cadbury* (1923), p. 126. Cf. R. V. Sires, 'The Beginnings of British Legislation for Old Age Pensions', *Journal of Economic History*, xiv (1954).

[3] Rogers, *Labour, Life and Literature*, p. 257.

Lab' M.P.s to press the question in Parliament, or to demand the retention of existing taxation levels in order to introduce Old Age Pensions.[1] Of the 1906 election, Rogers wrote: 'We had no reason to believe that the Liberals would give us pensions for the aged, any more than the Tories had.'[2] Somehow, an astonishing conversion of the Liberal Party had taken place by 1908, and the principle of state pensions was accepted by M.P.s who had previously ignored the subject. As F. H. Stead, also an officer of the Old Age Pensions Committee, put it: 'It was a curious experience. . . . Our thunderbolts were being hurled by alien hands. The amusing thing in many of the speeches was the air of discovery with which were announced the platitudes of our agitation worn with continual use.'[3]

What had happened between the general election of 1906 and the spring of 1908 to change the minds of so many Liberals? There were two main developments. The first was that Asquith as Chancellor of the Exchequer had discovered that he could both reduce taxes and lay the foundations for an expensive social reform. In the 1907 Budget he cut the income tax by 3d. for earned incomes of less than £2,000, and also announced that he was proposing to put £2¼ million aside for a scheme of non-contributory Old Age Pensions. The main reason for this loosening of the Treasury's purse strings was the temporary lull in the naval building race, which was due to the destruction of Russian battleships in the Russo-Japanese War. Even if such unlikely combinations as France plus Germany, or Germany plus the United States, were contemplated as opponents for Britain in a naval war, it was still impossible to maintain that the two-power standard required much naval building by Britain in the immediate future. Thus in a sense it was Admiral Togo, the victor of Tsushima, who laid the groundwork of Old Age Pensions and deserves to be remembered as the architect of the British Welfare State.

The second important development was the reconstruction of the Cabinet on Campbell-Bannerman's retirement in the spring of 1908. This brought Lloyd George to the post of Chancellor of the Exchequer and Winston Churchill, a newcomer to the Cabinet, to the post of President of the Board of Trade. These two men, the

[1] Ibid., p. 261.   [2] Stead, *How Old Age Pensions Began to Be*, p. 160.
[3] Ibid., p. 260.

youngest in the new Cabinet, were keen to undertake social reform, whether or not the electorate clearly indicated its support for it, because they believed it desirable. It did not need the sensational upset of the Colne Valley by-election in July 1907 – when an independent Socialist won a Liberal seat – to persuade either of them that a far-reaching programme of social reform needed to be set on foot.[1]

Although the beginnings of this programme were evident by 1910, its development had been held up by the opposition of the House of Lords to the 1909 Budget, and so the two general elections of 1910 were not held directly on the question of social reform. In January 1910 the principal issue was the constitutional one of whether the Lords were entitled to reject the Budget. The landlords, it is true, were upset by the details of proposed new taxation, but these did not directly affect the wider public. The second election in December was fought on the more general question of the right of the Lords to delay any legislation from the Commons, including Home Rule for Ireland. In both elections, Tariff Reform was an issue – less so, however, in December than in January, for Balfour's pledge not to introduce it until after a referendum took a good deal of the significance out of its advocacy. The question of naval building had now become urgent once more: but it was distinctly more important in December than in January. At both elections, Liberal candidates sought to claim credit for Old Age Pensions, and the Unionists found it desirable to announce that they had no intention of rescinding the Liberal Government's legislation on this matter. But in 1911, when the Insurance Bill was under discussion, popular feeling appeared to be against it, and two referenda of electors at Walsall and Rutland – conducted, admittedly, by the Unionists – showed large hostile majorities.[2]

From this survey of the progress of social reform as an electoral issue, we may, I think, draw three conclusions.[3] The first is that

---

[1] This argument is developed in Ch. 8.   [2] *The Times*, 6 Dec 1911.

[3] I have not attempted to draw conclusions from the results of local elections. But if Newcastle under Lyme municipal politics were in any sense typical, working men were just as hostile to increased activity by local authorities as to increased activity by the state. See F. Bealey, 'Municipal Politics in Newcastle-under-Lyme, 1872–1914', *North Staffordshire Journal of Field Studies*, v (1965), esp. p. 69.

the progressive legislation of the period was in great measure sponsored by middle-class reformers, partly for humanitarian reasons, partly because they thought that social reform would be electorally popular. Secondly, there is no evidence that social reform was in fact popular with the electorate as a whole until *after* it had been carried out. The non-contributory Old Age Pensions scheme was already popular in 1910, when the villagers said 'God bless that Lord George' for making their old age more cheerful;[1] but National Insurance, as even Lloyd George admitted, was unpopular for some time after its enactment.[2] Thirdly, the working class, while rarely willing to express an emphatic demand for social reform, was always concerned about unemployment and higher prices and often expressed this in its political behaviour: indeed this concern led, not only to the defeat of any government which sought a new mandate during a period of trade depression, but also to the rejection of Tariff Reform as a panacea, except in the most distressed industries. Before proceeding further, however, it is necessary to turn aside to examine the new phenomenon of the period, the Labour Party, and its attitude to social reform.

The Labour Party before 1918 was not a Socialist party, but it was a party which contained Socialists. The Socialist societies had helped to bring the party into existence and they were permitted to affiliate to it on the same basis as working-class organisations such as trade unions and co-operative societies. Some historians of the recent past, especially those who were active Socialists themselves, such as the Webbs and G. D. H. Cole, tended to assume an identity between Socialist and working-class organisations. They imagined that Socialist societies, because they advocated state activity to aid the working class, were necessarily popular with that class; and they readily came to the conclusion that trade unions, because they bestowed a collective benefit upon their members, were in tune with the idea of national collectivism – or if not already so, were becoming more so all the time.

In fact, the early Socialist societies of the 1880s were largely founded by middle-class people who were worried about Britain's

[1] Flora Thompson, *Lark Rise to Candleford* (1948), p. 89.
[2] Lloyd George, quoted *Daily Citizen*, 14 Oct 1912.

position in the world at a time of increasing trade competition, or who had taken to heart the record of popular distress revealed by the social investigators of the period. They made a few converts in the working class, but on the whole they remained electorally insignificant. H. M. Hyndman, the founder of the Social-Democratic Federation, told Marx at the beginning of his agitation in 1881: 'At times ... I must confess it seems hopeless to attempt to found a Labour party here. The men are so indifferent, so given over to beer, tobacco, and general laissez-faire.'[1] Twenty years later he was still 'quite astounded at the ignorance and apathy of my countrymen'.[2] Meanwhile, a modified form of Socialism had spread in the 1890s to a section of the lower middle and upper working class in the northern counties, but not even the foundation of a new organisation with the title 'Independent Labour Party' in 1893 really gave the movement a mass base. After its electoral defeat in 1895, the I.L.P. declined and by 1900 was heavily dependent upon the subsidies of a few middle-class sympathisers such as George Cadbury, and upon the lecturing activities of a few men on the verge of the middle class, such as Ramsay MacDonald, Philip Snowden and Bruce Glasier (all of whom were married to middle-class women). Apart from Keir Hardie himself, a journalist who had been a miners' leader, the links with genuine working-class life were comparatively weak at the time of the foundation of the Labour Party in 1900. Frederick Rogers, the first chairman of the L.R.C., disliked the I.L.P. 'because of the large middle-class element in it',[3] and it was significant that Ramsay MacDonald, one of the party's leaders, became secretary of the L.R.C. without opposition, because he was the only candidate who could afford to take the honorary post.

Still, the trade unions were apparently willing to collaborate with Socialist organisations in the formation of the L.R.C. in 1900. How was this possible? The collaboration does not make sense until we realise that the trade unions – or some of them – came in for strictly limited purposes. (It is necessary to say *some* of them, because others did not join at all.) Those which joined, did so in order to defend themselves at Westminster against legislation or judge-made law which they regarded as hostile to

[1] Hyndman to Marx, 29 Oct 1881, quoted E. Bottigelli, 'La rupture Marx–Hyndman', Istituto G. Feltrinelli, *Annali*, iii (1960).

[2] *Justice*, 10 Aug 1901.   [3] Rogers, *Labour, Life and Literature*, p. 210.

the principles of unionism. Unlike the Socialists, their interests were in the *status quo*, rather than in social change; they were politicians from fear of adversity, rather than through hope of improvement. Adversity soon took the form of the Taff Vale decision, which had the effect of rapidly increasing the membership of the L.R.C. and strengthening the members' willingness to pay for their own M.P.s.

But the trade-union leaders who joined the Labour Representation Committee were not, for the most part, Socialists. They were Liberals – sharing Liberal party views on questions of the day such as Tariff Reform, Education and Temperance. For them, it was the most natural thing in the world to fight elections in alliance with candidates standing as Liberals – as they were in fact required to do by the electoral *entente* of 1903, which Mac-Donald had made on their behalf. They had no policy which was in advance of Liberalism; indeed, they tended to follow the Liberal lead rather than to force the pace in all matters except those directly affecting trade unions. It was in deference to their views that the Labour Party remained, in the years before the First World War, uncommitted, not merely to Socialism, but to any programme whatsoever.

In its complete freedom from commitment to ideas or programme, the Labour Party was truly representative of the working class of its day. Its Members of Parliament rarely admitted to having read any work of Socialist doctrine, whether by Marx or by any other author. Jealous as it was of the rights of the trade unions, it could only be induced to support National Insurance by the bribe of payment of M.P.s from the Exchequer – a great convenience at the time owing to the crippling effects of the Osborne Judgment on the party finances. As the government's Chief Industrial Commissioner, George Askwith, put it, the parliamentary Labour Party was 'a force to be reckoned with, but they were not constructive. Their chief influence consisted in the desire which the government had to bring in bills which they would not oppose, or to carry on administration without being subjected to too many unpleasant questions.'[1]

It should perhaps be added that the degree of liaison between the leaders of the Labour Party and the Socialist intellectuals of the Fabian Society was at this stage of their history extremely

[1] G. R. Askwith, *Industrial Problems and Disputes* (1920), p. 352.

limited. The Fabian role in the making of Balfour's Education Act had alienated Nonconformist sympathisers in the Labour ranks, and the Fabians for their part had little expectation that the Labour Party could ever replace the Liberals in the two-party system. With the accession of the Miners Federation to membership of the Labour Party in 1908–9, the prospect of winning the party for Socialism seemed more remote than ever. When Bernard Shaw heard of this increase in Labour Party membership he shook his head and said 'What then becomes of Socialism?'[1] Some attitudes were to change in later years, especially as far as the miners were concerned; but even after the adoption of the Socialist constitution of the Labour Party in 1918 there were strong forces of conservatism within the party. As R. H. Tawney pointed out in the early 1930s, the process of making Socialists through membership of the Labour Party resembled the proselytising activities of Feng Yu-hsiang, the 'Christian general', who baptised his troops with a hose.[2]

Once we accept that the pressure for social reform from the working class was politically negligible in the years before the First World War, we can look at the general politics of the period in a new light. We can see, for instance, that Randolph Churchill did not need to adopt a social programme in order to attract Conservative voting in the working class. It has been said that he 'fell short of greatness' because he 'failed to supply his party with a new and live programme'.[3] It might be maintained, on the contrary, that this was an indication of his real understanding of popular political attitudes. The working man who freely voted Conservative did so either because he was what is now called a 'deference' voter or because he was motivated to do

[1] *Fabian Quarterly*, Apr 1944, p. 2. Quoted in A. M. McBriar, *Fabian Socialism and English Politics, 1884–1918* (Cambridge, 1962), p. 340. Shaw's query was a reasonable one, for some of the miners who were in favour of joining had argued that it would be a good way of 'controlling' the Socialists in the Labour Party: Miners Federation of Great Britain, *Annual Conference Report, 1907*, p. 52. But see Ch. 6 below.

[2] R. H. Tawney, *The Attack* (1953), p. 59.

[3] C. Howard, 'Lord Randolph Churchill', *History*, xxv (1940), p. 27.

so by the prejudices or interests of his nationality, religion or employment. There was a great deal of Conservative voting in the working class in East London, for instance, and in Lancashire, where the employment and housing standards of the working class, such as they were, appeared to be threatened by the influx of immigrants. Similarly, there was Conservative voting among the ribbon workers of Coventry, who were suffering so much in the 1880s from Free Trade, and among the workers of Woolwich Arsenal, who looked to Tory policies of rearmament in order to secure work for themselves. From the reappearance in 1903 of Tariff Reform as a major political issue, the sectional interest of particular trades became even more obvious.

At the same time, we obtain a fresh view of the career of Joseph Chamberlain. Had his advocacy of social reform been generally popular in the working class, one would expect him to have secured wide support for his policies outside Birmingham as well as inside. But in fact in 1886 he was unable to wrest control of the working-class membership of the Liberal Party from Gladstone, and he only began to gain real influence in the Black Country as well as in Birmingham after 1903, when Tariff Reform made an appeal to workers in the depressed trades of that area. Yet the general prosperity of the country as a whole in 1906 and again in 1910 doomed him to failure at general elections. The working class was essentially conservative (with a small 'c'), and although the unemployed wanted employment, the employed feared the higher prices which the Liberals, with some justification, asserted would be the effect of tariffs.

In the long run – let it be repeated – the most popular leader among the working class was Gladstone, and he was more hostile than almost anyone else to the extension of the power of the state. Under him, the Liberal Party increasingly became a working man's party, as much of a working man's party as the Labour Party is today; after him, it returned to power only on the strictest Gladstonian programme – Free Trade, retreat from Balfour's Education Act, the *status quo ante* Taff Vale, the repudiation of the consequences of the South African War. In so far as the Labour Party won seats at the 1906 election, it did so by sharing this programme, which was almost an antithesis of the objects of Socialism.

Some historians, following the lead of Marx and Engels, have used the concept of the 'labour aristocracy' to explain the hostility of the British working-class organisations to social change in this period.[1] The difficulties of applying this concept are discussed in another chapter;[2] it is enough to say here that the evidence suggests that skilled workers were individually more radical in politics than the unskilled, if only because they were more literate and so more open to rational or quasi-rational argument. This is, on the whole, the impression obtained by Charles Booth in his survey of the people of East London.[3] The poorer sections of the working class were those most easily influenced by xenophobia, and the immigrants themselves, who were usually even poorer, often reacted by an exaggerated loyalty to their own nationality or religion. The most 'class-conscious' workers were perhaps those who were geographically most isolated, in particular the miners: and they adhered solidly to the Liberal Party until after the 1906 election. On questions of social reform, as was clear in the case of the abolition of the half-time system, the leaders of the unions and the politicians of the Labour Party, cautious though they were, were in fact more progressive than their rank and file. The members of the working class as a whole, cynical about the character of society as they knew it, were yet fearful of change which they thought would more likely be for the worse than for the better.[4] They advanced into the twentieth century with little expectation of social improvement being engineered by political means, and none at all of the 'Welfare State' as we know it today.

[1] E. J. Hobsbawm, *Labouring Men* (1964), ch. xv; Royden Harrison, *Before the Socialists* (1965), pp. 25–30.

[2] See Ch. 3, below.

[3] C. Booth, *Life and Labour of the People of London*, i (1892), p. 51.

[4] 'The labouring classes are always sceptical of good to accrue to them from any quarter.' Mackerness, *Journals of G. Sturt*, i, 222 (2 Dec 1892).

2 Popular Attitudes to Religion

It is disappointing how little we yet know about the relationship between organised religion and the working class in the Victorian and Edwardian era. The trouble has been that historians both of Church and of Chapel have been intent on telling the story of the foundation and early growth of their respective denominational institutions, and on explaining their subsequent development, from the point of view of the loyal, usually the ordained, believer. Doctrinal changes and disagreements are well treated, but little attention is paid to the composition of the lay membership and its occupational or class characteristics, the degree of its religious commitment, and its numerical relationship to the total population of the country. Even Professor K. S. Inglis's book, *The Churches and the Working Classes in Victorian England*, excellent in many ways though it is, does little more than outline the need for research in the fields just indicated.[1] And Dr Wearmouth's work on Methodism and the working class consists largely in cataloguing the names of trade-union leaders who had a Methodist upbringing, without making any systematic attempt to distinguish the reasons for the extent and limits of Methodist influence, or the local and occupational pattern of the various sects concerned.[2]

The religious historian ought really to bear in mind that the ordinary working-class population was too preoccupied with the needs of day-to-day living to spend much time on the niceties of religious doctrine. People's denominational sympathies, therefore, were likely to be determined by such practical matters as the location of churches and chapels in relation to their homes, the extent of religious charities, the availability of schools for the children, and the degree of influence exerted by landlords, farmers, and employers. The growth of new sects would owe much

[1] Published in 1963. Reviewed by me in *Past and Present*, no. 27 (1964).

[2] R. F. Wearmouth, *Methodism and the Struggle of the Working Classes, 1850–1900* (Leicester, 1952), and *Methodism and the Trade Unions* (1959).

to the personality of particular evangelists, but however good the seed, if it 'had no root, it withered away'.

This is not the place to attempt a rigorous analysis of denominational development. Some of the main lines on which the ecological pattern of the Methodist revival may be traced are, however, clear enough to be stated briefly. The Anglican parish system, on which the whole system of local government was still based in the eighteenth century, remained virtually unchanged in a period of rapid growth of industry in various parts of the country. Populous mining or textile manufacturing districts such as Cornwall, East Lancashire, West Yorkshire and Durham were 'good ground' for the Wesleyans, because the Anglican clergy, however devoted to their duties they might be in some cases, clearly could not cope with the need.[1] In agricultural districts the difficulties of proselytisation might be greater, particularly in 'close' parishes where a single landowner, commonly in close contact with the parson, could deny the use of land for building a chapel. Rural Methodism consequently developed most readily in the 'open' parishes, where no one landlord was supreme, and where the labourers lived a more independent life. Even in the late nineteenth century an Anglican incumbent could stress the disadvantages that his work suffered from the fact that his village (Rillington, near Malton in Yorkshire) was 'for the most part freehold': 'As a consequence ... there is a constantly changing population, outcasts coming from other parishes.... Three chapels, Congregational, Wesleyan and Primitive Methodist.'[2]

Working-class religious commitment in the nineteenth century seems to have been most complete in isolated single-occupation districts, where a new sect could secure a high degree of identity with the entire community, and some of the community's natural leaders could serve as its evangelists. This seems to have been the case with the Primitive Methodists among the miners of Durham and fishermen of East Yorkshire and perhaps with the Bible Christians among similar communities of the West Country.[3]

[1] Maldwyn Edwards in *History of the Methodist Church in Great Britain*, ed. R. Davies and G. Rupp, i (1965), 59.

[2] V.R. York, 1900: Borthwick Institute, York, R.Bp.e.

[3] On the fishermen of the Yorkshire coast, see, e.g., A. N. Cooper, *Across the Broad Acres* (1908), p. 224. Cooper was Vicar of Filey. On the Durham miners, see E. Welbourne, *Miners' Unions of Northumberland and Durham* (Cambridge, 1923), pp. 30, 57 f.

By mid-century, the Primitive Methodists or 'the ranters' as the clergy called them had also made substantial inroads in rural districts, where they satisfied the desire of many an active village craftsman or agricultural labourer to show his qualities of leadership and earnestness. The quarrel with the Church was not doctrinal but organisational: in the 'radical' sects, a man could play an active, perhaps even a key, role without having to be ordained or formally to qualify as a minister. It was quite in keeping that the Vicar of Sparsholt in Berkshire should have reported to the Bishop of Oxford in 1854 that 'Some of the Ranters have told me, they would willingly come to Church, if I would allow them to "speak" in the Church.'[1] One of the greatest weaknesses of the Church of England at this time was its failure to provide any means whereby men of humble origin could play an active part in its religious life or for that matter in its social work. The question of how large a say the laity should have in the control of church organisation was also a cause of disruption among the Methodists – although as a recent historian of Methodism has justly pointed out, 'The flexible polity of Methodism and its control of cadres of lay helpers were to prove the mainspring of its success during the Industrial Revolution.'[2]

But as the nineteenth century went on the 'activists' among the working class seem to have found other outlets for their energy. As communications improved, so did opportunities for social expression – trade unionism, politics, organised sport and entertainment. There were no noteworthy religious revivals in England after the 1860s – though as we shall see, there were in Wales – and even strictness of sectarian behaviour was rapidly in decline, surviving only in isolated pockets such as the Peculiar People of Prittlewell in Essex, who could boast in the 1880s 'that no member of the sect has ever received parochial relief of any description'.[3] The distinction which the farmhand Coggan drew in Thomas Hardy's *Far from the Madding Crowd* was gradually losing its force: 'There's this to be said for the Church, a man can belong to the Church and bide in his cheerful old inn, and never

[1] V.R. Oxford, 1854: Bodleian Library, Oxford Diocesan Papers, d. 701.

[2] John Walsh in Davies and Rupp, *History of the Methodist Church*, p. 312.

[3] *The Times*, 20 Jan 1888.

trouble or worry his mind about doctrines at all. But to be a meetinger, you must go to chapel in all winds and weathers, and make yerself as frantic as a skit.'[1] Something of the same contrast existed in the towns in the early nineteenth century: an artisan who wrote his autobiography in 1853 commented: 'Among the denizens of the workshop, to dissent is at least to have the character of being religious to a certain extent, while to belong to the Established Church is too often to have a character for no religion at all.'[2] But the growth of suburbs and the closing of chapels in the dingier districts of the cities as the middle-class Nonconformists moved away showed how little permanent strength there was in the religious commitment of the working class to any Protestant denomination.[3]

The lack of sectarian loyalty even on the part of those who did go to church or chapel is seldom commented on by religious historians. Halley, who chronicled the development of Lancashire Nonconformity, was an exception. Writing of East Lancashire, he declared:

That the Calvinistic Baptists and the Arminian Methodists have, notwithstanding their conflicting doctrines, produced good results in the hearts and lives of the multitudes of the working classes of Lancashire, as effectively as if they had preached one and the same doctrine, shows how small among uninstructed people is the effect of dogmatic theology . . .[4]

This absence of firm conviction about the merits of a particular version of the Christian faith was both very widespread and very worrying to clergy and ministers, at a time when 'strait is the gate

[1] Ch. xlii. The novel was first published in 1874 but relates to an earlier part of the century.

[2] 'A Journeyman Printer', *The Workingman's Way in the World* (1853), p. 318.

[3] Wesleyan Connexion, *Minutes of Conference, 1873*, p. 278. I owe this reference to the valuable chapter on religion in G. Kitson Clark, *Making of Victorian England* (1962).

[4] R. Halley, *Lancashire: Its Puritanism and Nonconformity* (Manchester, 1869), ii, 482.

and narrow is the way' was the motto of most of them. The evidence of it is to be found more often in private than in public utterances. It comes out, for instance, in Episcopal Visitation Returns, when incumbents volunteered, for the eyes of their bishop only, their frankest opinions of their parishioners.

Thus even at mid-century, when the Bishop of Oxford asked his parish clergy for information on the relative strength of Church and Dissent, he received numerous comments to the effect that among the poor, there was little real distinction.[1] At Bletchingdon the Rector reported that 'many of the poor here as elsewhere will attend both Church and Meeting'. At Idbury it was stated that several who attended Church also attended chapel 'during that part of the day in which there is no service in the P[arish] Church'; the same was true at Wroxton. At Letcombe Basset in Berkshire it was said of the poor that 'they are not decidedly dissenters nor church people'.

A considerable number of the incumbents sought in their returns to distinguish between the 'real' or 'professed' dissenters and the remainder. At Sonning it was pointed out that while there were few 'professed' dissenters, 'two of the chapels are ... well attended occasionally by those living near, in consequence of their distance from the Parish Church'. At Calverton in Buckinghamshire, 'the lower orders run about after any preaching of any kind that offers whether they go to Church or not', and at Drayton Parsloe, 'Too many are to be found ... who divide their religious worship between the Church & "Conventicle" & think no harm in doing so, notwithstanding the oft repeated remonstrances of their Pastor – the Rector.'

It is not to be supposed that these characteristics were confined to the diocese of Oxford, or that they became less marked in later years. Whenever a bishop invited his clergy to tell him the relative proportions of churchgoers and dissenters in their parishes, he received spontaneous comments of the same nature. The Vicar of Felmersham in Bedfordshire reported to the Bishop of Ely in 1897: 'There is this peculiarity about our Dissenters that they come to Church for their Baptisms, Marriages and Burials. They seem to draw the line of separation at Confirmation & Holy

---

[1] V.R. Oxford, 1854. The returns for the Archdeaconry of Oxfordshire only have been edited and published by E. P. Baker, *Oxfordshire Record Society*, xxxv (1954).

Communion. They come to the Church on great days.'[1] At Newton near Sudbury in Suffolk: 'There is no strict line of demarcation between Church and Chapel. In the same household some go one way, some another & some attend both. In bad weather the Chapel has the advantage because it is closer.' And at Little Stukeley in Huntingdonshire it was remarked that 'the habit of the people is to attend Church & Chapel alternately'. At St Nicholas at Wade in Kent in 1893: 'Of those who are "chapel goers" many are baptised by the Church of Eng. and bring their children to be baptised by the Church, and their dead to be buried by the Church of England. With the question, "Why am I, or why am I not a Churchman", the labouring man unfortunately concerns himself but little!'[2]

It might be supposed that in the diocese of York, where dissent was relatively stronger than in most of the southern counties, the loyalty to the chapel would be greater. In many parishes, however, we find a similar tolerance of attitude on the part of the poor. At Holtby in the North Riding, for instance, in 1900: 'Except a retired tradesman and his wife . . . no parishioner is above the rank of working farmer. With the exception noted all the families are more or less dissenters and "give the chapel a turn".'[3] This last expression was in general use: at West Heslerton in the East Riding the Rector felt that an impediment to his work was 'the rooted opinion that not to "give the chapel a turn" is a breach of Christian charity'.[4] At Amcotts in Lincolnshire in 1895 'nearly all the inhabitants attend both Church and Chapel';[5] the same was true elsewhere in the county, for instance, at Cumberworth. At Holton-le-Moor: 'Nearly all are labourers and farmers who do some labour on their farms. No chapel. A room is lent for an occasional prayer meeting. . . . They all attend Church occasionally – and they on special occasions nearly all would attend a "Camp Meeting" or special gathering of Dissenters elsewhere.'

It might be supposed that this eclecticism was simply for the sake of diversion in rural parishes, where entertainment of any

[1] V.R. Ely, 1897: Ely Diocesan Papers, Cambridge University Library, Mss. C3/36–9.

[2] V.R. Canterbury, 1893: Lambeth Palace Library, vi.ii.

[3] V.R. York, 1900.   [4] Ibid.

[5] This and the two succeeding citations are from V.R. Lincoln, 1895: Lincolnshire Archives Office, Lincoln.

kind was sorely lacking. No doubt there would be some truth in this; but it is also likely that the lay population were frequently more genuinely tolerant of their fellow-Christians than were the clergy and ministers. At Codford St Peter in Wiltshire in 1909 the Rector noticed a friendliness to himself among the dissenters and 'a tendency to the "many ways to heaven" formula'.[1] Probably he returned the friendliness without sharing the formula. At Pertwood in the same county a number of Primitive Methodists were: '*Personally* most friendly and regularly attend the Sunday service joining reverently in the service there being no chapel within easy reach. But they do not accept the Church's claims in teaching.' But then, who among the poor laity did 'accept the Church's claims'? At Damerham in Hampshire the Vicar complained that the existence of four chapels as well as the church for only 110 families 'tends to distract the mind and begets the habit of wandering from one to another – and a spirit of inquisitiveness and at the same time indifference to the character of the teaching given'. At Southbroom in Wiltshire it was reported that the dissenters were friendly, but 'with mixed feelings that there is no difference of teaching in the Church of England from that of Baptists, Congregationalists, etc. Any Church teaching as of the discipline of the Church is regarded by Dissenters & taught by some clergy to be Popery'.

So far, the question of non-attendance has not been considered, but the Visitation Returns even of rural districts show that there was a great deal of this. Rural attendance was always very patchy, and hardly better than in the towns, as has been shown in a recent study of Cheshire in the period 1750–1850.[2] In a mid-nineteenth-century study of Suffolk we are told: 'That the main portion of these non-attendants [*sc.* at religious services] belong to the artizan and labouring classes, the testimony of all observers will prove.'[3] It appears that the attendance was proportionately better

---

[1] This and the three succeeding quotations are from V.R. Salisbury, 1909: Diocesan Record Office, Salisbury.

[2] R. B. Walker, 'Religious Changes in Cheshire, 1750–1850', *Journal of Ecclesiastical History*, xvii (1966).

[3] J. Glyde, *Suffolk in the Nineteenth Century* (1856), p. 279.

in the smaller rural parishes than in the larger ones – which suggests that people were likely to be discouraged from worshipping if they lived some distance away from the church. The Visitation Returns of half a century later reveal, for other rural parts of the country, a similar tendency of the population to be discouraged by distance and other purely secular factors. The incumbents of the diocese of York were specifically asked in 1900: 'Is there anything which specially hampers your parochial work?' The Vicar of Aughton with East Cottingwith pointed out that 'The majority of the population is $3\frac{1}{2}$ miles away from the Parish Church and Vicarage, and have no resident gentlemen or clergymen.' At Kirkdale, also in Yorkshire, the incumbent complained of: '1. The isolated position of the Parish Church and its condition; 2. The size of the Parish, about 9 mile by 3, and the consequently scattered population. Some people are 4 miles away from either of the Churches. The income being at present less than £200 does not allow of a pony being kept and it is therefore impossible to keep up sufficient personal intercourse with many outlying houses.' At Blacktoft the Vicar pointed to 'Frequent changes of servants (boys & men) at the farmhouses. Also the indifference of employers as to how their servants spend Sunday.' This complaint about the regular changing of farmservants was made elsewhere. Another factor, recorded at Pocklington but often mentioned by clergymen as a serious discouragement to worship by the poor, was the system of appropriated pews. Yet another factor was the discomfort of the church, as at Hedon where it was 'frightfully cold and large'.

One cannot help feeling that all these factors are really excuses for a basically indifferent people. If a few miles' travel put them off, or if they would only attend at the behest of 'gentlemen' or employers, or if they broke off from churchgoing whenever they moved, could they be regarded as in any real sense loyal members of the Church? We may recall that Horace Mann, in his analysis of the findings of the religious census of 1851, found that the rural districts were really only a little better at church attendance than the towns ($28 \cdot 1\%$ at the best-attended services, as against $23 \cdot 9\%$).[1] The conclusion must be that the problems even of urban religious apathy could not be solved by church-building. The proof of the pudding was in the eating: the churches in the cities

[1] H. Mann, *Religious Worship in England and Wales* (1854), p. 90.

were built, and yet at the turn of the century the population still did not attend them. This was not a matter of the habit of non-attendance becoming established after immigration to the cities from the countryside: most of Birmingham's 1900 population, it has plausibly been argued, must have arrived at a time when adequate church accommodation and 'pastoral care' was already available in the city.[1]

It is sometimes maintained that the urban working class was positively anti-religious. Dr Hobsbawm has gone so far as to say that 'the British labour and socialist movements, like those on the continent, were dominated by the secularist-radical tradition'; but this seems to be an exaggeration, except perhaps in relation to London.[2] Putting aside the labour and socialist movements for the moment – for we are considering the working population as a whole, and not just the politically or industrially active elements of it – it is difficult to find evidence of a strong atheist or for that matter anti-Christian feeling even in London, although to be sure there was a good deal of anti-clericalism there early in the nineteenth century. In 1847 the purchasers of George Jacob Holyoake's *Reasoner*, whose total number did not run far into four figures, were 'more than a third . . . of the middle and educated classes'.[3] Horace Mann summed up the general situation at mid-century:

Probably, indeed, the prevalence of *infidelity* has been exaggerated, if the word be taken in its popular meaning, as implying some degree of intellectual effort and decision; but, no doubt, inert indifference prevails, the practical effects of which are much the same. . . . They are *unconscious secularists* – engrossed by the demands, the trials, and the pleasures of the passing hour, and ignorant or careless of a future.[4]

This view is confirmed by evidence given to the 'Select Committee on the Means of Divine Worship in Populous Districts', which reported in 1857–8. The Rev. T. F. Stooks, for instance, who was

[1] R. H. T. Thompson, 'The Church and the Proletariat', *Theology*, lxi (1958), p. 183.

[2] E. J. Hobsbawm, *Primitive Rebels* (1959), p. 128. Dr Hobsbawm's essay is nevertheless an interesting study in religious sociology.

[3] Holyoake, cited F. B. Smith, 'The Atheist Mission, 1840–1900', in *Ideas and Institutions of Victorian Britain*, ed. R. Robson (1967), p. 224.

[4] Mann, *Religious Worship*, p. 93.

secretary of the London Church Building Society, said: 'I think there is a good deal of floating doubtful scepticism, chiefly from the poor people not having been better taught. I do not think, generally speaking, there is anything like systematic infidelity.'[1] Similarly the Rector of St Philip's, Birmingham, the Hon. and Rev. G. Yorke, reported on his city: 'I am afraid that indifference is [increasing]; I do not think that there is any systematic teaching of infidelity.'[2]

It may be that 'systematic infidelity' got a certain slight boost with the foundation in 1866 of the National Secular Society – a body which included a mixed bag of atheists, deists and agnostics who were agreed only on the desirability of attacking organised religion. But the membership of the society even in 1880, when it must have been at its peak, was no more than six thousand.[3] Charles Booth, commenting on London in the 1890s, declared that secularist propaganda was 'not a very powerful influence'. What he called 'pronounced atheism' was rare.[4] It may well be, as George Haw maintained, that: 'The aggressive agnostic belongs more to the middle class than to the working class.'[5] – although recent research has suggested that the N.S.S. membership was predominantly working class.[6]

On the other hand, the general indifference to worship is fully attested by the investigations made by Booth in the 1890s and by the *Daily News* census of attendance in 1902–3. Booth's conclusion was that 'the bulk of the regular wage-earning class' was 'untouched' by religion, with one important qualification, namely, that 'their children attend Sunday School'.[7] The *Daily News* census – the most precise religious census ever undertaken in Britain – found that 'the poorer the district the less inclination is there to attend a place of worship'.[8] Perhaps just for the sake of

[1] *P.P.* 1857–8, ix, 97.   [2] Ibid., p. 370.

[3] J. E. McGee, *History of the British Secularist Movement* (Girard, Kansas, 1948), p. 73.

[4] Booth, *Life and Labour of the People in London*, ser. 3 (1902), vii, 424.

[5] G. Haw, *Christianity and the Working Classes* (1906), p. 1.

[6] S. Budd, 'The Loss of Faith in England, 1850–1950', *Past and Present*, no. 36 (1967), p. 122.

[7] Booth, *Life and Labour*, ser. 3, vii, 400.

[8] R. Mudie-Smith (ed.), *Religious Life of London* (1903), p. 26.

the spectacle, the most popular services in poor parishes were the most pagan ones – New Year's Eve and the Harvest Thanksgiving.[1] It might be that the Harvest Thanksgiving, at any rate, would be accompanied by a distribution of largesse. Charles Masterman, an observer by no means hostile to the Church, thought that the hope of material gain was an important factor in bringing the poor to Sunday services: 'The poor (except the Roman Catholic poor) do not attend service on Sunday, though there are a few churches and missions which gather some, and forlorn groups can be collected by a liberal granting of relief.'[2]

If such was the position in London, can a better report be made upon the provincial cities? Unfortunately the high quality of evidence which, thanks to Charles Booth and the *Daily News*, we have for London is not available for other cities. There was, it is true, a veritable rash of local censuses of religious attendance, particularly just after the 1881 general census, but the results, which were summed up in a special issue of the *Nonconformist and Independent* and also in a pamphlet by Andrew Mearns, are hardly sufficiently precise and detailed for us to draw any particular conclusions about the behaviour of the working-class population. It was reckoned that out of seventy-eight places – mostly urban – where attendance was measured the average proportion of separate worshippers to the total population was 25·4%.[3] This figure was slightly better than that worked out by Horace Mann as a national figure for the large towns in 1851; but it was only a partial result, and it included a number of small market towns and some rural districts which, on the whole, tended to take the average up. It was noteworthy that the largest industrial towns, such as Liverpool, Newcastle and Sheffield, were distinctly below average; so too were smaller but even more distinctly working-class towns such as Gateshead and Widnes. Obvious middle-class towns, on the other hand, such as Bath or Scarborough, were above the average for attendance. There were a few exceptions to these general rules. Bristol, which had a large number of churches and charities dating from its historic prosperity, had a high attendance (35·6%) in relation to its population. There is,

[1] Ibid., p. 30.   [2] Ibid., p. 201.

[3] *Nonconformist and Independent*, 2 Feb 1882; A. Mearns, *Statistics of Attendance at Public Worship* (1882).

however, independent evidence that churchmen in Bristol were as worried as those elsewhere about the shortage of working-class worshippers.[1] The survey was almost entirely confined to England; but a few Welsh towns were included – Conway, Llanelly and Wrexham – and each of these towns had remarkably high attendance figures, even when compared with that for Bristol. But the special characteristics of churchgoing in Wales must be treated separately. We may simply conclude that so far as England was concerned, the general picture was one of non-attendance by the working-class population in the main centres of industry. Booth's view that 'the bulk of the regular wage-earning class' was 'untouched' seems to find confirmation outside London.

It will be recalled, however, that Booth made one significant exception, to the effect that 'their children attend Sunday School'. The working-class population outside London also sent their children to Sunday School; and their willingness to do so, and their lack of concern about the character of the religious instruction given, is further evidence of their tolerance, at all events as between the varying sects of Protestantism. Le Play, the French sociologist who investigated behaviour in various provincial towns at mid-century, found that 'In general, parents are completely indifferent on the subject of the religious instruction given to their children: the chance which places the family close to a particular chapel or school is usually the circumstance which has most influence on the choice of doctrine which the family favours.'[2] A few years later an official enquiry, the Commission on Popular Education, reported that parents' choice of schools in general bore little relation to sectarian loyalty: 'Their selection of schools, in so far as it is affected by the character of the instruction, seems rather to be determined by the efficiency with which such things as tend to the advancement in life of their children are taught in it, and by its general tone and discipline.'[3] The only exception was that, if not themselves Catholics, they were reluctant to send the children to a Catholic school.

After another half century the same attitudes were prevalent.

[1] *Report of the Committee to Inquire into the Condition of the Bristol Poor* (1885), pp. 192 ff.

[2] M. F. Le Play, *Les Ouvriers Européens* (Paris, 1855), p. 193. My translation.

[3] *P.P.* 1861, xxi, 34.

Miss M. Loane, the district nurse who wrote several books about working-class attitudes, commented:

Few of those who fling themselves into the conflict as to what religious instruction should be given in primary schools, seem to be aware that enormous numbers of children . . . are in the habit of attending chapel Sunday Schools in the morning and Church Sunday Schools in the afternoon, and no doubts or difficulties seem to be roused in the scholars' minds.[1]

The advantages, both for the parents and for the children, in the latter attending at least one Sunday School regularly are briefly but clearly indicated by Stephen Reynolds, who lived in a Devon fishing community early in the twentieth century:

The children go to Sunday School, of course; it is convenient to have them out of the way while Sunday's dinner is being cooked and the afternoon snooze being taken. Besides, though the Sunday School teaching is a fearful hotch-potch of heaven, hell and self-interest, the tea-fights, concerts and picnics connected with it are well worth going to.[2]

But the household religion, he indicates, was a form of agnosticism. The Sunday School teaching, if absorbed at all, was forgotten when the children grew up. A Birmingham investigator reported: 'My own enquiries . . . fully confirmed . . . that almost every boy gave up Sunday School and Church when he left the Day School. In his pride of manhood he "puts away childish things".'[3] Can there be any clearer indication of the 'benevolent neutrality' of the English working man and his wife in their attitude to religion than is shown in their use of the Sunday Schools?

Let us now turn to the areas where a different pattern may be observed – in particular, the behaviour of the Catholics and their relationship to the rest of the working class; and the distinctive situation in Wales. We shall find that these examples of variant

[1] M. Loane, *The Queen's Poor* (1906), p. 32. For a similar view, see R. A. Bray, *Labour and the Churches* (1912), p. 35.

[2] S. Reynolds, *A Poor Man's House* (1911), p. 104.

[3] A. Freeman, *Boy Life and Labour* (1914), p. 126.

behaviour help us to form a consistent picture of working-class motivation whether in going to church or in failing to attend.

In this period, the working-class Catholics were nearly all Irish immigrants or their children or grandchildren. Coming to the English towns with virtually no industrial skills, they could naturally compete only for the humblest jobs; and in a period of constant heavy unemployment, they competed in rivalry with the poorest of the indigenous population. Like more recent immigrants, they encountered much xenophobia, and rioting between the English and the Irish was by no means uncommon. A major distinctive feature of the bulk of the Irish was their Catholicism: indeed they looked to their priests both to remind them of their community life in Ireland and to guide them in the day-to-day problems of making a living in England.

Under these circumstances it is clear that the Catholic Church provided a social service for its members which went far beyond what the Protestant sects could do for the indigenous population. It is true that in the districts where Irish settlement was heaviest – and in particular in Lancashire – the English population also tended to make fuller use of the Church for social purposes than they did elsewhere, presumably for the sake of emphasising their own national identity. Church schools, Sunday schools, and other voluntary organisations such as the Church Lads' Brigade were markedly stronger in Lancashire than in other English counties, and the Church assumed a militant Protestantism which was clearly due to the need to assert its distinctive character in the face of the Catholicism of the Irish.[1]

It must also be said that the Catholics had their own problems of apathy and non-attendance – 'leakage' as it was called.[2] It is difficult to estimate how large the Catholic population of Britain ought to have been, compared with the number of the faithful. Dr Vaughan, Bishop of Salford in the 1880s and later Archbishop of Westminster, said of a Catholic population of 75,000 in his part of

---

[1] An interesting recent study of the distinctive character of the Church in Lancashire will be found in P. F. Clarke, 'Elections and the Electorate in North-West England, 1900–1914' (Ph.D. thesis, Cambridge, 1967).

[2] There is a valuable treatment of this topic in Inglis, *The Churches and the Working Classes*, pp. 122 ff. See also J. A. Jackson, *The Irish in Britain* (1963), pp. 140 ff.

Lancashire that there were some 10,000 in spiritual need, of whom 5,400 were 'in extreme danger of loss of faith or practically lost to the faith'.[1] It was thought that the loss was principally of the children of the poor, especially just after they left school, an important factor being the 'Protestant or infidel atmosphere in which these children live'.[2] When Vaughan moved to Westminster he instituted a census of his new diocese, which was held in 1893–4. This reported a known Catholic population of only 130,817, although on a calculation based on the number of Catholic baptisms, it should have been almost 200,000. Further, of the known population, 24,262 did not attend Mass, and 27,863 did not attend their Easter duties. The total number of known apostates, however, was small – only 670. The problem was one of apathy. The survey concluded that less than half the total of baptised Catholics were 'leading practical Catholic lives'.[3]

Yet if the Catholics were less loyal to their Church than has sometimes been supposed, it should not be pretended that their loyalty was anything like as weak as that of the Protestants. In a community that was – in spite of a proportion of wealthy English Catholics – for the most part desperately poor, what is impressive is the way in which they built up the number of their churches and schools, and while these were still in very limited numbers, made excellent use of what accommodation they had – for instance, by holding numerous services in the same church on Sundays. In the years after 1900, when the more efficient Council Schools began to make great headway and the voluntary schools went into decline, it was only the Catholic schools among the latter which continued to expand.[4] The Catholic Church determined to educate its own children; and the laity supported it. In the last analysis, the failure of the Anglican and Nonconformist schools was due to the lack of loyalty of their members. As Booth put it, the Catholic poor 'constitute a class apart, being as a rule devout and willing to contribute something from their savings

[1] C. G., 'The Leakage of the Catholic Church in England', *The Month*, lix (1887), p. 181.

[2] Ibid., p. 182.

[3] Diocese of Westminster, Census 1893–4: Lancashire Record Office, Preston.

[4] For the statistics, see M. Cruickshank, *Church and State in English Education* (1963), p. 191.

towards the support of their schools and the maintenance of their religion'.[1]

It may seem odd to pass from the consideration of the Irish immigrants to that of the Welsh nation as a whole, for there were many contrasts in their condition and in their religious attitudes. Nevertheless, there was this similarity, that they were much more devout than the mass of the English, and also that they had national aspirations still to satisfy in the conditions of the late nineteenth century. The Welsh had been conquered by the English in the Middle Ages, yet to a surprising degree they had retained their national characteristics and in particular their language. But the Church of Wales had really become an alien Church, for in its many years of intercommunion with the Church of England it had become Anglicised: there was, for instance, no Welsh-speaking bishop in any of the four Welsh sees for a period of over 150 years. The result was that Protestant Nonconformity had a unique opportunity in Wales, particularly among the Welsh-speaking population; Welsh Nonconformity became a vehicle of Welsh nationalism; and the disestablishment of the Church of Wales became the political object of the great majority of Welshmen.

It has already been pointed out that in the religious census movement of 1881 the few Welsh towns included were remarkable for their high proportion of attendances at worship. There is plenty of evidence to show that people in all parts of Wales were much more inclined to attend either Church or Chapel on a Sunday than in England. The Churchgoers were, for the most part, an upper crust of English or Anglicised middle-class people: the Chapelgoers were the remainder. South Wales was the last region of Britain to experience a religious revival on a large scale – that launched by Evan Roberts in October 1904.[2] But even without the revival, Wales would have been quite distinctive. The Royal Commission which looked into the state of religion in Wales in the early twentieth century could report: 'We think from the evidence adduced before us that the people of Wales show a marked tendency to avail themselves of the provision made by the Churches of all denominations for their spiritual welfare . . .'[3] This

[1] Booth, *Life and Labour*, ser. 3, vii, 401.
[2] On this see C. R. Williams, 'The Welsh Religious Revival, 1904–5', *British Journal of Sociology*, iii (1952).
[3] *P.P.* 1910, xiv, 23.

was particularly significant as the accommodation available in churches and chapels was far greater in proportion to the population than it was in England. The Commission did distinguish between rural and industrial districts: 'The evidence as to agricultural districts, especially Welsh agricultural districts, was quite conclusive that very few habitually absent themselves from Divine Service. As to industrial districts the evidence varies . . .'[1]

The agricultural districts, it must be borne in mind, were much more purely Welsh than the industrial districts. In the mining valleys the rapid expansion of the pits had led to a considerable immigration from England: but as there were jobs for all, there was little conflict between the two communities. It may be surmised, however, that the English immigrants were, at least to begin with, less accustomed than the Welsh to regular worship on Sundays. All the same, the Welsh mining villages were, by and large, noteworthy for chapel attendance on Sundays. In the early twentieth century there was a decline in the number of 'hearers' or 'adherents' – that is, attendants who were not members, most of them working miners.[2] This change was thought to presage the class war in the valleys, and the abandonment of Liberalism for Socialism. And indeed, we may well believe that in the case of the Welsh, as with the Irish, religious attendance was an expression of national feeling – and when the wrongs of Wales ceased to be the primary instinct of the working-class population, and the grievances of the working class under Capitalism took their place, the chapel ceased to have the significance that it had so long maintained.

We may conclude, therefore, that in Victorian Britain religious feeling needed the additional spur of an association with thwarted nationalism in order to secure the loyalty of the working class. In spite of a certain residual anti-Catholicism which re-emerged when Irish immigrants were present (and to some extent also in the face of Anglo-Catholicism) the English worker had little cause to feel

[1] Ibid., p. 55.
[2] E. T. Davies, *Religion in the Industrial Revolution in South Wales* (Cardiff, 1965), pp. 151, 155.

that church or chapel attendance was of any particular value to himself for the purposes of social identification.[1] Partly for this reason, worship was a primarily midddle-class affair in England, and English Christianity was, as Edward Miall, the mid-Victorian dissenting leader, put it, 'essentially the Christianity developed by a middle-class soil. . . . It puts orthodoxy in place of reverence for truth, and substitutes pecuniary subscriptions for active personal exertions'.[2] And the reaction of the ordinary working man to the tenets of middle-class orthodoxy was very much as Stephen Reynolds described it: ' "Us can't 'spect to know much about it. . . . Tain't no business o' ours. Maybe as they says; maybe not. It don't matter, that I sees. 'Twill be all the same in a hunderd years' time when we'm a-grinning up at the daisy roots".'[3]

[1] This seems also to have been true of Scotland. See A. A. Maclaren, 'Presbyterianism and the Working Class in a mid-nineteenth century City', *Scottish Historical Review*, xlvi (1967), esp. p. 134.

[2] A. Miall, *Life of Edward Miall* (1884), p. 151.

[3] Reynolds, *Poor Man's House*, p. 103.

3 The Concept of the Labour Aristocracy

THE concept of the labour aristocracy is increasingly being used as a tool in the analysis of British politics and society in the period since the impact of the industrial revolution and up to the First World War. What follows is an attempt to subject the concept to close examination in the light of the evidence, and to define the limits of its value, both for the economic and social historian and for the student of politics.

Although the word 'aristocracy' was already in the 1830s occasionally being applied by analogy to the highest ranks of manual workers,[1] the term 'labour aristocracy' really derives its significance from its use by Marxist writers in their efforts to reconcile the observable phenomena of Victorian and Edwardian life with the Marxist theory of economic development. Marx expected that the further growth of capitalism would result in the increasing impoverishment of the working class, but was confounded by the emergence in Britain, particularly after about 1850, of a comparatively prosperous and, in his view, regrettably self-satisfied body of workers, devoid of Socialist aspirations and anxious only to develop trade unions and co-operative societies, as it appeared, along a line of narrow respectability in imitation of capitalist enterprises. Engels agreed with him, writing in a letter of 1858 that 'The British working class is actually becoming more and more bourgeois'.[2]

[1] W. B. Adams, *English Pleasure Carriages* (1837) has been cited, e.g., by E. P. Thompson, *Making of the English Working Class* (1963), p. 237. A usage closer to that of today is to be found in Select Committee on Combinations, *P.P.* 1837–8, viii, 134, where the Sheriff of Lanarkshire, Archibald Alison, refers to the trade unions as creating an 'aristocracy of skilled labour'.

[2] Engels to Marx, 7 Oct 1858, quoted K. Marx and F. Engels, *Selected Correspondence* (Moscow, 1956), p. 133.

There had to be an explanation of this change which would fit in with Marx's general expectation of the impoverishment of the workers under capitalism. The obvious interpretation – that a certain share of the new wealth created by the development of industry under capitalism went to the mass of the workers – had to be rejected. The solution lay in the elaboration of a theory about a working-class élite, who obtained most of the benefit and who set the tone of contentment and respectability in working-class organisations. The theory is expounded by Engels in an article in *Commonweal* in 1885.[1] Entitled 'England in 1845 and 1885', the article is an attempt to describe the changes that had taken place in the condition of the working class since he wrote his important study of *The Condition of the Working-Class in 1844*. In the article, Engels makes four points: first, that factory hands had benefited somewhat in the period, but only as a result of the intervention of Parliament to reduce hours and to improve conditions; secondly, that in other trades in which 'the labour of *grown-up men* predominates' – in particular, the engineering and building trades – there was a trade-union 'aristocracy' which was much more prosperous than the great body of the working class; thirdly, that the 'great mass' of the working class was as badly off as ever; and fourthly, that the workers' acquiescence in these conditions was due to a purely temporary state of affairs, namely, the prosperity that Britain acquired from her world industrial monopoly.

For the Marxist, committed both to a belief in the evils of capitalism and to the expectation that the final crisis of the system was about to take place, this theory had many comforting features. It explained the signs of comparative affluence in the working class, and also the presence of non-revolutionary sentiments among the workers, as both partial and temporary phenomena. It was important, of course, that the labour aristocracy should be shown to be a limited section of the working-class – say, not more than 10% – and that it should be regarded as being very sharply divided off from other strata.

Engels lived to see the emergence of the 'New Unionism' of the unskilled at the end of the 1880s, and also the beginnings of the Independent Labour movement in the industrial North. He

[1] Reprinted in K. Marx and F. Engels, *On Britain* (Moscow, 1953), pp. 23–31.

regarded these developments as a confirmation of his belief that the day of the labour aristocracy would soon be over, and associated the changes with the increasing competition which British industry suffered from foreign countries. Had he lived, his impatience would no doubt have mounted, for British industry on the whole succeeded in adjusting itself to the first challenges from the United States and Germany, and by and large the Edwardian era was a period of renewed domestic prosperity, in which the new political Labour movement appeared to have reached an accommodation with the Liberals.

But whether Engels would have modified his views quite as Lenin did is of course impossible to determine. Lenin associated the concept of labour aristocracy not so much with industrial monopoly as with imperialism – the possession and consequent exploitation of colonial territories. He implicitly abandoned Engels's view that the challenge to Britain's industrial monopoly would be enough to destroy the labour aristocracy; and he found no comfort in the existence of the Labour Party. So long as the British Empire existed, thought Lenin, there would be at any rate a proportion of the British working class which would 'enjoy crumbs from colonial advantages'. He regarded the I.L.P., and its parliamentary expression the Labour Party, as 'the party of Liberal–Labour politics', and thus an expression of the 'petty bourgeois craft spirit that prevails among the aristocracy of labour'.[1]

It is not surprising that the concept of the labour aristocracy has in recent years received closest attention from Marxist historians. The most careful and well-informed attempt to establish its validity for Britain is that made by Dr E. J. Hobsbawm, the versatile champion of Marxist historical interpretation in many fields.[2] Dr Hobsbawm speaks of the labour aristocrats as being in their 'classical period' in the period 1840–90. Yet he does not find it easy to define who they were: 'there is no single, simple criterion of membership of a labour aristocracy'. Various factors should be considered – prospects of social security, conditions of work, relations with other social strata, general conditions of living and the prospects of advancement for a man and his

[1] *Lenin on Britain* (1934), pp. 67, 99.

[2] 'The Labour Aristocracy' (1954), reprinted in E. J. Hobsbawm, *Labouring Men* (1964), pp. 272–315.

family. But 'incomparably the most important' factor is the 'level and regularity of a worker's earnings'. Dr Hobsbawm relies principally upon wage figures to identify the aristocrats, maintaining that this is in any case the only type of evidence which is reasonably comprehensive. On this basis, he finds that the labour aristocracy is not easily separable on the one side from the lower middle class; but that 'If the boundaries of the labour aristocracy were fluid on one side of its territory, they were precise on the other.' He adds that 'an artisan or craftsman was not under any circumstances to be confused with a labourer'. He admits that there were some workers who were neither labourers nor aristocrats in the strict sense, but implies that this does not seriously qualify his general statement.

It soon becomes evident that even with the help of the wage figures it is by no means easy for Dr Hobsbawm to distinguish the labour aristocrats, except by making a series of additional assumptions. Even for the 'classical period' of 1840–90, he is able to operate only on the basis of 'more or less plausible guesses'. From these, he arrives at the conclusion that the labour aristocrats were about 10% of the working class. They were more or less coincidental with the membership of trade unions in 1892, if we deduct the women and 'many miners' and the members of the new unskilled unions. After 1890 'genuinely useful statistics' begin to appear, but Dr Hobsbawm does not seem to be markedly more happy with them. Taking the wage census of 1906, he produces a table of industries with a high proportion of workers earning high wages, but he describes them as a 'super-aristocracy', presumably to indicate that this is only the top section of the labour aristocracy. The unions of these workers, he asserts categorically, with few exceptions 'had an unbrokenly conservative record'. Few 'aristocratic' trade unions joined the Labour Representation Committee in its first year of existence (1900–1), and those that did had special, perhaps temporary, reasons for feeling industrially insecure at that time. In the period up to 1914, he concludes, the labour aristocracy as a whole remained much the same in type and composition as in the third quarter of the nineteenth century, though 'its centre of gravity shifted further towards the metal industries'. The development of the white-collar occupations, and the increasing scale of industry, however, had widened the 'gap above the labour aristocracy, though that below it had not significantly narrowed'. During and after the First World War there was a 'collapse of the old labour aristocracy comparable to the collapse of the old skilled handicrafts', but Dr Hobsbawm does not develop his argument about this period very fully, and we need not pursue it, except to note that he regards the period before 1914 as a 'deceptive Indian summer' for the labour aristocracy, and indeed for British capitalism as a whole.

The difficulty about the Marxist labour aristocracy is that it means something slightly different in almost every context. As we have seen, Dr Hobsbawm's criterion is primarily one of wages, but he assumes that this will correspond closely to the membership of the old trade unions in 1892. Engels clearly thought of it in terms of the trade unions of the skilled trades – or, to be precise, of those trades in which 'the labour of *grown-up men* predominates'. By implication and context he excluded the factory population, and he mentioned specifically the engineers, the carpenters and joiners and the bricklayers. It seems clear that he was thinking primarily of those crafts in which, by means of the system of apprenticeship and the control of entry into this system, the artisans secured an effective bargaining position *vis-à-vis* their employers. This could only be done, of course, in trades which were not adversely affected by rapid technical change.

To postulate the absence of such change, however, is to remind ourselves of the precariousness of the position of the artisan in nineteenth-century Britain. Only the engineering craftsmen, whose manufactures were doing much of the damage to the position of craftsmen in other industries, were able to benefit in status and income from the early impact of the industrial revolution. Elsewhere, if the craftsman survived with his position unscathed or improved, it was either because his trade still lay beyond the fringes of the revolutionary changes which were occurring, or because his exceptional scarcity-value or his exceptionally well-established bargaining position enabled him to adapt the new technology to suit himself – or possibly even to keep it at bay altogether, at least for a time.

The conditions which favoured the craftsman were really much more those of the period just before the industrial revolution than those of the nineteenth century. For it was not merely new inventions and their application which endangered his position; it was also the different systems of manufacture encouraged by the rapid growth in the size of markets, which was in turn due to urbanisation and improved communications. The widening of the labour market, which was effected by the improvement in communications, particularly the spread of the railway network, also created great difficulties for the maintenance of trade-union control over apprenticeship, for small firms in the country still remained ununionised and could compete with manufacturers in larger centres the more effectively by using a large number of apprentices. When the apprentices completed their term, they were obliged to migrate to the larger towns, where they could hardly be denied admission to the union. It was partly because apprenticeship in many trades was already breaking down that Parliament in 1814 repealed the clauses of the Statute of Artificers which gave legal sanction to the apprenticeship system; but the repeal naturally weakened the system in those trades where it still remained effective.

It is generally recognised that one of the most striking features of the early years of the industrial revolution was the rapid destruction of the privileges of craftsmen in some industries, and the gradual erosion of their privileges in other industries. The story has been well documented by social historians, particularly by the Hammonds, and in more recent years and with fresh evidence, by Mr Edward Thompson.[1] The great bulk of the evidence of decline which is presented by these writers refers to the various branches of the textile industry, in which old domestic crafts, such as shearmen and croppers, hand-workers in calico printing and woolcombing and fustian-cutting, were gradually driven to the wall and replaced by factory operatives. Yet the total employment in the textile trades even as late as 1831 was less than that in the building trades, and there were large bodies of craftsmen in shoemaking, tailoring, cabinet-making, printing, and a vast number of lesser trades. There were distinctive village trades, such as the blacksmiths, wheelwrights and saddlers, probably largely self-employed. Joe Gargery in Dickens's *Great*

[1] J. L. and Barbara Hammond, *The Skilled Labourer, 1760–1832* (1919); Thompson, *Making of the English Working Class*.

Expectations is a good example of the type. The process which brought each of these occupations in turn into travail was a gradual one; and the one city in the United Kingdom which seemed to contain the most effectively organised crafts, with the strongest control over apprenticeship, was Dublin – also the one city which did not grow rapidly and which was least affected by all the changes resulting from industrialisation.[1] So too, one of the sharpest descriptions of the barriers separating the craftsman from the labourer is that given by Alexander Somerville, writing of his own early life in a rural part of the Scottish Eastern Lowlands in the period before 1832.[2]

London was in an intermediate situation between Dublin and, let us say, Manchester, the hub of the factory district. On the one hand, its industries were for the most part either connected with the port, where there were comparatively few craftsmen anyway, or they were engaged in manufacture for the luxury market of the West End, on which industrialisation had little impact. But on the other hand the city was growing rapidly, and both the supply of labour and the market for goods were uniquely large. Craftsmen like William Lovett, who picked up cabinet-making in the West Country and who then 'worked five years to the business' in London before becoming a member of the Cabinet-Makers Society, must have been by no means unusual.[3] The size of the market encouraged the sub-division of work usually done by the properly trained craftsmen, and this in turn meant that men of limited skill could be employed more readily, thus undercutting the regular journeymen. Henry Mayhew reckoned that in the London of the 1840s there was only about 10% of 'society men' in each trade, the remainder being non-society men working for cheaper wages and in most cases either specialising or simply producing inferior work.[4]

We know less about the situation elsewhere at this period, but evidence available for the later part of the nineteenth century

---

[1] For the strength of Dublin trade unionism, see Select Committee on Combinations, pp. 501, 514; National Association for the Promotion of Social Science, *Transactions*, 1860, *passim*.

[2] A. Somerville, *Autobiography of a Working Man* (1950), p. 86. The work was first published in 1848.

[3] R. H. Tawney (ed.), *Life and Struggles of William Lovett* (1920), i, 33.

[4] H. Mayhew, *London Labour and the London Poor* (1861), iii, 221.

suggests that what happened in London was gradually repeated in other large towns. The Royal Commission on Trade Unions in 1867–9 found that most of the societies of the building trades had no clear national rules governing apprenticeship, the local branches being left to do what they could about restricting entry into the trade.[1] Often they could do little. Dr Royden Harrison, who broadly shares Dr Hobsbawm's views about the labour aristocracy, quotes the reminiscences of a young builder's labourer who looked on the bricklayers 'almost as demi-gods'; he does not mention that in three years the same man was a journeyman stonemason. As for the 'demi-gods', he tells us elsewhere: 'The strangest thing to me at that time was that they were all, without exception, from the country, and I have found it so all through life.'[2] This movement 'from the country' was something that the unions were trying to control throughout the remainder of the century – usually with no success at all. The Royal Commission on Labour in 1891–4 received many complaints from trade union leaders about the continued immigration into the larger towns of journeymen from small towns or country districts where there was no control of apprenticeship.[3] The description by the French observer de Rousiers, written at just this time, is not inappropriate:

The trade union movement still clings in many instances to the defence of positions which can no longer be defended under modern conditions. . . . These workers of the old type are in the position of a nation which persists in defending itself behind the fortifications of Vauban . . . while the latest modern artillery renders their protection vain.[4]

The situation in London was so bad by this time that it was difficult to discover more than a very few trades in which it was worth while to undertake an apprenticeship. By that time it was 'scarcely known' in cabinet-making: 'the trade is picked up', declared one union leader.[5] In the precious-metal trades it was

[1] Royal Commission on Trade Unions, *P.P.* 1868–9, xxii, 45 (masons), 59 (bricklayers), 82 (painters).

[2] 'A Working Man', *Reminiscences of a Stonemason* (1908), p. 76.

[3] E.g. *P.P.* 1892, xxxvi, 578 (tailors) and 802 (cabinet-makers); *P.P.* 1893–4, xxxiv, 69 (lithographic printers).

[4] P. de Rousiers, *Labour Question in Britain* (1896), p. 250.

[5] *P.P.* 1892, xxxvi, 802.

said to be 'breaking down'; in bricklaying it was 'practically extinct, at any rate in London and most of the large towns'.[1] In 1912 a manual on *Trades for London Boys* produced a sadly attenuated list of occupations in which it would be to a boy's advantage to undertake an apprenticeship.[2] Composing and machine-minding in the printing industry; brushmaking; glass bottle making and silk hatting – these appeared to be the only trades where it was definitely recommended.[3] In the building trades, bricklayers could 'enter the trade after having served as labourers'; in carpentry or masonry lads might 'have a chance of picking up the trade'; there were no apprentices taken in painting; plastering was 'as a rule picked up by boys without regular apprenticeship', and the same was at least partly true of plumbing.[4] In the furrier's trade and in upholstery apprenticeship was only to be found in the West End. For goldsmiths and silversmiths it was 'said to be dying out' in the one case and 'not at all an invariable rule' in the other. Machinery had just been introduced into coopering, and although there was scope for 'intelligent boys', there was no talk of apprenticeship. It might very well be, of course, that substantial differentials would still exist in these trades between the wages of the adult artisans on the one hand and the labourers on the other, the latter often being young lads 'picking up' the trade. But there would be little 'aristocratic' about an occupation which could be entered in this way, and the wage level of the adult worker would owe more to custom or to the gradually rising national standard of living of the working class than to the peculiar scarcity value of the trained craftsman.

It is important to appreciate how it was that the processes of change gradually invaded separate crafts one after the other, reducing them all, or nearly all, to a situation in which the skill of

[1] F. W. Galton (ed.), *Workers on Their Industries* (1896), pp. 43, 182.

[2] Apprenticeship and Skilled Employment Association, *Trades for London Boys* (1912). Cf. also R. A. Bray, *Boy Labour and Apprenticeship* (1911), pp. 135 ff.

[3] For a delightful picture of the hatters, see F. Willis, *101 Jubilee Road* (1948), pp. 88 ff.

[4] For the impact of technical change in plumbing, see de Rousiers, *Labour Question*, pp. 68 ff.

the worker was something that could readily be 'picked up'. Naturally the process was most devastating in the early years of the industrial revolution, when the living standards of the ordinary worker without a craft were close to a subsistence level. In the cotton industry, as Engels pointed out in 1844, the skilled spinner disappeared with the introduction of the factory system. The same thing happened to the weaver, though at a somewhat later date. It is true that in the factories there was a class of highly-skilled spinners, who were comparatively well paid, and who were the employers of the less skilled piecers who performed the simpler tasks. This, together with the well-known fact that many Lancashire spinners were Conservative in politics, has led some historians to regard the spinners as labour aristocrats. But there was no apprenticeship in the industry, and no skill other than manual dexterity. Furthermore, the piecers do not correspond to a depressed class of labourers. D. J. Shackleton pointed out at the 1898 T.U.C. that the half-timers were the children of men earning 30s., 35s., and £2 a week;[1] and a government enquiry a few years later confirmed that they mostly came 'from families that are earning good wages'.[2] This, of course, was because the spinners themselves were recruited from the ranks of the piecers, the latter being nearly all below the age of twenty-one. According to James Mawdsley, the secretary of the spinners' union, the piecers were divided into two groups, the little piecers who were aged less than sixteen, and the big piecers, who were mostly aged between sixteen and twenty-one. Those who did not become spinners – and the selection was made on the basis of their ability as piecers – were obliged to seek other occupations, but did not necessarily become labourers.[3]

Wages were comparatively high in the cotton industry in the middle and late nineteenth century, and the fact that there was employment for all members of the family meant that family incomes could be substantial. It was this which enabled so many people of the working class to buy their own homes and even to invest in shares.[4] But it had not started like this; the first effects

[1] T.U.C. *Report, 1898*, p. 76.   [2] *P.P.* 1909, xvii, 746.

[3] *P.P.* 1892, xxxv, 746.

[4] House ownership in Oldham: A. Shadwell, *Industrial Efficiency* (1906), i, 92. Share ownership: S. Webb and H. Cox, *The Eight-Hour Day* (1891), p. 125; J. Haslam in *Clarion*, 26 Jan 1912.

of the factory system were indeed to depress the standards of the craftsmen. The long hours of work in the factory, even for the youngest children, interfered sadly with education and resulted in a marked decline in literacy.[1] Only in the 1840s and later did the situation begin to improve markedly; and the class which now emerged into comparative prosperity was not an élite of labour aristocrats, but a more homogeneous class of factory workers – a body whose discipline in strikes and in the adversity of the cotton famine won the praise of Charles Dickens, W. E. Gladstone, and many other observers.[2]

In the mining industry it would be still more difficult to speak of an élite of labour aristocrats confronting a mass of labourers, although Dr Hobsbawm, by including 'some miners' in his labour aristocracy of the 1890s, appears to have attempted to do this. It is true that in the early stages of the growth of the industry, the 'butty' system was commonly employed, whereby some skilled miners employed a number of less skilled men to work for them. By the later nineteenth century, however, this.type of employment was obsolete except in a few Midland pits. The hewers were the most highly paid men in the industry, those engaged in putting or hauling being less well paid, and the trappers, who were usually young boys, getting very little indeed. The hewers, however, were not distinct from other workers except in being fitter and more powerful. This was as much a matter of age as of physique. In a mining village any reasonably strong boy could expect to become a hewer in his young manhood and to stay in that capacity, if he survived, until at least his mid-forties. There was no apprenticeship system, and all students of mining villages have stressed their extraordinary social cohesion, which must be ascribed in part to their isolation and concentration upon one type of employment, in part to the common dangers of the miner's life, and in part to the absence of social cleavage such as might apply where a labour aristocracy existed.[3]

[1] This is well documented in J. M. Sanderson, 'The Basic Education of Labour in Lancashire, 1780–1839' (Ph.D. thesis, Cambridge, 1966).

[2] Dickens in *Household Words*, 11 Feb 1854; Gladstone's speech, 6 Apr 1866, quoted J. Morley, *Life of Gladstone* (1908), i, 567.

[3] The best discussion of this subject is to be found in R. G. Gregory, 'The Miners in Politics in England and Wales, 1906–14' (D.Phil. thesis, Oxford, 1963).

The pattern was not so very different in the manufacture of iron and steel. Already by 1860 workers in the pig or wrought iron manufacture at Sunderland were reported to require no apprenticeship, 'the work requiring strength and endurance, rather than skill'.[1] It was a very strenuous occupation, and led to a fairly early retirement to lighter work. A representative of the South Staffordshire ironworkers told the Royal Commission on the Aged Poor (1895) that puddlers tended to 'break down' at the age of 55.[2] Charles Booth noted at about the same date that 'ironworkers rarely save, and early cease to get employment'.[3] The headmaster of Consett Iron Company's British School, giving evidence to another government enquiry, that on Pupil Teachers, refused to describe the ironworkers as artisans, even though they were earning 'from £4 ... to as much as £10' a week. As he put it, 'their merit is mere animal strength, such physical strength is required'.[4] Consequently, boys leaving this school refused to accept the sacrifice of income which was involved in being apprenticed to a trade or in becoming pupil teachers. Dr Hobsbawm found the wages of iron and steel puddlers on piecework to be so high in 1906 that he was constrained to put them in his 'super-aristocracy'; yet these were the workers of the type investigated by Lady Bell at Middlesbrough, subject to constant risks of accident and illness, and facing grim prospects of reduced income in their later years, because all too frequently they saved nothing and belonged to no friendly society.[5] The iron and steel industries did contain one major group of skilled craftsmen, the moulders, whose union, the Friendly Society of Ironfounders, remained strong, if not predominant, in the later nineteenth century, although threatened by the development of machine moulding and the growth of new unions of the less skilled.[6] There were also the various skilled trades of the light steel industry of Sheffield; but here, as Professor Pollard has pointed out: 'some trades such as file cutting and spring knife cutlery were depressed

[1] National Association for the Promotion of Social Science, *Transactions*, 1860, p. 318.

[2] *P.P.* 1895, xv, 814.

[3] C. Booth, *The Aged Poor in England and Wales* (1894), p. 112.

[4] *P.P.* 1898, xxvi, 846.   [5] Florence Bell, *At the Works* (1911), p. 173.

[6] H. J. Fyrth and H. Collins, *The Foundry Workers* (Manchester, 1959), pp. 92 ff.

by sweating employers to wage levels well below those of unskilled labour'.[1] A Sheffield master cutler maintained in the early twentieth century that apprenticeship was breaking down because boys could get better wages as semi-skilled workers;[2] and probably this had been the case for a good many years, for in 1892 file-cutters who had served a seven-year apprenticeship were getting only 24s., with about 2s. deduction for tools.[3]

There has been a tendency to write trade-union history of the mid-Victorian period from the point of view of the London-based 'new model unions', as if these bodies with their high fees, apprenticeship regulations and centralised finances were in some way the pattern of all the growing trade unions of the period. That this was not so has been well demonstrated by G. D. H. Cole in an important article.[4] It was not merely that the textile, mining and iron and steel industries followed distinctively different paths; it was also the case that in many trades the artisans, though they might endeavour to adopt the 'New Model', were quite unable to dominate their respective trades and found themselves defending a limited sphere or indeed forced to give up entirely. The Amalgamated Society of Tailors, for instance, was steadily undermined by the development of wholesale manufacture and the employment of many semi-skilled or sweated workers, and in 1905 a section of its London members split off and later joined the union of the wholesale trade, the United Garment Workers Union.[5] The old union of the shoemaking craftsmen, the Amalgamated Cordwainers Association, collapsed altogether in the 1870s, being replaced by a union of the machine-made boot and shoe trade, the National Union of Boot and Shoe Operatives.[6]

---

[1] S. Pollard, 'Wages and Earnings in the Sheffield Trades, 1851–1914', *Yorkshire Bulletin of Economic and Social Research*, vi (1954), p. 58.

[2] Albert Hobson, in *P.P.* 1910, xlviii, 486.   [3] *P.P.* 1892, xxxvi, 571.

[4] G. D. H. Cole, 'British Trade Unions in the Third Quarter of the Nineteenth Century' (1937), reprinted in *Essays in Economic History*, ed. E. M. Carus-Wilson (1962), iii, 202 ff.

[5] For an outline of unionism in the clothing trades, see S. W. Lerner, *Breakaway Unions and the Small Trade Union* (1961), pp. 85 ff. The great days of trade unionism among the handicraft tailors are recounted in F. W. Galton (ed.), *The Tailoring Trade* (1923).

[6] A. Fox, *History of the National Union of Boot and Shoe Operatives, 1874–1957* (Oxford, 1958), pp. 2 ff.

Even the building trades, which Engels regarded as one of the main resorts of the labour aristocracy, were not entirely immune from industrial change, and in the depression of the trades in the early twentieth century, they lost members rapidly. 'More serious than straightforward decline', wrote Raymond Postgate, 'was their utter inability to protect their members' standard of life.'[1] There was not much doubt about the raggedness of the 'ragged-trousered philanthropists'.

Engels spoke of the engineering industry as the other main resort of the labour aristocracy, and it would be impossible to deny that in this industry there was a remarkable growth of new trades which by virtue of their scarcity and skill were able to build up all the apparatus of the pre-industrial crafts, including a strict control over apprenticeship and the work done by labourers. It is paradoxical that the very workers whose industry contributed to the breakdown of other crafts were able to build up so strong a craft position of their own. Engineering expanded so rapidly in mid-century that almost as good wages could be secured by non-society men as by members of the Amalgamated Society of Engineers.[2] Nevertheless, the union continued to expand and only at the end of the nineteenth century began to run into real difficulties of the type which the products of their own industry had imposed upon other trades – namely, the application of machinery to replace their own skills.[3]

The engineers had an important role to play in the shipbuilding industry; but here also there were other unions of craftsmen who maintained their élite position with remarkable success throughout the period. The Boilermakers and the Shipwrights, the two most important, maintained a strict control of apprenticeship in the shipyards of the North-East and probably elsewhere as well. Sir Benjamin Browne, chairman of Hawthorn Leslie, told the Royal Commission on the Poor Law that 'all our mechanics serve their apprenticeship', and he was at pains to point out the contrast between the conditions that existed in his own industry and those that existed elsewhere.[4] All the same, there were

---

[1] R. W. Postgate, *The Builders' History* (1923), p. 371.

[2] M. and J. B. Jefferys, 'Wages, Hours and Trade Customs of the Skilled Engineer in 1861', *Economic History Review*, xvii (1947), p. 32.

[3] J. B. Jefferys, *Story of the Engineers* (1945), p. 136.

[4] *P.P.* 1910, xlviii, 407.

labourers in the Tyneside shipyards who earned as much as 29s.-
32s.;[1] and in Admiralty employment, where every established
employee including the unskilled was eligible for a pension, there
was said to be 'a very good opening for the unskilled labourer . . .
to become skilled'.[2]

Finally, we may consider the special problems of the railway
workers. There were many grades of responsibility and skill on
the railways, but throughout the nineteenth century the railway
companies refused to recognise any attempts at union organisation. The Amalgamated Society of Railway Servants, formed in
1872, contained a number of grades of railway workers, including
footplatemen.[3] It was only in 1880 that a separate union of
footplatemen was founded – the Associated Society of Locomotive
Engineers and Firemen – and even then many footplatemen
remained in the A.S.R.S. Non-recognition by the employers, the
successive all-grades movements, and finally the merging of three
unions into the National Union of Railwaymen in 1913 preclude
us from regarding railwaymen as part of an aristocratic élite,
although there were of course considerable differentials of reward
among the various grades. Nowhere, however, was there a system
of apprenticeship guarded by union restriction. Employment on
the railways, as in other sections of the transport industry, cannot
be said to have been of such a character as to fit in with the theory
of labour aristocracy.

This survey has by no means covered every occupation, but it
has touched on most of those in which large numbers of workers
were employed. In the later nineteenth century a secure body of
highly-paid artisans, protected by apprenticeship restrictions
enforced by their trade unions, was only to be found in a few
industries and then only in some centres of each industry: in
printing, where a highly literate class of workers was essential; in
engineering and in ship-building, where expansion was rapid and
skill was at a premium; and for the rest in a few small and static
trades such as silk hat manufacture, brushmaking, coachmaking,
and some but by no means all of the branches of the glass trade.
The building trades trembled on the edge of the aristocracy: their
members frequently dropped 'out of benefit' and they suffered

[1] *P.P.* 1893–4, xxxii, 38.   [2] *P.P.* 1893–4, xxxii, 380.
[3] The best study of railway trade unionism is P. S. Bagwell, *The
Railwaymen* (1963).

from the competition of the semi-skilled. There was no real labour aristocracy in the staple export trades – coal and the main branches of textile manufacture. And as more and more old crafts crumbled under specialisation or technical innovation, so the working-class became more homogeneous – a phenomenon which is generally accepted to have occurred, but which is rarely satisfactorily explained. It is time now to look at such figures as there are of the relative family incomes of the working class, to see whether we can generally separate out anything like Dr Hobsbawm's élite of comparatively prosperous earners against a background of the distinctly poor, or whether there was a substantial body of families which in terms of working-class income could be regarded as relatively comfortable.

The first point to be made is that the wages of the individual worker do not readily provide us with an index of his relative affluence, which must depend upon the size of his family, the earnings, if any, of his wife and children, the ability of his wife as a housekeeper, and his and her financial self-discipline, foresight, intelligence and temperance. Many knowledgeable observers of the nineteenth-century social scene made this caveat when they were asked to generalise about categories of workers. When David Chadwick, Treasurer of the Corporation of Salford, was asked by a member of the Select Committee on the Elective Franchise in 1860 to say whether a 'superior class' of artisans lived in houses rated at over £10, he replied: 'In one case [*sc.* a man] might be encumbered by a large family, and having to pay for their education and other things; in other cases men might be drunken, dissolute people; therefore there would be no criterion.'[1] So too almost a half-century later Lady Bell said of the workers of Middlesbrough:

Many of the men concerned are well off and prosperous; but not necessarily always those with the higher incomes. . . . The time when existence seems to press most heavily is during the first twelve or fourteen years after marriage . . . the income during these first years of married life being almost entirely

[1] Select Committee on the Elective Franchise, *P.P.* 1860, xii, 32.

dependent upon the health and physical condition of the bread-winner.[1]

It has already been pointed out that many of those whose earnings were highest for one reason or another made little or no provision for their old age; and in examining the records of the old people of Birmingham who were forced into the workhouse Joseph Chamberlain formed the decided impression that they constituted 'a very large and varied representation of all the trades of Birmingham', and were not by any means predominantly unskilled.[2] This may partly have been because the skilled man ran as great, or almost as great, a risk of unemployment as the unskilled. As W. H. Beveridge put it in 1909: 'It is by no means axiomatic that the proportion of unemployment is lower amongst skilled men as a whole than amongst unskilled, or amongst trade unionists than amongst non-unionists. The skilled man holds out for a job in his own particular line; the unskilled man will take anything he can do...'[3] The experience of unemployment insurance just before the First World War was that there was 'no substantial difference between the proportion of cases of unemployment among members of associations and among workmen who are not members of such associations'.[4] A further element of almost equal risk for both the skilled and unskilled was afforded by industrial injuries and disease. In the Potteries, for example, the Poor Law Commission found that: 'In a considerable number of individual cases pauperism is directly and distinctly due to ill-health produced by the conditions of the occupation.'[5]

It is better, therefore, to turn from the figures of average wage-levels by occupation to the social investigators' classification of households by family income. This will provide us with a cross-section of the entire population in a particular town or district, and will take account of the effect on standards caused by family size and by the number of wage-earners in each household. It will still leave out of account the important question whether these family incomes were spent wisely or not. It was calculated that in the latter years of the nineteenth century the average working-class family spent one-fifth of its income on alcoholic

[1] Bell, *At the Works*, p. 83.
[2] Royal Commission on the Aged Poor, *P.P.* 1895, xv, 670.
[3] W. H. Beveridge, *Unemployment* (1930), p. 21.
[4] Ibid., p. 271.   [5] *P.P.* 1909, xliii, 164.

drink:[1] but this proportion could obviously vary widely in particular cases; and intemperance, though often a result of poor housing and conditions, was also itself an important cause of poverty.

Charles Booth made a careful survey of the households of East London and classified them in an ascending scale from A to G and H, the last two being distinctly middle-class. According to Dr Hobsbawm we should find the labour aristocracy in Class F, which contained 12·5% of the total population, and was partly lower middle-class, partly upper working-class. But Booth goes out of his way to say that 'my classes E, F and G consort together in a free and friendly way' – and Class E contained no less than 42·3% of the total population.[2] This was apparently as true of the children as of the adult population: for although Booth found a tendency for the Board Schools to differ in social character he tells us that those of the 'upper grade' catered generally for Classes E and F and some of Class G.[3] The implication is that even in East London there was not so much a labour aristocracy of Dr Hobsbawm's size of 10%, but rather a very wide class of workers with some degree of comparative comfort (by the limited standards of the time). This impression is on the whole confirmed by the figures compiled by Seebohm Rowntree and others for households in provincial towns. Rowntree, in his survey of York in 1902, put 52·6% of the households in his highest class, namely, those in receipt of at least 30s. weekly and not burdened with particularly large numbers of dependants.[4] Using a slightly different method of calculation, Bowley and Burnett-Hurst provided figures for the weekly family income of working-class households in four industrial towns – Northampton, Warrington, Stanley (Durham) and Reading. Incomes were in excess of the Rowntree poverty level *by at least 20s. a week* in over half the households of Northampton and Stanley (a shoemaking and a mining town respectively), in well over a quarter at Warrington (mixed heavy industry) but in only about one-twelfth at Reading (light industry

---

[1] J. Rowntree and A. Sherwell, *Temperance Problem and Social Reform* (9th ed., 1900), pp. 10 f.

[2] C. Booth, *Life and Labour in London*, ser. i (1902), i, 34 f. and 99.

[3] Ibid., iii, 209.   [4] B. S. Rowntree, *Poverty* (1902), p. 65.

employing mostly unskilled workers).[1] Clearly only Reading could have corresponded to the pattern envisaged by Dr Hobsbawm, unless we are to suppose that the labour aristocrats formed only one of two or more classes of comparatively prosperous workers.

Nor is it true to suggest that the co-operative societies, friendly societies and other organisations of working-class origin were the exclusive preserve of the highly-skilled or even the highly-paid in the later nineteenth and early twentieth centuries. Co-operative societies tended to be most strongly established in the Lancashire towns, where the typical worker was not an artisan but a factory worker. In 1903 the secretary of the Co-operative Union reported that there were many members of the societies who earned less than £1 a week, and these members objected to the proposal that co-operative employees, who usually earned more than this, should receive an old age pension paid out of funds otherwise available for their dividends.[2] In the case of the friendly societies, we may notice the observation of E. W. Brabrook, the Chief Registrar, in 1895, to the effect that 'nearly all those who are in steady employment are members of some friendly society or another',[3] although we must place it against Lady Bell's remark, already quoted, that in Middlesbrough this was not necessarily true even of the most highly paid. Almost fifteen years later Brabrook said: 'I should certainly not say that they are exclusively taken from the ranks of skilled labour, because, for instance, the number of members in the agricultural districts is very large.'[4] Since the membership of friendly societies far outran the membership of trade unions it is very difficult, even if we allow for some overlap as well as for the insurance of several members of a man's family, to believe that it was even predominantly the preserve of the top 10% of the working class.[5] C. J. Drummond, a former President of the Hearts of Oak Benefit Society, told the Royal Commission on the Aged Poor in 1895 that 'There is a

---

[1] A. L. Bowley and A. R. Burnett-Hurst, *Livelihood and Poverty* (1915), p. 39.

[2] Select Committee on Aged Pensions Bill, *P.P.* 1903, v, 456.

[3] *P.P.* 1895, xv, 607.   [4] *P.P.* 1909, xl, 1000.

[5] As early as 1873 the total membership was estimated at 4 million: P. H. J. H. Gosnell, *Friendly Societies in England, 1815–75* (Manchester, 1961), p. 7. By 1909 it was 14 million: *P.P.* 1909, xl, 1000.

large number of the unskilled workers who are members of one or other of the friendly societies.'[1]

As for the trade unions themselves, we have already pointed to the significant differences between the exclusive artisans' societies and the more comprehensive unions of the miners and the cotton workers. In the later nineteenth century it was the latter which constituted the big battalions represented at the T.U.C. Perhaps if it had not been so, the 'new unions' of the unskilled would not have found it so easy to obtain membership of a body which, as we can tell from its name, was hardly expected to represent the entire working class. Not that, in point of fact, even its craft societies covered an economically distinctive section of the men in their trades. As the social worker Edith Simcox pointed out at the Industrial Remuneration Conference in 1885, there was no 'hard and fast line' of affluence between the trade unionist and the 'non-society man': 'Many a man drops his subscription when times are bad, and if there are workmen outside the trade societies who are as well off as any unionist, there are plenty of unionists who feel the pinch of want.'[2]

It is an essential feature of the Marxist theory of the labour aristocracy that this supposedly small section of the working class was conservative in politics, and imposed its conservatism upon working-class institutions, thereby concealing but by no means eliminating the underlying militancy of the mass of the workers. It may well be that this interpretation has some rough correspondence to the facts in the period of acute distress in the Chartist period, when the more moderate elements were to be found among the comparatively prosperous craftsmen, such as the members of the London Working Men's Association, while the 'physical force' men were mostly the unemployed factory operatives or dispossessed handloom weavers of the North. Later on, however, when 'physical force' was out of the question, the evidence almost invariably suggests that it was the more prosperous workers who were the more politically militant and radical, while the lower ranks displayed either apathy or conservatism.

[1] *P.P.* 1895, xv, 573.

[2] *Report of the Industrial Remuneration Conference* (1885), p. 90.

Henry Mayhew is an oft-quoted source on the characteristics of the London population in the middle of the nineteenth century. His testimony about the contrasts in political interest is particularly definite:

The artisans are almost to a man red-hot politicians. They are sufficiently educated and thoughtful to have a sense of their importance in the State.... The unskilled labourers are a different class of people. As yet they are as unpolitical as footmen, and instead of entertaining violent democratic opinions, they appear to have no political opinions whatever; or if they do possess any, they rather tend towards the maintenance of 'things as they are' than towards the ascendancy of the working people.[1]

We have seen that the engineering craftsmen were able to benefit from the industrial revolution, and to create a position of security for themselves at a time when the products of their industry were destroying the security of others. The 'Journeyman Engineer', who described their conditions in the 1860s, is often quoted by supporters of the concept of the 'labour aristocracy' to show the wide gulf which existed between artisan and labourer, as if it were as true of the whole working class as it was of the engineering shops. In other trades, incidentally, the 'Journeyman Engineer' perceived 'superseded artisans' who 'sink down into odd-job men or paupers, never to rise again'.[2] This is what he had to say about the politics of the artisan: 'He comes to entertain, either consciously or unconsciously, levelling doctrines.'[3] It is true that the 'Journeyman Engineer' also regarded the labourer as a leveller; in fact the only real distinction that he made in politics was between the generations – the 'old school' of working men retaining a 'feeling of class antagonism' that was not so strong among the young. But a later anonymous working-class author of the late 1870s said of the unskilled labourer that 'force of circumstances ... certainly tends to keep him quiescent'.[4]

Some recent historians of the mid-Victorian years have shown some impatience with the trade-union leaders of that period for the narrowness of their aims in both the industrial and the

[1] Mayhew, *London Labour and the London Poor*, iii, 233.

[2] 'Journeyman Engineer' (Thomas Wright), *Our New Masters* (1873), p. 146.

[3] Ibid., p. 7.

[4] 'A Working Man', *Working Men and Women* (1879), p. 107.

political sphere. The impatience would be more justified if any real alternative had existed at the time – if there was any prospect of the unions making rapid headway by a policy of continual militancy, or of working-class leaders securing election to Parliament as the candidates of independent labour. Those who belonged to trade unions were at least more militant than those who did not; and Mr R. V. Clements has shown that they were by no means so slavishly acquiescent in the tenets of middle-class economics as has sometimes been thought.[1] When conditions permitted they proved themselves perfectly capable of taking advantage of them to increase wages and to extend the membership of their unions. As G. D. H. Cole has pointed out, 'the late 1860s and early 1870s were in fact a period of very considerable trade-union militancy'.[2] In politics, although the majority of trade-union leaders were Liberals, they retained sufficient independence of mind to realise that at election times they could at least play off the candidates of the two major parties against each other. These tactics proved remarkably successful in securing trade-union legislation from the Conservative Government of 1874.[3]

When Socialism revived in Britain in the 1880s, it certainly had little support to begin with among the existing leaders of the working class. But this was probably more a matter of generations than of anything else. The first working-class Socialists tended to be young skilled men, especially engineers, such as John Burns, Tom Mann, and J. L. Mahon. A correspondent of the *Manchester Guardian* who was in touch with the foundation members of the Socialist League reported the view that the Socialists 'had never been able to touch the miserable poor, and had always been most successful in converting the well-to-do and intelligent artisans'.[4] A decade later, the Independent Labour Party appeared to secure the bulk of its membership from those who were distinctly above the level of ordinary unskilled labour. One or two quotations, taken almost at random, illustrate this. When the Birmingham

---

[1] R. V. Clements, 'British Trade Unions and Popular Political Economy, 1850–75', *Economic History Review*, xiv (1961).

[2] Carus-Wilson (ed.), *Essays in Economic History*, iii, 219.

[3] H. W. McCready, 'British Labour's Lobby, 1867–75', *Canadian Journal of Economic and Political Science*, xxii (1956), 155 f.

[4] *Manchester Guardian*, 26 Feb 1885.

Labour Church started a Cinderella Club to provide meals for needy children, 'our own members gave out the tickets, but the result was not satisfactory, we didn't get really poor children. Now we send the tickets to the Board Schools, and really get terribly poor children'. At Liverpool, where the same charitable work was undertaken, the Socialists tried the 'novel experience' of going into the alleys and courts to invite children promiscuously: 'It gave many of the members a glimpse as to how the poor live in the dilapidated, wretched hovels called houses.'[1]

These impressions from the North of England are paralleled for London by Booth's statement that his 'Class E' – the large section of the working class which had the advantage of 'regular standard earnings' – was 'the recognised field of all forms of co-operation and combination'. And he added 'Here, rather in the ruffianism of Class A [the lowest class], or the starvation of Class B, or the wasted energy of Class C, or the bitter anxieties of Class D, do we find the springs of Socialism and Revolution'.[2] The implication appears to be that it was only the better-off members of the working class who could really afford the time and energy for sustained political activity. A rather impatient Socialist writing at the time of the 1895 election came to the same conclusion:

Amongst the better-paid, better-fed, less hard-worked artisans, you find many who take an interest in social and political questions, and can discuss the same reasonably with you. But mix among the poorest workers, and you shall find that they are incapable of understanding or discussing the problems which concern them more nearly than any other.[3]

It was, of course, the ranks of the least skilled workers which contained the largest numbers of Irish immigrants. The Irish in Britain tended to vote Liberal for the sake of Home Rule, or sometimes Conservative for the sake of Catholic education; but they could rarely be induced to vote for independent Labour or Socialist candidates.

Dr Hobsbawm thinks that those trade unions which joined the Labour Representation Committee in its first year of existence – that is, before the Taff Vale decision in the House of Lords –

[1] *Scout*, i (1895), 32 f.   [2] Booth, *Life and Labour*, ser. i, i, 51 and 177.
[3] *Scout*, i (1895), 143.

must have been the most radical unions. As he points out, these unions were mostly organisations of the unskilled; and the few that were not he explains as having particular feelings of insecurity at the time. He regards this as confirming his view that 'The political and economic positions of the labour aristocracy reflect one another with uncanny accuracy.' It is perhaps surprising that a Marxist historian should regard joining the Labour Representation Committee (later the Labour Party) as a touchstone of militancy; after all, the Marxist organisation of the time, the Social-Democratic Federation, remained in affiliation to it for only a few months. But in any case, there were some non-political reasons why the new unions were more likely than the old unions to join the L.R.C. early rather than late. The new unions were more concerned than the old about the changes in the law of picketing which had been effected by legal decisions of the 1890s, thus slightly preceding the Taff Vale case which was also concerned with the question of trade-union funds.[1] On the whole, too, the new unions could make up their minds about joining the L.R.C. more quickly than the old could, because their decision-making systems were more centralised than those of the craftsmen's societies, which were often descended from amalgamations of trade clubs, and consequently had complicated constitutions. The general secretaries of the new unions were in several cases still the men who had founded the unions; they were men better at oratory than at administration, and so they more readily harboured political ambitions for themselves. Even at the turn of the century they were comparatively young men, not unwilling to take on extra responsibilities. As for the old unions, no doubt the officials and members of some of them were more than usually worried about particular problems of their respective trades;[2] but this could equally well be said of some of the unions which did not join the L.R.C. in the first year, for instance the Engineers. It can also be argued, as it was at the time, that the prosperity of a union was a very good reason for participating in politics. D. C. Cummings, the secretary of the highly aristocratic

[1] For an indication of the attitude of the older unions to picketing, see *Cotton Factory Times*, 28 Sep 1900; Friendly Society of Ironfounders, *Annual Report, 1901*, p. 3.

[2] I have myself made this point, which I now believe to be of only limited relevance, in my *Origins of the Labour Party* (1954), pp. 209 f.

Boilermakers, put this point to his members: 'Even the bitterest opponent of the Society will be forced to admit that a society nearly 50,000 strong, and then having over £415,000 to its credit, is indeed modest when it only asks for one or two representatives for the many and varied interests of so great a number of British citizens.'[1]

To sum up. The concept of the labour aristocracy has had its value in drawing attention to differences within the working class; but if it implies the existence in the late nineteenth and early twentieth century of a labour élite distinctly separated from lower strata and marked by political behaviour of an acquiescent type, then it is a concept that does more harm than good to historical truth. To be sure, in some industries the craftsmen did manage to perpetuate, sometimes even to extend, a tight control over entry into their trades. But the number of industries in which this was possible was constantly in decline after the onset of the industrial revolution. The growth of the factory and mining population in the nineteenth century meant the growth of a more homogeneous working class than had existed previously, and in this working class there was no aristocracy, unless we think of foremen, who, although they often appeared in wage statistics, did not normally belong to trade unions. As for politics, it is clear that the Marxist historians have completely got the wrong end of the stick: militancy was much more likely to be found among the better-off than among the poorer workers. We may notice, as a pendant to the discussion, that recruitment to the Communist Party, both in this country and in other countries of Europe, has been much more successful among more highly-paid manual workers than among those of lesser income. Thus we can agree after all with Professor Hugh Seton-Watson, who has examined this problem in an international context, that in its political application 'The theory of the labour aristocracy is as artificial as the theory of the class struggle within the peasantry.'[2]

[1] D. C. Cummings, *Historical Survey of the Boilermakers &c Society* (Newcastle upon Tyne, 1905), p. 163.

[2] H. Seton-Watson, *Pattern of Communist Revolution* (1953), p. 341.

4 Trade Unions, Workers and the Law

'LAWS grind the poor, and rich men rule the law', wrote Oliver Goldsmith; and his opinion could fairly be said still to represent the position in England in the Victorian era. The laws of the country were made by a Parliament of property owners, and the courts were controlled by men of the same class. The ordinary wage-earner could only hope that it would be his good fortune to avoid any entanglement with them.

Unless a working man were charged with a felony or worse, he was not likely in fact to come into contact with the higher courts of the realm, for he certainly could not afford to initiate a case before them. In all matters affecting his rights, therefore, he had to accept the decisions of the Justices of the Peace. The Justices, who were unpaid, part-time authorities, were persons of high social standing nominated for each county by the Lord Lieutenant, but actually appointed by the Lord Chancellor. In the towns, wealthier tradesmen often found a place on the bench, but the justices for the county jurisdiction until 1906 still required a property qualification of £100 rateable value, and in practice they were almost entirely drawn from landowning families.[1] Thus while a man charged with petty theft in a borough would appear before a bench of shopkeepers, those in the country who were accused of poaching were tried by the landowners whose game was at risk. Although a few trade-union leaders had been made J.P.s before the turn of the century, the general composition of the bench had changed but little by the time of the First World War. Ben Turner, the Yorkshire Weavers' leader, told the Royal Commission on the Selection of Justices in 1910 that in the West Riding there were eight 'representative workingmen' out of five hundred county magistrates, and in the towns the proportion was not much greater – five of 89 in Leeds, and five of 75 in Bradford.[2]

[1] L. Page, *Justice of the Peace* (1936); J. M. Lee, 'Parliament and the Appointment of Magistrates', *Parliamentary Affairs*, xiii (1959–60), p. 90.
[2] *P.P.* 1910, xxxvii, 896.

All this was bad enough; but if a poor man did have the misfortune to appear before a higher court he was even more at a disadvantage. It is true that the judges of the higher courts, being professionals, might be more disinterested than the local bench in particular cases with which they dealt; yet they too were drawn to an overwhelming extent from the higher ranks of society, and usually had little understanding of the mode of life and the way of thinking of the wage-earning class. Furthermore, the costs of actions, particularly in the High Court, were crippling. In criminal cases, if a man could at least raise a guinea fee, he could then plead poverty and obtain a free defending counsel on a 'dock brief'. In civil cases, there was a procedure known as the *in forma pauperis* procedure, but to obtain the benefit of free counsel by these means, a man had to show that he had disposable assets of less than £5 (raised to £25 in 1883) and also that he had a good *prima facie* case. This involved finding a solicitor to provide the necessary *affidavit* and to prepare the case for counsel.[1] These difficulties, coupled with the cost of travel and the loss of earnings for himself and his witnesses, made the whole business virtually prohibitive for the ordinary wage-earner. The establishment of County Courts in 1846 relieved the position only slightly: the *in forma pauperis* procedure was rarely used there, and it is generally agreed that the change helped the small tradesman to collect debts, but made little difference to the really poor man with a grievance.[2]

In the higher courts, the jury system was supposed to be the safeguard of the rights of the ordinary citizen. But in practice, juries included few representatives of the wage-earning class. The qualifications for a juror, as laid down by the Juries Act of 1825, were that he had to be a £10 freeholder, or a £20 long-leaseholder, or a householder of a house valued at £20 a year (£30 in London and Middlesex), or the occupier of a house with not less than fifteen windows.[3] This ruled out the great bulk of the working class. But as an additional safeguard, it might seem, for those of property and influence, many cases, including those for

[1] R. Egerton, *Legal Aid* (1945), p. 8.

[2] B. Abel-Smith and R. Stevens, *Lawyers and the Courts* (1967). p. 136n.

[3] R. M. Jackson, *Machinery of Justice in England* (Cambridge, 1960 ed.), p. 249.

sedition, were tried before 'special' juries, which were still more exclusive. By the 1825 Act, the members of a special jury had to be of the rank of esquire or higher, or a merchant or banker. In the civil trial brought by the Tichborne Claimant in 1870 the jury included among its eleven members no less than three Captains of the Royal Navy, as well as an officer of the Queen's Bodyguard and a partner of Coutts Bank.[1] It was no wonder that many people believed that the Claimant, who had temporarily at least abandoned the life of a gentleman, could never expect a fair verdict from such a jury. The popular enthusiasm for the Claimant derived its strength from a variety of sources, including anti-Catholicism; but the feeling that the legal system was heavily biassed against the poor man was perhaps the most important single factor. E. V. Kenealy, the Claimant's counsel, was actually elected to Parliament as a People's candidate at a by-election at Stoke in 1875, his platform being the demand for the release of the Claimant from imprisonment and a retrial of his claim. Stoke was already largely a working-class constituency, and five years later was to elect one of the first three trade-union M.P.s – Henry Broadhurst.

By the Juries Act of 1870 special juries were made somewhat less restrictive, but the change cannot be regarded as very drastic. Two additional qualifications were added: a special juror could now be a person either occupying a dwelling-house rated at not less than £100 in larger towns or £50 elsewhere; or occupying premises of £100 rateable value, or £300 if it were a farm. It is a curious feature of the system that special jurors were paid for attendance, while common jurors were not, so that poor people were especially anxious to avoid jury service even if qualified.

Early in the twentieth century all sections of the labour movement took up the demand for jury reform. In 1907 the Independent Labour Party at its annual conference passed a resolution demanding the payment of jurors, arguing that the existing system whereby 'workingmen are wholly or almost wholly excluded from juries has led to the gravest injustice'.[2] The Labour Party passed a resolution for the payment of jurors in 1908 and 1910, and the T.U.C. in 1910 and several later years described the existing system as 'unfair and partial', and demanded the

[1] D. Woodruff, *The Tichborne Claimant* (1957), p. 172.
[2] I.L.P. *Report, 1907*, pp. 65 f.

abolition of special juries and the payment of common jurors.[1] A Departmental Committee on Jury Law and Practice heard evidence on the subject in 1913, and W. J. Davis, a leading 'Lib-Lab', appeared for the T.U.C. to put its demands. He described the views of himself and his colleagues in these terms: 'We look upon the jury system as a nest-egg of the upper classes of this country. It is their protection; it is a rich man's asset.'[2]

Nor was this all. In several spheres of the law which were most important for the ordinary person, there was in the most literal sense 'one law for the rich and another for the poor'. One of these spheres was debt. Whereas the small debtor could be sent to prison for default – the more easily, as we have seen, after the establishment of the County Courts – the larger debtor, provided he owed at least £50, and provided he still retained or could obtain £10 to pay the necessary legal fees, could file a petition in bankruptcy, and thus obtain immunity from imprisonment.[3] Thomas Wright, the 'Journeyman Engineer', regarded this as one of the 'things that sting and rankle, that perpetuate and intensify class jealousy and hatred', when he discussed working-class grievances in the mid-Victorian era.[4] Wright might also have instanced the law of divorce and separation. Until 1857 divorce required a special Act of Parliament; so it was obviously a preserve of the very rich. By the Matrimonial Causes Act of 1857 a Divorce Court was established in London, and this measure, as has been said, extended opportunities for divorce 'from the very rich to the rich'.[5] For those without money, there could be no divorce and indeed no legal separation. Only in 1878 were magistrates given the power to make separation orders for women whose husbands had been convicted of aggravated assault. In 1895 this was extended to cases of cruelty and in 1902, under the Licensing Act, to cases

---

[1] Labour Party, *Report, 1908*, p. 79 and 1910, p. 97; T.U.C. *Report, 1910*, pp. 201–2.

[2] *P.P.* 1913, xxx, 629.

[3] E. A. Parry, *The Law and the Poor* (1914), pp. 52–6.

[4] T. Wright, *Our New Masters* (1873), p. 155.

[5] Abel-Smith and Stevens, *Lawyers and the Courts*, p. 42. Cf. Report of Committee on County Court Procedure, *P.P.* 1909, lxxii, 333.

of drunkenness. But even those who could obtain separation orders
were not free to remarry. The suffering which the system entailed
in many cases is well illustrated in the records of the Royal Commission on Divorce and Matrimonial Causes, which reported just
before the First World War.[1] It was still true at that time, as it
was expressed by a commentator of the period that: 'For the
majority of working people, divorce no more exists as a way out of
matrimonial difficulties than champagne as a morning pick-me-
up.'[2] The determined opposition of the Church, on grounds of
morality, and the Bar Council, on behalf of the vested interests of
London barristers, held up all reform until the social changes
effected by the First World War broke down some of the resistance.

Yet another sphere of the law where the wage-earner was at a
serious disadvantage was that about compensation for accidents.
In the case of injury at work, the employed person had limited
rights of recovery from his employer, but these lapsed if the
accident was the fault of a fellow-employee or employees. This was
due to the doctrine of 'common employment', which was not part
of common or statute law, but was first propounded in a judgment
by Baron Abinger in 1837, and subsequently accepted by the
courts. According to Abinger, it would be 'an absurdity' were it
the case that 'the footman . . . who rides behind the carriage, may
have an action against his master . . . for drunkenness, neglect, or
want of skill in the coachman'.[3] Nevertheless, the Abinger
doctrine led to even greater absurdity in large industrial concerns.
On the railways, for instance, although passengers could obtain
damages, the companies could usually escape liability for injuries
to their employees by pleading that an accident was the fault of
some person in 'common employment' with the victim – whether
it was an engine-driver, or a signalman, or even the superintendent
of the line. The Royal Commission on Railway Accidents reported
in 1877 that the men's interests were 'sacrificed from causes and
in circumstances which would clearly give a right to compensation,
were it not that the law refuses to regard in any other light than
as their fellow servants those to whom the company delegates the
master's authority'.[4]

[1] *P.P.* 1912–13, xviii, 197. For the letters, ibid., xx, 829–84.
[2] S. Reynolds, R. Woolley, and T. Woolley, *Seems So!* (1911), p. 247.
[3] Quoted Abel-Smith and Stevens, *Lawyers and the Courts*, p. 46.
[4] Quoted P. S. Bagwell, *The Railwaymen* (1963), p. 116.

The doctrine of 'common employment' was extended to Scotland in 1858 and remained in operation throughout Britain until the passing of the Law Reform Act of 1948. There was a limited improvement in 1880, when the Employers' Liability Act was passed, giving workers the right to claim damages from employers in a restricted range of accidents. But this measure proved to be ineffective, partly because firms could easily induce their workmen to 'contract out' of its provisions. Attempts by the Liberals to amend the measure in 1894 foundered on the opposition of the House of Lords. But Chamberlain's Workmen's Compensation Act of 1897 marked a substantial advance, for it gave an automatic right of compensation in industrial accidents, though it did not by any means apply to all industries or all situations within a particular industry. Thus, a workman injured while working on a building could obtain compensation if the building were thirty feet high or more, but not if it were less.[1] A man could get compensation if he contracted anthrax from wool which he was employed in sorting, for the House of Lords, on appeal, ruled that this was an accident; but if he contracted lead poisoning, which could not be linked with any particular incident of his working life, there was no compensation.[2] In a doubtful case it was difficult for a man to obtain fair treatment unless his case was taken up by his trade union. A government committee on the working of the Act reported that: 'The workman who has no organisation to resort to for advice and assistance is comparatively helpless.'[3]

A revised Act of 1906 removed many of the existing anomalies and also extended its provisions to an extra six million workers. But it still did not cover all casual workers, or outworkers, or policemen. And although the proportion of cases which involved litigation now declined considerably, there remained a rich practice for the legal specialist in this subject. The Court of Appeal was thought to be distinctly restrictive in its approach to cases which arose under the Acts; and for this reason, trade-union leaders were anxious that, expensive though it was, the

[1] Report of Departmental Committee on Compensation for Injuries to Workmen, *P.P.* 1904, lxxxviii, 795.

[2] Ibid., p. 787; *Law Journal*, xli, 4 (6 Jan 1906).

[3] *P.P.* 1904, lxxxvii, 785.

avenue to the highest judicial tribunal, the House of Lords, should remain open.[1]

The distinction between the treatment of the rich and that of the poor in so many spheres of the law helped to give the working man that characteristic bias against social legislation which observers so often noticed in this period. Lord Robert Grosvenor's Sunday Trading Bill, for instance, was much disliked because Sunday trading was largely a working-class necessity: it provoked the London riots of 1855.[2] So too, temperance legislation was looked upon with grave suspicion by working men because they realised that the rich man's private clubs would remain entirely unrestricted, while the public houses which were often the poor man's only resort for drinking would be closed.[3] Legislation of this discriminatory character existed in the case of betting, for the Betting Houses Act of 1853 left Tattersall's and the racehorse enclosures quite untouched. The Street Betting Act of 1906, in spite of Labour protests, followed the same pattern.[4]

In the early nineteenth century, life was made more tolerable for the poor by the fact that many of the laws which they found most oppressive could not be effectively enforced. Thus, trade unions flourished in spite of the law against combinations; unstamped newspapers – the only type which a poor man could afford – circulated widely throughout the country; and various local customs which gave the ordinary person an opportunity of enjoying himself for an interval, perhaps at the expense of other people's private property, prevailed in many places. In country districts there was a good deal of poaching, for which landowners could secure little redress. All these things were examples of the license that existed before the creation of proper police forces; and in

[1] Report of Departmental Committee on Compensation for Injuries to Workmen, *P.P.* 1920, xxvi, 195 and 490; J. Parris, *Under My Wig* (1961), p. 112; T.U.C. *Report, 1910*, p. 50.

[2] B. Harrison, 'Sunday Trading Riots of 1855', *Historical Journal*, viii (1965).

[3] At the 1895 election a placard headed 'Beer v. '47 Port' appealed to working men to vote against Sunday Closing. *Suffolk Chronicle*, 20 Jul 1895. Cf. Wright, *Our New Masters*, p. 155.

[4] See especially the debate on Clause 2 of the Bill, *H.C.Deb.*, ser. 4, clxii, 1159–70 (1 Aug 1906).

spite of the incidental disadvantages of managing without an effective system of law enforcement, the great bulk of English opinion was opposed to the introduction of police as an infringement of basic liberties, and as the thin end of the wedge of governmental despotism.

Unfortunately, the growth of towns posed ever-increasing problems of public control, and an efficient system of law enforcement became more and more essential. The need was felt first and most acutely in London, the largest city and the seat of government. Peel as Home Secretary determined to introduce a regular police force for the metropolitan area, and he secured the appointment of a Select Committee of the House of Commons to enquire into the matter. To his disappointment, the committee reported that: 'It is difficult to reconcile an effective system of police with that perfect freedom of action and exemption from interference, which are the great privileges and blessings of society in this country.'[1] Undeterred, however, he proceeded to the creation of the Metropolitan Police, which became known to the Radicals as 'Peel's Bloody Gang'.[2] Gradually, by careful training and effective discipline, the force commended itself at least to the governing classes and began to be used to suppress local disorders in the provinces. But there was an undercurrent of hostility to the force from humbler people, who felt that the police were depriving them of their liberties. The law that the police enforced, after all, was not a law which they had had a part in shaping. The Birmingham Chartists put the point clearly enough in 1839 when they resolved 'to have no Police whatsoever until the working classes had a voice in the making of the laws of the land'.[3] The Rural Police Act of 1839, which extended the system to the counties, was apparently largely responsible for the Chartist disorders of that year; and there is little doubt that the use of the Metropolitan Police for quelling disturbances in the provinces, which was a practice of the time, was particularly strongly resented.[4] The Chartist National Petition of 1842 listed as one of its grievances 'that an unconstitutional police force is

[1] Quoted N. Gash, *Mr Secretary Peel* (1961), p. 312.
[2] W. L. M. Lee, *History of Police in England* (1901), p. 251; H. Vizetelly, *Glances Back Through Seventy Years* (1893), i, 24, 59.
[3] F. C. Mather, *Public Order in the Age of the Chartists* (1959), p. 124.
[4] Ibid., p. 105.

distributed all over the country, at enormous cost, to prevent the due exercise of the people's rights'.[1]

The police were never sufficiently numerous, nor sufficiently centralised, to impose the despotism that Radicals feared. But they did enforce a state of order which had not previously existed, and which involved the elimination of many old local customs and pastimes. Street football, for instance, which was customary in various Midland towns on Shrove Tuesday, was permanently stopped, and survives only in the Staffordshire and Derbyshire custom of allowing the schoolchildren a holiday on that day. We know that in Derby the date of suppression was 1846.[2] In country districts the police were, not unnaturally, regarded as the agents of the landowners, who in their role as magistrates controlled the force and tried the cases which they brought to the sessions. By the Poaching Prevention Act of 1862 the police were given rights of search which were much resented by the labourers.[3] In any case, poaching was not generally regarded as anti-social behaviour. The result was a sort of guerilla warfare: a historian who has examined the records of the county police reports that 'there were not many county forces which had not lost one or more men killed or wounded at the hands of poachers in the thirty years after 1856'.[4] Even towards the end of the century, the village constable was, according to Flora Thompson, 'still regarded by many as a potential enemy, set to spy upon them by the authorities'.[5] A piece of children's doggerel reflected this hostility, and the feeling that the police prospered at the expense of the general population:

> There goes the bobby with his black shiny hat
> And his belly full of fat
> And a pancake tied to his nose.[6]

[1] S. MacCoby (ed.), *The English Radical Tradition* (1952), p. 137.

[2] A. W. Davison, *Derby: Its Rise and Progress* (1901), pp. 212–14; F. P. Magoun, *History of Football from the Beginnings to 1871* (Bochum-Langendreer, 1938), pp. 113–18.

[3] See Joseph Arch's evidence to Select Committee on Game Laws, *P.P.* 1873, xiii, 384.

[4] W. L. Burn, *The Age of Equipoise* (1964), p. 173.

[5] Flora Thompson, *Lark Rise to Candleford* (1948), p. 462.

[6] Ibid.; I. and P. Opie, *Lore and Language of Schoolchildren* (Oxford, 1959), p. 370.

A student of music-hall songs has recently pointed out that 'when the copper isn't portrayed as unscrupulous, he's considered comical', and that even in the apparently good-natured 'If you want to know the time, ask a p'liceman' there is a hint of corruption.[1] So too observers of working-class attitudes early in the present century could notice the 'dislike and distrust of the police, as such, which smoulders away always among working people', and could account for it by reason of the class bias of legislation and of the judiciary. In short, the function of the police was that 'At the bidding of one class, they attempt to impose a certain social discipline on another.'[2]

It is against this background that the attitude of trade unions to the legal system is to be measured. Involvement with the law meant, for them, as for the individual worker, exposure to a hostile environment, where the stakes were very high and where the dice might well be loaded. It is not very surprising that union leaders were inclined to steer clear of the law whenever they could.

It was only in the 1870s, however, that the unions secured legislation which appeared to provide them with the opportunity of keeping clear of the law. Previously they had run into difficulties because, under the common law concept of 'restraint of trade', trade unions were unlawful bodies. They had attempted to secure protection for their funds by registering as Friendly Societies under the Friendly Societies Act of 1855, but the decision of *Hornby* v. *Close* in 1867 showed that this subterfuge was unacceptable to the courts.[3] The appointment of a Royal Commission on Trade Unions in that year, and the urgent need to influence the Commissioners, Parliament and also public opinion in favour of trade unionism, led to the foundation of the Trades Union Congress in 1868, and to intensive lobbying by a Parliamentary Committee which the Congress set up.

[1] 'If drink you want and pubs are short / Go to the man in blue. / Say you're thirsty and good-natured and / He'll show you what to do.' Quoted Colin MacInnes, *Sweet Saturday Night* (1967), p. 96. For further evidence on this point see 'Journeyman Engineer' (Thomas Wright), *Some Habits and Customs of the Working Classes* (1867), p. 226.

[2] Reynolds *et al.*, *Seems So!* p. 85.   [3] [1867] 1 Q.B. 715.

It is remarkable how successful the Parliamentary Committee was in securing changes in the law to suit the wishes of the unions. By the Trade Union Act of 1871 the unions ceased to be unlawful on the grounds that their purposes were in restraint of trade; and consequently they were enabled to sue for the protection of their funds. On the other hand, because they were not corporations, they could not in the existing state of the law be sued in tort. By the Conspiracy and Protection of Property Act, 1875, peaceful picketing was legalised and trade disputes were exempted from the law of conspiracy unless the acts concerned were intrinsically criminal. Also in 1875, the Employers and Workmen Act removed the old injustice of the Master and Servant law, whereby workmen, but not employers, could be sent to prison for breach of contract – a provision that had been effectively used by employers in the preceding years in order to break strikes.[1]

Probably the union leaders' success was due in part to the great expansion of trade unionism in the period, which enabled the membership represented at the T.U.C. to reach a peak of almost twelve hundred thousand in 1874 – a figure not again attained until the 1890s. In part, too, the extension of the franchise in 1867 was responsible for an increased concern, perhaps even an exaggerated concern, among the politicians about the electoral danger of defying the unions. Yet another factor, possibly the most important one, was the comparative weakness of employers' organisations, which might have provided a counterweight to the influence of the unions in the Westminster lobbies and in the constituencies.

By the 1890s, however, the situation was changing. The size of firms was growing; there were more effective employers' combinations; and the rise of the militant 'new unions' led to more vigorous attempts to circumscribe union rights. The lawyers had found a way to make ordinary companies suable for the actions of their officers, by the device known as the 'representative action'. The case of *Temperton* v. *Russell*[2] appeared to suggest that this procedure could not be applied to trade unions; and the Royal Commission on Labour, in its report in 1894, accepted this interpretation. Some of the members of the Commission took the

[1] D. Simon, 'Master and Servant', in *Democracy and the Labour Movement*, ed. J. Saville (1954), p. 168.

[2] [1893] 1 Q.B. 435.

view that it would be desirable if the trade unions were given a
'legal personality', so that they could enter into agreements which
could then be enforced against them. This would, they thought,
be a necessary preliminary step if a system of compulsory
arbitration of trade disputes were to be brought into operation.[1]

There were four trade union leaders on the Royal Commission
on Labour, and they signed a joint rebuttal of this proposal. They
assumed, as did the other Commissioners, that the trade unions
were not under the existing law suable in tort. Their view was that
the unions were obviously better off if they could keep out of the
courts: 'If every union were liable to be perpetually harassed by
actions at law on account of the doings of individual members; if
Trade Union funds were to be depleted by lawyers' fees and costs,
if not by damages and fines, it would go far to make Trade
Unionism impossible for any but the most prosperous and
experienced artisans.'[2] This standpoint was endorsed by the
Parliamentary Committee of the T.U.C. and by the Congress
itself at its next meeting.[3] As the employers were also no more
than lukewarm about the idea of compulsory arbitration, which
would of course have involved the recognition of unions in many
industries where they were not yet recognised, the Salisbury
Government decided to do no more than encourage the conciliation
of disputes by voluntary means, which it did by the Conciliation
Act of 1896.

In the later 1890s, however, a section of trade-union opinion
began to see some merit in the idea of compulsory arbitration.
This was in large part the result of events in New Zealand. In that
country trade unionism was very weak, but the Liberal Government in 1894 passed an Industrial Conciliation and Arbitration
Act, which was designed, as its preamble said, 'to encourage the
formation of industrial unions and associations and to facilitate
the settlement of industrial disputes by conciliation and arbitration'.[4] The Act, which was the work of a Minister under the

[1] Final Report, Royal Commission on Labour, *P.P.* 1894, xxxv, 62.
[2] Ibid., p. 154.　　　　　[3] T.U.C. *Report, 1894*, pp. 49–50.
[4] There is a copy of the text in *Report of the Industrial Commission on
Labor Organisations* (Washington, D.C., 1901), pp. 522–32, and this is
followed by a discussion of its success in the early years. See also W. B.
Sutch, *The Quest for Security in New Zealand, 1840–1966* (Wellington,
N.Z., 1966), pp. 99 ff.

influence of Fabian Socialism, William Pember Reeves, contained provisions whereby disputes which were not solved by voluntary conciliation could be determined by compulsory arbitration.[1] The Act in its early years certainly did encourage the growth of unions and this was also accompanied by a rise in wage levels and a general freedom from strikes. As a result of this early success it was copied by legislation in Western Australia in 1900 and in New South Wales in 1901.

The principal supporter of the proposal to introduce this system to Britain was Ben Tillett, secretary of the London Dockers, and it seems that he thought that the major advantage of the system would be that it would force the employers formally to recognise his own and other as yet comparatively weak unions. Tillett visited New Zealand in 1893-4 and again in 1897, and he could argue his case from study of the New Zealand scheme in operation. At a long succession of annual meetings of the T.U.C., beginning in 1899, he proposed a resolution in favour of compulsory arbitration. On each occasion he secured support from the leaders of other unions which had not won the employers' recognition, such as the Railway Servants, the Shop Assistants and the Postal Telegraph Clerks. But he had to face the scepticism of the unions which had already achieved a satisfactory bargaining status, such as the Miners, the Boilermakers and the Compositors. It was unfortunate for Tillett that his campaign coincided with a number of legal decisions adversely affecting the rights of the unions. Thus in 1898 the case of *Lyons* v. *Wilkins*,[2] which considerably limited the rights of picketing, was principally responsible for a resolution of the Congress deploring the 'unsatisfactory decisions recently given by many of our judges in cases affecting trade unions and their officials, such decisions being in opposition to the spirit and intentions of the Acts, and involving many unions in heavy and unnecessary expenditure'.[3] The Parliamentary Committee had intended to take the case of *Lyons* v. *Wilkins* to the House of Lords, but the solicitors failed to put in the appeal in time, partly owing to a mistake in their office, and partly because the union involved in the case had been unable to pay them for services already rendered.[4] Right from the start,

[1] For Reeves's career see K. Sinclair, *William Pember Reeves* (Oxford, 1965).

[2] [1899] 1 ch. 255.   [3] T.U.C. *Report, 1898*, p. 50.   [4] Ibid., *1900*, pp. 33 ff.

therefore, Tillett was on the defensive about the legal system; and in the 1899 debate he had to admit that the judges had displayed hostility to the unions. He explained it by saying that it was 'simply due to their ignorance of economic questions and their class bias'; but he did not say how these difficulties would be overcome in the arbitration court.[1]

The debate on Tillett's resolution in 1900 is an instructive one, for it shows a succession of delegates – by no means all of the skilled and successful unions – declaring their concern about the partiality of the judges. John Ward, of the Navvies' Union, for instance, had this to say: 'There was a great difference between the condition of things in the United Kingdom and those which prevailed in New Zealand, and there should not be considered to be any fair analogy between the two. He should like to know how the delegates would like Mr. Justice Grantham appointed arbitrator in any dispute between employer and employed.'[2] Grantham was a former Conservative M.P. who had been promoted to the Bench by Salisbury's Lord Chancellor, Halsbury, as a reward for political services. Not in any way a distinguished lawyer, he became well-known for his tactless and partisan *obiter dicta*. His career in this respect was as yet by no means at its peak, for he was to occasion a debate in the House of Commons after his failure to convict in a case of Corrupt Practices at Great Yarmouth at the 1906 general election; and in 1911 he was actually publicly rebuked by the Prime Minister for a further indiscreet observation from the bench.

Another of the delegates referred to a different sphere of judicial bias. This was W. Mosses, of the Pattern-makers, who said:

Candidly speaking, he could not trust the judges of this country to give a fair and impartial verdict on any question as to the conditions of labour which might be remitted to them. When they considered the decisions under the Workmen's Compensation Act, what did they think would happen when they had to settle the complex questions raised by arbitration?[3]

James O'Grady of the London Cabinet-makers put the point more generally: 'There they had an absolutely new country, with new ideas, where such an experiment stood a much greater chance of success than in the old country, which was weighed down by

[1] Ibid., *1899*, p. 73.   [2] Ibid., *1900*, p. 77.   [3] Ibid.

centuries of tradition.'[1] The resolution had been defeated in 1899, without a card vote, by 131 to 62. The 1900 resolution was defeated by 939,000 to 246,000.

Even while the 1900 Congress was meeting, the first decision of the Taff Vale case by Mr Justice Farwell was announced;[2] and thereafter this case, with its threat to the liability of the union funds, increasingly dominated the thinking of the union leaders. But they were at first by no means agreed as to what policy they ought to adopt. The secretary of the Railway Servants, whose funds were directly exposed to an action for damages by the Taff Vale decision, was Richard Bell, Labour Member of Parliament for Derby. He thought that the judgment would be 'a useful influence in solidifying the forces of trade unionism and in subjecting them to wholesome discipline'.[3] By this he meant that the rank and file would in future have to adhere to the rules of the union and to the decisions of the executive. He continued to believe in industrial arbitration as the best thing for the unions, and he thought that the judgment would improve the chances of success for a Compulsory Arbitration Bill which he had drafted. At the 1901 T.U.C. the resolution for compulsory arbitration in fact picked up some support and was defeated by a majority of less than two to one – 676,000 to 366,000.[4]

Gradually after this, however, opinion began to harden in favour of the establishment of complete freedom from liability in tort, as had been assumed to be the position before Taff Vale. The reaction was already noticeable at the 1902 T.U.C., when compulsory arbitration was rejected by a margin of over three to one – 961,000 to 303,000.[5] One reason for the shift may have been a growing recognition of the scale of damages which unions might have to pay if their officials were found guilty. The Taff Vale damages case had not yet been completed, but it was known that the Company was asking for £20,000.

At the end of 1902 the T.U.C. Parliamentary Committee

---

[1] Ibid.   [2] [1901] A.C. 426 (contains a summary).

[3] *Clarion*, 27 Jul 1901, quoted F. Bealey and H. Pelling, *Labour and Politics, 1900–6* (1958), p. 75.

[4] T.U.C. *Report, 1901*, p. 69.   [5] Ibid., *1902*, p. 68.

arranged a joint meeting with the executives of the General Federation of Trade Unions – the unions' mutual insurance organisation – and the Labour Representation Committee in order to discuss the terms of a bill which would suit the unions. The bill which was finally agreed gave the unions freedom from liability only in cases where the damages were the result of action which had not been authorised by the union executive. This was, in fact, an acceptance of union liability, very much on the lines which Richard Bell favoured.[1] But when the Labour M.P. David Shackleton came to introduce the bill, for which he had won Private Member's time, he was told by the Speaker that he must drop the clauses referring to union liability as they went beyond the title of the bill which he had earlier submitted – 'A Bill to Legalise the Peaceful Conduct of Trade Disputes'.[2] The bill, in its truncated form, was debated in May 1903 and was defeated by the surprisingly narrow majority of thirty votes.[3] As it turned out, the dropping of the extra clauses was an advantage to the T.U.C.'s cause, for it saved the T.U.C. leaders and its parliamentary spokesmen from some embarrassment in the succeeding months when they changed their official view on the type of measure that was required.

The change in the T.U.C. attitude was effected at the September meeting of Congress. In the preceding few months there had been several events to cause the delegates to be more hostile to union liability in any form. First, in January 1903 there had been the conclusion of the Taff Vale damages case, which resulted in a payment by the union of no less than £23,000 damages and costs.[4] It was known that the South Wales Miners were fighting a case involving even larger damages against the Glamorgan Coal Company – a case later decided against the union by the Lords.[5]

---

[1] According to MacDonald, only one person on the sub-committee which drafted the bill favoured a stronger measure – himself. But he did not approve Hardie's action in attacking the bill in the *Labour Leader*. MacDonald to Glasier, 24 Jan 1903, Glasier Papers.

[2] T.U.C. *Report, 1913*, p. 52.

[3] *H.C.Deb.*, ser. 4, cxxii, 204 ff. (8 May 1903). The bill was originally reported as having been defeated by only twenty votes, but the error was later corrected.

[4] Bealey and Pelling, *Labour and Politics*, pp. 70 f.

[5] [1903] 2 K.B. 545; [1905] A.C. 239.

There was also a dispute at the Denaby and Cadeby Main Collieries in Yorkshire, where an injunction similar to that at the beginning of the Taff Vale case was granted in February 1903.[1] But in addition to this litigation, there was the fact that after the emergence of the Tariff Reform issue in the spring and early summer of 1903 the government appeared to be on the point of collapse, and on the eve of a general election which the Liberals seemed likely to win, some union leaders probably decided to pitch their demands rather higher than they would otherwise have dared. Consequently a resolution instructing the Parliamentary Committee to draft a bill 'which will definitely secure the immunity of Trade Union funds against being sued for damages' was proposed. Bell and Tillett favoured an amendment to endorse the previous session's bill, but this was defeated by 276 votes to 28. Shackleton did not vote. The usual resolution in favour of compulsory arbitration also lost support, being defeated by 899,000 to 251,000.[2]

This was the turning-point for British industrial relations in the early twentieth century. The new, much stronger Trade Union Bill was accepted by the Liberal leadership and carried, on a free vote, by a majority of 39.[3] As John Burns noted in his diary, 'Good result but insincere majority. One on the nose for Halsbury.'[4] Certainly, the upshot was quite contrary to Halsbury's policy as Lord Chancellor; and certainly, too, the Liberals were insincere in their support of the new T.U.C. bill, as became evident in 1906, when they framed legislation on the lines of that which they had supported in 1903. But by that time it was too late. The Labour Party demanded full freedom from liability for union funds, and there were enough Liberal M.P.s committed to it by their election promises to ensure its substitution for the less drastic measure.

As for compulsory arbitration, this retained a certain degree of support, notably among the intellectuals, but it was less and less successful at the annual T.U.C. meetings. Its advocates tried to ensure the success of their annual resolution by weakening its

[1] The employers eventually lost the appeal for damages. [1906] A.C. 384. The original injunction was given by Mr Justice Grantham.

[2] T.U.C. *Report, 1903*, pp. 67–71, 84.

[3] *H.C.Deb.*, ser. 4, cxxxiii, 1007 (22 Apr 1904).

[4] John Burns's Diary, B.M. Add. Mss. 46322 (22 Apr 1904).

content – in particular, by making it possible for the employers and unions in particular industries to opt out if they wished. Even this emasculated resolution, however, did not pass. Sidney Webb, who was in favour of compulsory arbitration, served on a Royal Commission on Trade Disputes which the Unionist Government appointed in 1903, and with which the T.U.C. refused to co-operate, on the grounds that no trade-union leader was to be appointed as a Commissioner.[1] Webb signed the Commission's report, which favoured the retention of union liability, and he added a rider pointing to the desirability of arbitration on the model of New Zealand and the Australian states.[2] Pember Reeves, the architect of the New Zealand legislation, was now in England, first as the colony's Agent-General and later as the Director of the London School of Economics; and he publicised the idea of arbitration within the British Labour movement, and particularly through the Fabian Society.

After 1903, however, and even more after 1906, there was little prospect of the adoption of compulsory arbitration in Britain. The strong unions had won the day for the policy of complete freedom from the law; and as the weaker unions came also to be strong, they accepted this attitude. It is possible that the T.U.C. might have voted in favour of arbitration if they had had a little more faith in the existing legal system and in the judges who administered it. But Lord Halsbury, whose political partisanship in appointing judges had actually aroused a gentle rebuke from his own Prime Minister, Lord Salisbury, had seen to it that the bench was overwhelmingly Conservative.[3] This meant sometimes that men who were not particularly good lawyers were elevated to the bench.

This is not to say that the Taff Vale Judgment, or any other

[1] T.U.C. *Report, 1903*, p. 53.

[2] Report of Royal Commission on Trade Disputes and Trade Combinations, *P.P.* 1906, lvi, 22. He had already expressed similar views in S. and B. Webb, *Industrial Democracy* (1902 ed.), xlii ff.

[3] 'The judicial salad requires both legal oil and political vinegar; but disastrous results will follow if due proportion is not observed.' Salisbury to Halsbury, Nov 1897, quoted R. F. V. Heuston, *Lives of the Lord Chancellors* (Oxford, 1964), p. 57.

decision of the period, was 'bad law', resulting from a conspiracy of lawyers and employers against the unions. The Osborne Judgment, perhaps, was 'bad law', but this occurred after the decisive period that we have been considering. The judges did not always decide against the unions, and even when they did, as over the liability of union funds, the decision seemed to be the result of a long process of change in legal procedure which had in origin little to do with trade unionism – in particular, in the development of the procedure of the 'representative action'. The Court of Appeal was certainly extraordinarily restrictive in its Workmen's Compensation decisions early in the century; but this had the effect of making the House of Lords appear liberal on this subject, so much so that they actually obtained approval even at the T.U.C. It was their *obiter dicta* that condemned the judges, as much as their actual decisions; and they aroused the hostility, not just of Socialists, but of trade unionists who were otherwise the mildest of Liberals.

The lines of division among the union leaders about arbitration and about union liability provide a striking illustration of the way in which the needs of their particular organisations, rather than any general political bias, could determine their attitude. The supporters of arbitration and of making the best of the Taff Vale Judgment ranged from 'Lib-Labs' like Bell to Fabian Socialists such as Sidney Webb and Independent Labour men such as Tillett. The opposite view, on the other hand, was taken not only by Keir Hardie and others, who hoped to make some advantage out of it for the sake of building up the Labour Representation Committee, but also the miners' leaders, who were predominantly loyal to the Liberal Party.

Nor is there anything surprising about this. The theoretical claims of Socialism were here in conflict with the practical questions of union rights and working-class militancy. Liberal-Labour men could be just as militant as Socialists in situations which were not concerned with the substitution of one entire economic system for another. And Socialists who were in positions of responsibility in the unions could feel acutely the tug of their rival loyalties. George Barnes, the secretary of the Engineers and a member of the I.L.P. (he was later to be a member of the War Cabinet in 1917–18) expressed his own dilemma in a letter to Sidney Webb in 1903:

Are we to try to get back to ante-Taff Vale, or should we have some closer connection with the law? My inclinations are to the latter, but I must say that the difficulties and complexities of the situation seem to me almost unsurmountable, and that possibly the best thing for propaganda purposes at present is ante-Taff Vale. But here again I am landed in a difficulty, as it seems to me that ante-Taff Vale is after all anti-social and but a glorified individualism, inasmuch as it seeks to get for groups of men anti-social rights.[1]

So too in the later twentieth century there is a conflict between the national, and perhaps also the Socialist, interest on the one hand, and the interests of particular trade unions on the other. If the unions still remain largely loyal to what Professor Kahn-Freund has called their tradition of 'collective *laissez-faire*',[2] this is not least because the legal system itself remains, in spite of certain changes, about as much out of touch with the realities and need of contemporary British life as it was over half a century ago.

[1] Barnes to Webb, 9 Jun 1903, Webb Papers, British Library of Political and Economic Science.
[2] O. Kahn-Freund in *Law and Opinion in England in the Twentieth Century*, ed. M. Ginsberg (1959), p. 227.

5 British Labour and
British Imperialism

It is sometimes maintained that the British working class in the generation before the First World War was largely infected with Jingoism, or Imperialism, and was consequently inclined to abandon what otherwise should have been its natural political attitude – namely, a desire for international tranquillity, coupled with an emphasis on the need for domestic social change. We may have our doubts whether social change was a deeply-felt concern of the working people in this period.[1] Let us, however, put them aside for present purposes, and engage in an examination of the evidence for Jingoism or Imperialism as a popular sentiment in the late nineteenth and in the early twentieth century.

It is clear at the outset that Imperialism as an intellectual theory was a matter for the middle class, or at any rate for those who were sufficiently well educated to read comparatively abstract books. It was the same, of course, with Socialism. Seeley's *Expansion of England* was no doubt more intelligible, if less profound, than Marx's *Capital*; its working-class readership was probably no larger. Just as, for the masses, Socialism arrived in the somewhat bowdlerised and sentimental form of Blatchford's *Merrie England*, so too Imperialism could reach down only in the catchy slogans of Kipling's verse and in the leaders of Harmsworth's *Daily Mail*. Yet even the halfpenny *Daily Mail* was a paper for the lower middle class, rather than for the manual worker;[2] and Imperialism had even less success than Socialism in influencing the spokesmen of labour. Of the dozen trade-union leaders who were in the House of Commons at the outbreak of the South African War – all of them members of the Liberal Party – only one, Havelock Wilson, the seamen's leader, was inclined to take the 'imperialist' side on the issue of the South African War.[3]

[1] See Ch. 1. [2] F. Williams, *Dangerous Estate* (1957), p. 143.
[3] He had been called 'Havelock' after General Sir Henry Havelock, of Indian Mutiny fame. See his autobiography *My Stormy Voyage Through Life* (1925), p. 6.

After the 1900 election there were to begin with only nine trade-union leaders in the new Parliament, but they were all opposed to the war, Havelock Wilson having been one of those defeated.

It is instructive to observe that these 'Lib-Labs', as they were called, based their opposition to the war on grounds which were in some ways distinctive, and which were likely to appeal strongly to people of their own social origin. The actual breach between Britain and the Transvaal Republic in 1899 had come about over the unwillingness of the latter to give the franchise to recent British immigrants, of whom there were a substantial number at the Transvaal mines. The 'Lib-Labs', in their assessment of the causes of the war, naturally pointed to the contrast between the Unionist Government's concern to enfranchise these immigrants in South Africa and its evident lack of interest in the question of enfranchising the British working class at home: for it was still the case that only a little over half the adult male population of Britain was on the register of electors. W. C. Steadman made this point to the 1899 Trades Union Congress: 'With our present electoral system not one-half of the million and a quarter workers whom this Congress represents would have a vote if an election took place on the morrow.'[1] And W. M. Thompson, the editor of the popular weekly *Reynolds's Newspaper* – which must be added to Halévy's very inadequate list of those newspapers which opposed the war[2] – wrote in October 1899, just as it broke out: 'If the war . . . has no other use it will at least have taught people this great lesson – that where in any country the franchise is denied, even to foreigners, it is not only just, but it is an absolute duty to use force to acquire it.'[3]

If then the franchise was simply a trumped-up excuse for war, what was the real cause? Here the 'Lib-Labs' drew upon that suspicion of capitalist motivation which was common to working men of all political views. According to Fred Maddison, one of their number who was much criticised by the Socialists as being a hanger-on of Liberalism, 'It was not a desire for political power, but for Stock Exchange purposes, that the agitation against the

[1] T.U.C. *Report, 1899*, p. 85.

[2] É. Halévy, *History of the English People: Epilogue,* i (1929), 95. To Halévy's list should also be added the *Morning Leader* and the *Star*.

[3] *Reynolds's Newspaper,* 8 Oct 1899.

Boer Government was started.'[1] The view was shared by the other
'Lib-Labs'. According to Ben Pickard, the Yorkshire Miners'
leader, 'this Transvaal crisis was a matter of money and land,
rather than the seeking of the franchise for people who did not
want it'. He urged the 1899 Trades Union Congress to declare:
'We are not going to vote for the capitalists of this country to
make millions to squander, and become monopolists in every
department of trade.'[2]

But the suspicions of the 'Lib-Labs' did not stop at the
suggestion that the capitalists wanted war for the sake of profit.
They also held that the profit was to be made at the expense of the
working man, whose wages and conditions in the Transvaal were
to some degree being protected by the Boer Government. Thus
John Burns, speaking in Battersea Park only a few days after the
relief of Mafeking in May 1900, maintained that the war presaged
a decline in the conditions of labour in South Africa. It was part
of his argument that the capitalist interests working under the
cover of the British flag were themselves alien, and hence all the
less likely to treat British labour with respect: 'The South
African Jews have . . . no bowels of compassion. . . . The slave of
the centuries, the persecuted of all time, released from the
restraint of disciplined control, gained a cash ascendancy.' Yet in
spite of this, for a time 'the British workman made good wages'
because: 'The alien capitalists were kept in check by Kruger, and
the workmen were able to hold their own.'[3] The same point, with
its flavouring of the anti-semitism that was so widespread at this
time, was made at the 1900 Trades Union Congress by at least two
of the delegates speaking about South Africa. One of them was
John Ward, the Navvies' leader and from 1906 onwards a 'Lib-
Lab' M.P., who said:

Practically £100,000,000 of the taxpayers' money had been spent
in trying to secure the goldfields of South Africa for cosmopolitan
Jews, most of whom had no patriotism and no country. . . . There
was also a question from the labour point of view. Did they
imagine that the wages on the Rand under Rhodes, Beit and

[1] F. Maddison, 'Why British Workmen Condemn the War', *North
American Review*, clxx, 523.

[2] T.U.C. *Report, 1899*, p. 86.

[3] J. Burns, *War Against the Two Republics* (1900), p. 4.

Eckstein would be as high as those which prevailed under the old farmers?[1]

Just at this time there were reports that Rhodes was in favour of importing Chinese labour into the Transvaal mines; and these reports provided some substance for the fears of the 'Lib-Labs'. The same Congress carried by a large majority a resolution condemning the proposal, which it described as 'to the detriment of British subjects both here and in South Africa'.[2] It became a key issue in at least one constituency at the 'khaki' general election which ensued. This was the Cornish division of Camborne, where many of the electors were tin-miners contemplating migration to the gold-mines of South Africa owing to the depression in Cornish tin. The retiring Unionist member, A. Strauss, in his election address denounced his Liberal opponent's 'political dodge' of suggesting that Chinese labour was to be used in the Transvaal;[3] and Rhodes was induced to send a message denying any intention of seeking to import Chinese into South Africa.[4] In the upshot, Camborne swung heavily to the Liberals (a 4·8% swing, at a time when the national swing was going the other way). But there were other factors to account for this, and since miners elsewhere in the country seem to have shown less loyalty to Liberalism on this occasion than in any other election of the period, it cannot be said for certain that Strauss was a victim of the first 'Chinese labour' scare.

Clearly, however, as early as the first year of the war there had emerged a distinctive working-class standpoint on its origins. To be sure, many of the arguments used were common to middle-class Liberal spokesmen also: but the emphasis was different. Moreover, this was a standpoint held by the great majority of politically active trade-union leaders. It is possible to find the occasional union leader who supported the war. W. J. Davis of the Birmingham Brassworkers was one: and according to his biographer he lost his seat on the Parliamentary Committee of the T.U.C. as a result.[5] Since Birmingham was the centre of Chamberlain's influence, there must have been many supporters of the war in Davis's own union, and his attitude may have been dictated by this fact. Alexander Wilkie of the Shipwrights, who fought

[1] T.U.C. *Report, 1900*, pp. 54 f.   [2] T.U.C. *Report, 1901*, p. 91.
[3] *Cornish Post*, 20 Sep 1900.   [4] Ibid., 11 Oct 1900.
[5] W. A. Dalley, *Life Story of W. J. Davis* (Birmingham, 1914), p. 294.

Sunderland as a candidate of the newly-founded Labour Representation Committee, shared his platform with a Liberal Imperialist candidate in this two-member constituency, but it is by no means clear that he himself was inclined to support the war, as he did everything he could to avoid discussion of the matter. It is difficult to discover any other prominent union leaders who openly supported the war. Obviously the 'little England' attitude was unpopular among workers of certain occupations which benefited from a strong foreign and defence policy, as for instance shipbuilding and the Birmingham metal trades. There was also a good deal of long-term sympathy for Unionism among working-class electors in Glasgow and Liverpool, where the rivalry of the Orange and the Green was strong. Professor Frank Bealey's study of popular reactions to the South African War suggests that in Scotland, where the trades councils took a definite line on the war, there was a marked contrast between Glasgow and other cities. Whereas the Edinburgh and Aberdeen trades councils declared their opposition to the war, the Glasgow organisation was in support.[1] Indeed, 400 Clydeside shipwrights marched to Glasgow University to demand the expulsion of a pro-Boer professor.[2]

Yet among the organised workers, these manifestations of support for the war were exceptional. Obviously, once war had broken out, there were those who thought that it was wrong to provide comfort for the enemy or embarrassment for British troops. There were also those who thought that too emphatic a political participation by the unions at a time when people's views were sharply divided would be bad for the unions' industrial functions, which after all deserved first place in their deliberations. All the same, the T.U.C. committed itself against the war to a considerable degree. In 1899, in a rather hurried debate on the last day of the meeting, Congress passed a resolution demanding a peaceful solution to the conflict, which had not yet reached the stage of hostilities.[3] In 1900 a resolution condemning the war was carried by a small majority, with a large body of delegates refusing to vote.[4] In 1901 a resolution calling for immediate peace negotiations was moved, but it was held to be contrary to Con-

[1] F. Bealey, 'Les Travaillistes et la Guerre des Boers', *Le Mouvement Social*, no. 45 (1963), pp. 56 f.

[2] S. C. Cronwright-Schreiner, *The Land of Free Speech* (1906), p. 75.

[3] T.U.C. *Report, 1899*, pp. 85–7.   [4] T.U.C. *Report, 1900*, pp. 54 f.

gress's new standing orders, and it was decided by a considerable majority not to discuss it further.[1] In 1902 a move to amend the Parliamentary Report in order to brand the war as 'unjust' was carried, on a card vote, by 591,000 to 314,000. On the latter occasion W. J. Davis was one of two speakers against the proposal.[2] On the whole, the record justifies the view expressed by Fred Maddison in the first year of the war that: 'Among what may be called the regular body of workmen there has never existed anything which could fairly be called enthusiasm.'[3]

But it is clear that we have to distinguish between the 'regular body of workmen' – that is, the trade unions and their spokesmen – and the remainder of the working class, whose sentiments we can measure only in more indirect ways. The evidence for popular sympathy with Imperialism is based upon five distinct phenomena, each of which deserves separate examination. These are, first of all, the expression of imperialist feeling in music-hall songs of the period; secondly, the flood of recruits for the army during the South African War; thirdly, the enthusiasm in popular demonstrations at notable events during the war, and particularly after the relief of Mafeking in May 1900; fourthly, the breaking-up of anti-war meetings during the first year of the war; and finally, the Unionist election victories of 1895 and 1900.

J. A. Hobson, the leading critic of Imperialism, described the art of the music hall as 'the only popular art of the present-day',[4] but popular though it was, there are still great difficulties in assessing its significance. Thus, for instance, a song such as 'Beer, glorious beer', which was sung in the 1890s, may be taken as some evidence of the general popularity of the beverage concerned, but it does not necessarily indicate a rising consumption of beer in that decade as opposed to the 1880s, nor does it imply much as to the proportion of heavy drinkers to teetotallers in the working class as a whole. So far as Imperialism is concerned, we must distinguish between this and 'Jingoism' – a term derived directly from a music-hall song – and also between both of these and the sentiment of songs which simply reflect the soldier's courage or the

[1] T.U.C. *Report, 1901,* pp. 37, 81.   [2] T.U.C. *Report, 1902,* p. 36.

[3] Maddison, *North American Review,* clxx, 519.

[4] J. A. Hobson, *Psychology of Jingoism* (1901), p. 3.

seafarer's enjoyment of distant ports. The song which caused the coining of the nouns 'jingo' and 'Jingoism' was one sung at the time of the crisis of the Eastern Question in the late 1870s:

> We don't want to fight, but, by jingo! if we do,
> We've got the ships, we've got the men, we've got the money too.
> We've fought the Bear before, and while Britons shall be true,
> The Russians shall not have Constantinople.

It will be apparent that while these words form a strident assertion of British power in the Mediterranean and its approaches, they also indicate an unwillingness to initiate hostilities, and imply a conception that, if hostilities do take place, they will be confined to a conflict at sea, the issue being the protection of Turkish sovereignty. It is difficult to see anything here distinctively 'imperialist', in the late nineteenth-century or twentieth-century understanding of that word. The most careful recent study of popular opinion at the time of the Eastern Question crisis tells us that it is impossible to 'sustain a generalisation' as to whether the working class was stronger in the support of Gladstone or of Disraeli at this juncture.[1]

Of course it is true that songs relating in some way to expansion overseas were popular in the late nineteenth century; but this had long been the case. Kipling's *Road to Mandalay* is an example, but its theme, the attractions of a Burmese maiden to a visiting British soldier, hardly seems to fit in with the idea of the 'White Man's Burden'. When the South African War broke out, naturally there were soldiers' songs, though a recent student of the subject suggests that by comparison with the Crimean War a 'marked element of satire' had crept in with the military sentiment.[2] It may also be significant that the most popular song sung by Leo Dryden, sometimes called 'the Kipling of the Halls', was *The Miner's Dream of Home* – hardly a song of imperial purpose.[3]

If the evidence from 'the halls' is somewhat dubious, it may be argued that enthusiasm for the South African War was shown by the large-scale voluntary enlistment in the army. But recruits join up for a variety of reasons, of which unemployment is one of the most important. In 1899 and 1900 the patriotic motive could be combined with the hope of finding a job in South Africa without

[1] R. T. Shannon, *Gladstone and the Bulgarian Agitation* (1963), p. 234.
[2] C. MacInnes, *Sweet Saturday Night* (1967), p. 75.   [3] Ibid., p. 81.

the need to pay any passage money to get there. Even so, however, the great bulk of recruits in the early stages of the war appear to have been of relatively high social status. The Imperial Yeomanry, the Duke of Cambridge's Own (who paid the cost of their own passage to the Cape), Lovat's Scouts, the Honourable Artillery Company, the City Imperial Volunteers – these were typical units which went out after the regulars, and it appears that a majority of all those who embarked in the first six months of 1900 were of the upper or middle classes.[1]

It was partly for this reason that the relief of Mafeking occasioned such remarkable demonstrations of enthusiasm in Britain. Working-class people were always willing to display their emotions in public, if given the opportunity by those guardians of law and order, the middle classes. The exceptional feature of the 'mafficking' was that the middle classes, who normally kept a 'stiff upper lip', joined in. All the reports comment on the fact that people of every social class participated in the celebrations, and, as the *Annual Register* put it, fraternised 'in a way so opposed to our national coldness and reserve that a foreigner might have thought that some crowning victory had been achieved. From a military point of view the event was a small one. . . .'[2]

The relief of the beleaguered town was in fact acclaimed by all who respected individual achievement against odds, as is shown by the comments of Keir Hardie, one of the most determined of the 'pro-Boers':

The cheery courage and never-failing resource with which Baden-Powell had met the seven long and weary months during which he was shut up in the small brick town evoked the heartiest appreciation, and appealed to everything that is most likeable in human nature. Small wonder, therefore, that after hope had almost deserted the British people the news of the relief should have sent all classes literally mad with joy.[3]

Hardie perhaps had an axe to grind in suggesting that the enthusiasm was not in itself an indication of support for the war as such: but as it happens the verdict of Joseph Chamberlain's official biographer, J. L. Garvin, is on the same lines: 'The pluck and wits of a British handful had won against the odds'.[4] Such a

---

[1] R. Kruger, *Goodbye Dolly Gray* (1959), pp. 151 f.
[2] *Annual Register, 1900*, p. 127.   [3] *Labour Leader*, 26 May 1901.
[4] J. L. Garvin, *Life of Joseph Chamberlain*, iii (1934), 550.

victory against superior numbers was reassuring after so much bad news, which had given the impression that the Boers were the only people who really knew how to fight. It was not realised at the time that the survival of the Mafeking garrison was due more to good luck than to good management.[1]

The imponderables in assessing popular feeling are such that one cannot but feel misgiving when confronted by statements such as this one, offered by Koebner and Schmidt: 'As 1898 was drawing to a close, Imperialism had reached its zenith of respectability and popular acclaim.'[2] The only evidence which they adduce to support this statement is the fact that the year 1899 saw the development of criticism of Imperialism, and particularly of South African policy, by politicians such as John Morley and Lloyd George, and by journalists such as W. T. Stead and J. A. Hobson. Yet in 1897–9 the by-elections went heavily against the Unionists;[3] and in March 1898 Chamberlain could warn that: 'A war with the Transvaal, unless upon the utmost and clearest provocation, would be extremely unpopular in this country.'[4] During the war itself, however, the breaking-up of anti-war meetings may suggest a much more active 'popular acclaim' for Imperialism than anything that had taken place previously. It would be difficult to maintain that the war was unpopular in its early stages, or that politicians and newspapers opposing it were likely to gain greater influence as an immediate result.

Nevertheless it seems constantly to have been people of the middle and upper classes who led the way in attacking the anti-war minority. This even applies to physical force at pro-Boer meetings. There is a good deal of evidence that those who led the disturbances were of fairly high social status. The biographer of Thomas Burt, who chaired an anti-war meeting at Newcastle on the very day of Kruger's ultimatum, has a circumstantial account which puts the prime responsibility on medical students.[5] S. C.

---

[1] See B. Gardner, *Mafeking* (1966) for a critical account.

[2] R. Koebner and H. D. Schmidt, *Imperialism* (Cambridge, 1964), pp. 219 f.

[3] J. P. D. Dunbabin, 'Parliamentary Elections in Great Britain, 1868–1900: A Psephological Note', *English Historical Review*, lxxxi (1966), 93.

[4] Garvin, *Chamberlain*, iii, 366.

[5] A. Watson, *A Great Labour Leader* (1908), p. 198.

Cronwright-Schreiner, the South African 'pro-Boer' who spoke at a series of meetings in Britain in the early months of 1900 and who later wrote a most detailed narrative of his experiences, repeatedly blamed students, and particularly medical students, for leading the uproar when he tried to speak in public in Scotland, whether at Glasgow, at Edinburgh or at Dundee.[1] By contrast, his more distinctively working-class audiences, as at Canning Town and at Battersea, were quiet and attentive[2] – though this may have owed something to careful organisation of the meetings concerned by Radical or Socialist bodies which knew by long experience how to deal with rowdyism. The evidence perhaps affords some justification for J. A. Hobson's view that the most striking feature of popular reaction to the war was the 'credulity displayed by the educated classes'.[3] Compared to this the fact that many uneducated persons were 'misled' was altogether less remarkable.

But the only way of obtaining some sort of statistical expression of people's feelings on imperial questions is by looking at the election returns. Here again, however, a preliminary note of caution is necessary. In the 1895 election, in particular, various domestic questions played a more important part in determining people's voting behaviour than the issue of imperial expansion. Koebner and Schmidt tell us, without quoting evidence, that: 'The election of 1895 gave Salisbury and Chamberlain a majority which could be interpreted by contemporaries as a large vote for Empire expansionism and a defeat of the "little Englanders".'[4] It is not clear why contemporaries should have interpreted it in this light. Rosebery as Liberal Foreign Secretary and, after Gladstone's retirement, as Prime Minister, had insisted on a complete continuity of foreign policy with the Unionists; and the occasion of Gladstone's retirement had been the Cabinet's insistence upon a considerable expansion of naval building (the Spencer programme). What was much more an issue between the parties was the Liberal attempt to secure a measure of temperance reform, involving Local Option on the closing of public houses – a proposal which aroused much hostility not only on the part of the powerful pressure-group of brewers and licensed victuallers, but also, it would appear, among a large section of the working class who were

---

[1] Cronwright-Schreiner, *Land of Free Speech*, pp. 64, 79, 98, 122.
[2] Ibid., pp. 15–18, 284.   [3] Hobson, *Psychology of Jingoism*, p. 21.
[4] Koebner and Schmidt, *Imperialism*, p. 207.

most likely to suffer under the restrictions. There was also a
tendency in late nineteenth-century elections, unreasonable
though it may have been, to blame the outgoing government for
any trade depression which had occurred within a few months of
the dissolution; and times had certainly been bad in 1893–4. In
the background of the election there loomed the issue of Irish
Home Rule, but this was not a novel issue in the 1895 election,
nor did it bulk quite as large then as in 1886 or in 1892. In all these
elections the greatest strength of the Unionist Party was in
middle-class constituencies rather than in working-class ones,
though there were also marked regional differences. Taken as a
whole, Wales and Scotland continued to favour Liberalism, while
England was strongly Unionist.[1]

In 1900 the Unionists again won a general election – the 'khaki'
election which was fought after the military successes of the
summer of 1900. There is little doubt that the war was the major
issue of the election, and we may concede that had it not been for
the war the Unionists might well have been defeated. Salisbury
said after the election: 'That the love of justice should have
overborne the great law of the pendulum I confess puzzles and
bewilders me.'[2] One factor that he might have taken into account,
before putting the 'love of justice' as the main reason, was the
tendency of war to overcome the downswing of the trade cycle,
thus depriving the electorate of a customary grudge against the
government. Another factor was that the Liberals were seriously
divided in their attitude to the war, and practically leaderless as a
result. There were personal quarrels involved in this: Rosebery's
touchiness and egotism were matched by Harcourt's incapacity
for working in harness with colleagues.[3] Campbell-Bannerman,
who assumed the leadership in 1898, was a less outstanding
personality than either Rosebery or Harcourt, but, as time was to
show, a better man for reconciling the factions of the party. By
the time of the 1900 election, however, he had hardly had time
to assert himself as a national leader.

In view of this it is remarkable that the Liberals performed as

[1] See my *Social Geography of British Elections* (1967) for further
documentation of these points.

[2] Quoted in J. P. Mackintosh, *The British Cabinet* (1962), p. 198.

[3] For an account of the difficulties of the Liberal leadership, see P.
Stansky, *Ambitions and Strategies* (Oxford, 1964).

well as they did in the 1900 election. The party funds were in low water, and many seats had to be left uncontested simply for financial reasons. Yet they actually secured seven more seats than they had won at the 1895 election, though that still left the Unionists with a substantial majority. Comparing the median constituency vote in the two elections, we find that there was a slight overall swing to the Unionists in Britain as a whole. Wales, however, inclined to sympathise with the Boers who were felt to be fellow-victims of English aggrandisement, and the median constituency vote for the Unionists declined there from 43·6 to 35·0.[1] In England it went up from 54·0 to 57·0, and in Scotland, where English attitudes to Empire were more or less shared, it went from 48·5 to 50·4. For the first time Scotland returned a majority of Unionist members.

Not all of these shifts of opinion, however, are to be put down to the South African War. There is some evidence that the behaviour of the Irish voters was an important determining element in British urban constituencies which showed a considerable swing. The question of Irish Home Rule was not felt to be as immediately relevant in 1900 as in 1895, and the Irish Nationalist Party had not yet recovered from its divisions. The Catholic priests were urging their flocks to vote in support of any candidates who were willing to pledge themselves in favour of a Catholic University for Ireland. This proposal commended itself to a good many Unionist candidates, some of whom won Irish Catholic support as a result. Among those to benefit was Bonar Law, in the Blackfriars division of Glasgow.[2] This appears to be the main explanation of a strange feature of the elections, namely, that the larger towns swung towards the Unionists, while the countryside swung against: for the Irish vote was predominantly urban.

Contemporaries were much impressed with the success of Unionist candidates in working-class constituencies of large towns, and ever since it has been accepted that the working class gave a striking vote of approval to the government for its conduct

[1] Dr K. O. Morgan thinks that Wales's support of the Boers is a 'myth of modern Welsh history'; but his evidence, that *some* Welshmen supported the war, and that *many* engaged in 'mafficking', is not in my view conclusive. *Wales in British Politics, 1868–1922* (Cardiff, 1963), pp. 178 f.

[2] *Scotsman*, 5 Sep 1900.

of the war. The success of Unionism in East London, where in fact Irish voters were not particularly numerous, has been especially remarked.[1] But a careful examination of the East End contests indicates yet another important component in the campaign. This was the issue of Jewish immigration, which was reaching a peak at this time, and which aroused considerable xenophobia among the indigenous population owing to the rising rents and the competition for jobs which it occasioned. The East End Unionists promised legislation to reduce immigration, and won many votes thereby. In due course the promises were fulfilled, in the form of the Aliens Act of 1905.[2]

The evidence that opponents of the war did particularly badly at the polls is by no means convincing, except for constituencies in the remoter parts of Scotland and in the English North-East. The Scottish crofters were often Naval Reservists, and the crofting counties also supplied many army regulars. In North-East England, seafaring and shipbuilding combined with a military tradition to make for strong support for the war. Hence Dr G. B. Clark, a leading pro-Boer, was easily evicted from the representation of Caithness by a Liberal Imperialist; and Thomas Burt and Charles Fenwick, the Northumberland miners' leaders, without losing their seats both suffered serious wastage of their usually massive majorities. Among the pro-Boer 'Lib-Labs', W. C. Steadman and Fred Maddison were defeated, at Stepney and Sheffield, Brightside, respectively; but W. R. Cremer, who had similar convictions, won back the seat which he had lost in 1895 at Shoreditch. At Merthyr Tydfil the 'pro-Boer' I.L.P. leader Keir Hardie defeated a sitting Liberal Imperialist; and Havelock Wilson, in spite of his support for the war, was defeated at Middlesbrough. The swing against John Burns at Battersea and Labouchere at Northampton was well below the national average, though both were 'pro-Boers'; and another leading opponent of the war, F. A. Channing, actually increased his majority at Northamptonshire East.

It is true that the opponents of the war, and particularly those who had witnessed the violence at anti-war meetings, were distressed by what they regarded as the failure of democracy in

[1] *Annual Register, 1900*, p. 207; S. MacCoby, *English Radicalism, 1886–1914* (1953), p. 302.

[2] See my *Social Geography of British Elections*, pp. 44–6.

re-electing the Unionists; and J. A. Hobson wrote his book *The Psychology of Jingoism* to explain what another 'pro-Boer', G. P. Gooch, called 'the spiritual demoralisation which war brings in its train, the clouding of the mind, the paralysis of the critical faculties'.[1] But the Unionists, although they rejoiced in what they took to be the popular mood, were very soon doubtful how long they could rely upon it as a lasting characteristic. Alfred Milner, the High Commissioner in South Africa, thought that the election had taken place only 'in the nick of time',[2] and by early 1901 was expressing to Chamberlain his fears of a 'wobble' in public opinion. Chamberlain, in writing to reassure him, nevertheless admitted that: 'If some progress is not made before long I think public dissatisfaction may become serious and threaten the position of the Government in spite of its enormous majority.'[3]

Nor were these premonitions unjustified. By 1902 by-elections were going heavily against the government, and from then until the general election of 1906 it was evident that Unionism had lost the confidence of the country. For the final defeat, Chamberlain was inclined to blame factors outside the sphere for which he was responsible: he thought that the Education Act of 1902 alienated large numbers of Nonconformists and really turned the country. It was partly because of his feeling that it was necessary to 'change the issue' that he introduced his proposals for Tariff Reform, with their emphasis on the needs of imperial consolidation.[4] Whether or not he misjudged the impact of the Education Act – and there is room for doubt here – it is quite clear that he grossly miscalculated the popular reaction to Tariff Reform. Only a minority of people felt that their economic circumstances would be benefited by the fiscal changes he proposed: the great majority felt that the result would be, not only damage to major exporting industries, but also a sharp increase in the cost of living. The old slogans of fiscal controversy which had served the Liberals many times in the past – in particular 'the Big Loaf versus the Little Loaf' – were resurrected once again and had a powerful effect at the 1906 election. If one thing was clearly demonstrated by that

[1] G. P. Gooch, *Under Six Reigns* (1958), p. 87. Cf. also 'Ralph Lane' (Norman Angell), *Patriotism under Three Flags* (1903).

[2] Garvin, *Chamberlain*, iii, 621.

[3] J. Amery, *Life of Joseph Chamberlain*, iv (1951), 27 f.

[4] Ibid., p. 514.

election, it was that the electors were not prepared to pursue the hope of imperial consolidation if it involved any diminution of their immediate standard of life.

The question of Tariff Reform was without doubt the most important issue in 1906. There was, however, a secondary issue of imperial significance: the issue of Chinese labour in the South African mines. We have already seen that locally at least this issue had proved a tender one at the 1900 election, and that the repudiation of the proposal by Cecil Rhodes had been solicited by supporters of the Unionist cause. At that time, it seems clear, Rhodes was in fact hostile to the proposal.[1] It gained popularity only two or three years' later, when it became apparent that there was a shortage of labour in the mines. The mine-owners argued that white workers were too expensive for the unskilled work, and in any case they refused to undertake what was known as 'Kaffirs' work'. There was a shortage of native labour which, it was argued, could only be made up by recruiting abroad – and the best place to get a cheap labour supply would be China. In order to ensure that the Chinese did not become a permanent element in the South African population, they were to be kept in compounds at the mines, and were to bring no women or children with them.[2]

There were many critics of the policy of the mine-owners. The Boer population of the Transvaal feared the introduction of a new element into their country, and mineworkers of all races were concerned about the impact of the Chinese upon their own jobs. It was difficult to argue with the mine-owners at the level of management policy, but one experienced manager, F. H. P. Creswell of the Village Main Reef Gold Mining Company, maintained that there was no acute shortage of labour and that in any case the mines could gradually be taken over by white labour, particularly if machinery were introduced to eliminate the more unskilled jobs. Both in California and in Australia gold-mines were able to pay their way although entirely worked by white labour.[3]

[1] J. G. Lockhart and C. M. Woodhouse, *Rhodes* (1953), p. 453.

[2] For the evolution of the policy see C. Headlam (ed.), *The Milner Papers*, ii (1933), pp. 438 ff.; G. B. Pyrah, *Imperial Policy and South Africa* (Oxford, 1955), pp. 188–98.

[3] F. H. P. Creswell, 'The Transvaal Labour Problem', *Independent Review*, ii (1904).

The question became a burning political issue in Britain in 1903 when Milner, in spite of local opposition in the Transvaal, decided in favour of the scheme and secured the approval of Alfred Lyttelton, Chamberlain's successor as Colonial Secretary. Milner argued that the introduction of the Chinese for a limited period would in fact stimulate the flow of British immigrants to take the more skilled jobs at the mines, as the demand for skilled workers expanded with the supply of unskilled. But the policy was highly vulnerable on two grounds. In the first place, the conditions in which the Chinese were to live were degrading: they were to be second-class citizens in a sense in which native labour was not, for native labour was at least free to enjoy ordinary family life. Secondly, after having given people in Britain the idea that a main purpose of the war was to open up the whole of South Africa to British immigration, it was very difficult to explain the need for Chinese labour instead. As we have seen, it had been argued by the opponents of the war that it was being fought solely for the benefit of the mine-owners, who simply wanted to reduce the cost of labour.

It was the humanitarian aspect of the proposals which was taken up most strongly by Liberal politicians. They spoke of the conditions of work for the Chinese as 'slavery'. The Unionists replied that the conditions in the compounds were good, and that it was hypocritical to denounce a form of indentured labour which in fact existed elsewhere in the British Empire without attracting unfavourable notice.[1] But the Unionist case suffered a heavy blow just before the 1906 election, when it was revealed that Milner had authorised the infliction of corporal punishment on the Chinese without due process of law. Even Balfour described this privately as an 'amazing blunder, which seems to violate every canon of international morality, of law, and of policy'.[2]

The reaction of British labour was quite as strong as that of the Liberal Party as a whole. But it was also significantly different, in that the emphasis was less on the humanitarian side and more upon the disappointment felt by British labour that the jobs available in South Africa were not for themselves, but for cheap, alien labour. Charles Fenwick, the Northumberland miners' M.P.,

[1] Conservative Central Office, *Notes for Speakers no. 11: Chinese and 'Slavery'* (1906).

[2] A. M. Gollin, *Proconsul in Politics* (1964), p. 71.

put the case in a nutshell when he declared, in a Commons debate in February 1904:

Towards the close of the late unhappy war supporters of the government pointed out to the working classes in this country what a happy hunting ground South Africa would be for the British labourer, and what a splendid outlet it would be for the surplus population of this country. Now it turned out that this country had shed the blood of tens of thousands of its subjects not in the interests of British labour but in the interests of Chinese labour.[1]

A resolution denouncing the new policy was carried unanimously at the conference of the Miners Federation of Great Britain later that year, and one of the delegates who spoke in support emphasised the contrast between Chamberlain's description of the war as being 'waged in the interests of the miners of this country' and the existing state of affairs, in which every issue of the *Labour Gazette*, the official Board of Trade publication, was warning intending migrants not to go to South Africa, as there were no jobs there and many unemployed.[2]

It would be wearisome to continue quoting evidence to show the strength of this reaction against Chinese labour among British working-class spokesmen of all occupations. That already provided indicates clearly that the Chinese were regarded as competitors, quite as much as and indeed rather more than as objects of sympathy. Graham Wallas tells us that 'Anyone ... who saw anything of politics in the winter of 1905–6 must have noticed that the pictures of Chinamen on the hoardings aroused among very many of the voters an immediate hatred of the Mongolian racial type. This hatred was transferred to the Conservative party. . . .'[3] The reaction had a slightly more rational basis than Wallas, who apparently saw only the humanitarian angle, is prepared to allow.[4] Even Leopold Amery, a

[1] *H.C.Deb.*, ser. 4, cxxx, 71 (17 Feb 1904).

[2] Miners Federation of Great Britain, *Annual Conference Report, 1904*, p. 68.

[3] G. Wallas, *Human Nature in Politics* (1908), p. 107.

[4] Another writer to miss the significance of Chinese labour as competition for British labour was R. C. K. Ensor: see his *England, 1870–1914* (1936), p. 377. But Halévy has it right: *English People: Epilogue*, i, 376.

protégé of Milner's, was prepared to admit that the attitude of
the British working men was 'ignorant perhaps, but sincere, that
the government was helping greedy capitalists to supplant
Englishmen'.[1] A surprising number of Conservative politicians,
however, thought that the whole agitation was 'a discreditable
party fraud' by the Liberals – a view which shows no appreciation
of the force of popular feeling.[2] For the ordinary man, what was
the value of Empire if it did not mean more jobs?

This enquiry into the British workman's attitude to imperialism
has concentrated on the South African War and its repercussions:
not inappropriately, I believe, for imperial questions were of less
moment for the ordinary person at other times in the period I have
been considering. The enquiry has suggested that whatever the
spontaneous and temporary enthusiasm developed in the course
of the South African War, there is no evidence of a direct
continuous support for the cause of Imperialism among any
sections of the working class. There was some indirect continuous
support, for instance among Ulstermen and Irish Protestant
immigrants in Britain, who always voted Unionist for the sake of
the maintenance of the Protestant ascendancy in Northern
Ireland; and among members of certain occupations, such as
soldiers and sailors and shipbuilding workers, who favoured a
strong defence policy and the building of battleships. In 1894–5
the question of the Indian Cotton Duties – a revenue tariff
imposed on cotton goods imported into India – agitated the
Lancashire constituencies and resulted in a heavy swing to the
Unionists in the 1895 election, in order to ensure their removal.[3]
But the trade-union leadership, overwhelmingly Liberal as it was,
always adhered to the 'little England' view; and Lenin's view that
the 'upper stratum' of the working class was politically corrupted
by Imperialism is demonstrably false.[4] As for the bulk of working-

[1] L. S. Amery, *The Times History of the War in South Africa* (1909), vi, 124.

[2] The phrase is from A. S. T. Griffith-Boscawen, *Fourteen Years in
Parliament* (1907), p. 294.

[3] See P. Harnetty, 'The Indian Cotton Duties Controversy, 1894–6',
English Historical Review, lxxvii (1962).

[4] *Lenin on Britain*, pp. 64, 67.

class opinion, although it may perhaps have shared the expansionist optimism of the first months of the South African War, it was soon veering away on a calculation of the immediate short-term disadvantages of Empire. The disappointment of immediate hopes of migration, and the threat of a rise in the cost of living, at once induced the 'wobble' of which Milner was afraid. Milner was indeed right to come to the conclusion that democracy was no way to run an Empire.

6 Labour and the Downfall
   of Liberalism

T H E decline of the Liberal Party and its replacement by Labour is one of the most remarkable transformations in British political history, and it is surprising that the reasons for it have not given rise to more discussion and debate. Since the 1920s, there have in fact been two quite irreconcilable interpretations of the course of events, but these two interpretations are hardly ever put in confrontation, let alone systematically examined. On the one hand, there is the view that the Liberal Party suffered an unexpected and almost accidental setback as a result of the conflict between Asquith and Lloyd George in 1916, and the subsequent split which proved so damaging at the 1918 election. This view has always been popular among the Liberals themselves, for it has the obvious implication that there was no reason why the party should not revive in the more normal conditions of peacetime. It carries the corollary that the Liberal Party had been doing perfectly well before 1914, and that the threat from the Labour Party, if of any significance at all, was nevertheless quite satisfactorily contained. Thus J. A. Spender in a study of twentieth-century history pointed out that the Labour Party secured 53 members at the 1906 election – a figure that dropped to 40 in January 1910 and rose only to 42 in December 1910.[1] And Ramsay Muir in a similar work mentioned a Labour Party total of 51 in 1906.[2] Since only 29 members of the Labour Representation Committee were elected in that year, it is clear that the total is obtained by putting together all those M.P.s who were of working-class origin, regardless of whether they regarded themselves as members of the Liberal Party or not. It is not surprising that Liberal authors could thus conclude that the threat from Labour was not very serious between 1906 and 1914, as the party seemed in this period, numerically at least, to be in decline. Thus Spender could put the blame for the Liberal collapse squarely on

[1] J. A. Spender, *Short History of Our Times* (1934), p. 81.
[2] R. Muir, *Brief History of Our Own Times* (1934), p. 151.

the wartime Coalition: 'That one or other of the parties which entered a Coalition would be crippled for life before it came out had always been the prediction of old Parliamentary hands, but it was an evil chain of circumstances which gave all the disadvantages and none of the benefits to the Liberal Party.'[1] It does not seem to occur to Spender that the Labour Party had also been a party to the Coalition and that serious disagreements had occurred among its leaders as well as among those of the Liberals.

Diametrically at odds with this interpretation is that which was offered in the 1920s by the supporters of the Labour Party. Looking at the figures of members elected to Parliament under the party's auspices, they saw the regular increase from 29 in 1906 to 40 in January 1910, 42 in December 1910 and 57 in 1918. In 1922 the figure was 142, and in 1923 it was 191.[2] It was at this point that Sidney Webb made his well-known remark at a Labour Party conference, to the effect that if the poll of the party went on rising at the same ascending rate, by about 1926 there would be a Labour Government elected by a clear majority of the voters.[3] His prediction was belied by events, and indeed the Labour Party has never yet secured a majority of the votes polled in a general election. All the same, until 1931 it did secure an increasing total of votes, and, what was more important, an increasing proportion of the total poll. From this point of view it was difficult not to see the Labour Party as pursuing an inexorable advance from its foundation in 1900 onwards – an advance which was certainly hastened by the events of 1914–18, but which would have taken place with or without the interlude of war. As R. H. Tawney put it in his American lectures published in 1925, 'In a country where social organisation is as tough and tradition as powerful as in England, national habits are not altered even by an earthquake.'[4]

In 1936 the view that the decline of the Liberal Party was already evident before 1914 received fresh support from the somewhat melodramatic prose of a young Oxford scholar, George Dangerfield. His book was entitled *The Strange Death of*

[1] J. A. Spender, *Life of Lord Oxford and Asquith* (1932), ii, 341.

[2] See Arthur Henderson's article in *The Book of the Labour Party*, ed. H. Tracey (1925), i, 12–14.

[3] Labour Party, *Annual Report, 1923*, p. 175.

[4] R. H. Tawney, *British Labour Movement* (New Haven, Conn., 1925), p. 33.

Liberal England, and although he saw the signs of mortality principally in the violence of the years 1910–14, when, as he put it, 'fires long smouldering in the English spirit suddenly flared up', he traced the Liberal Party's parliamentary decline to the 1906 election.[1] Thereafter, in Dangerfield's words, the party was 'doomed': 'It was like an army protected at all points except for one vital position on its flank.' On the flank, he tells us, were 'twenty-nine professed Socialists'.[2] This of course is a mistake: there were twenty-nine members of the Labour Party, but only about eighteen were members of Socialist organisations, in most cases of the Independent Labour Party. The Labour Party was as yet in no way committed to Socialism, and even in policies of social reform was entirely eclipsed by Lloyd George and Winston Churchill.

Later historians of twentieth-century British history have had little to say on this question of Liberal decline. Perhaps this is because many histories tend to end in 1914, while others begin at that date. It has thus rarely been possible for historians to contemplate the twentieth century as a whole. Then again, some authors, such as Mr A. J. P. Taylor, are more interested in narrative than analysis, and do not always consider problems over the long period. We have had to wait until 1966 for a scholarly account of the decline of the Liberal Party in the twentieth century, and this book, Dr Trevor Wilson's *Downfall of the Liberal Party*, devotes nearly all its attention to the Coalition and the post-war years, dismissing the need to examine the pre-war period in a few pages of its introduction.

Dr Wilson's case on the pre-war period may be summed up as follows. The Liberal Party had its greatest success in 1906 and continued to form the government after 1910; and there is strong evidence that it was not losing working-class support to Labour before 1914. First of all, Liberalism showed no lack of *rapport* with working-class aspirations, for 'the social reforming wing of the Liberal government was making the running'. Secondly, the Labour Party was not supplanting the Liberal Party at the polls: 'in the general elections of 1910, and in by-elections from 1911 until the outbreak of war, Labour fared abysmally in contests with the Liberals'. As for the 'pattern of violence' discovered by

[1] G. Dangerfield, *Strange Death of Liberal England* (1936), p. vii.
[2] Ibid., p. 10.

Dangerfield in the years 1910–14, this was no more than an 'accidental convergence of unrelated events'. In short, the Liberal Party had no reason to fear for the future until the First World War, for which the Liberal Government was in no sense responsible, disrupted the life of a political organism that had previously had only the mildest symptoms of ill-health. The Liberal Party was like a pedestrian involved in a motor accident. 'A rampant omnibus (the First World War) . . . mounted the pavement and ran him over. After lingering painfully, he expired.'[1]

It is high time, I think, to turn from assertions of this sort to an analysis of the long-term changes involved in the transformation of politics. If we compare the major left-wing party of 1930 with that of 1890 we notice three main differences in its character. In the first place, a body in which a preponderantly middle-class band of politicians – businessmen, Nonconformist ministers, and professional men – held the key offices had been replaced by one in which the man or woman of working-class origin, and particularly the trade-union officer, was predominant. Secondly, although the parliamentary Labour Party was by 1930 clearly asserting its independence of the extra-parliamentary party, the latter was still much more powerful in the movement as a whole and also much more centralised than the extra-parliamentary Liberal Party – whether we mean by this the Liberal Whips' Office, or the National Liberal Federation or both together. Thirdly, we notice that the Labour Party had acquired a Socialist constitution, whereas even the National Liberal Federation never had any formula of principles – as opposed to legislative proposals of a limited character – to which its members were theoretically committed.

The question is, how far could these changes have taken place within the Liberal Party, so as to avoid the painful complication of replacing one political organisation with another? To be sure, the Liberal Party after 1886 – the year of the Home Rule split – did secure the votes of the great bulk of working-class electors; and the occasional trade-union leader found his way into Parliament through the Liberal Party. There were 'Lib-Lab' M.P.s in

[1] T. Wilson, *Downfall of the Liberal Party* (1966), pp. 16–18.

Parliament from 1874 onwards, but never any 'Tory-Labs' – though one man of the latter type, James Mawdsley, was very nearly elected for Oldham in the double by-election which he fought in 1899 in harness with the young Winston Churchill. But the 'Lib-Labs' were not very numerous, and they were nearly all miners, who could most easily dominate particular constituencies by the weight of their union organisation. If the Liberals were to give up other working-class constituencies to be fought by working-class candidates, they had to be persuaded to do so by a combination of trade-union interests at the local level, which had clearly to indicate, not only that they could provide the votes, but also that they could find the financial support for their candidates' election expenses and maintenance in Parliament. Until this were done, working-class candidates could not secure adoption for mixed working-class constituencies; and many of the later leaders of the Labour Party – Keir Hardie, Ramsay MacDonald, Arthur Henderson – went away disappointed when they applied for Liberal candidatures in seats which they thought would suit them very well.[1]

It was not the national leadership which was responsible for rejecting these men as candidates. Gladstone said he would be happy to see more working men M.P.s; and there is little reason to doubt his sincerity. The difficulty lay in the local Liberal associations. In some cases, no doubt, the middle-class men who controlled these associations rejected Labour candidates because they feared that such men would represent their own middle-class interests poorly or not at all; but in other cases, they simply refused to contemplate shouldering the burden of expense which fell upon a constituency association whose member could not pay his own way. In this situation the Whips and the National Liberal Federation, short of money as they were, were rarely able to help more than marginally.

The difficulty was that M.P.s had to find, not only their own and often much of their party's election expenses in their respective constituencies, but also a share of the returning officer's expenses, and – worst burden of all – their own upkeep while in Parliament. One or two exceptional 'Lib-Lab' M.P.s, most notably John Burns, were able to survive on a special 'wages fund' for

[1] For evidence of this see my *Origins of the Labour Party* (new ed., Oxford, 1965), pp. 164 f., 222 f.

which contributions were constantly being solicited. But it is not surprising to find that demands were made for the payment of M.P.s and election expenses by the state, and the National Liberal Federation in its election programme before the 1892 election adopted a clause in favour of the state payment of M.P.s. Unfortunately the Liberal government of 1892–5 gave the matter little priority. When a resolution in favour of payment of members 'forthwith' was proposed in the Commons in 1893, Sir William Harcourt, who was Chancellor of the Exchequer, accepted the proposal upon his own construction, saying that it needed an Act of Parliament for 'a proposal . . . of serious constitutional change'. He interpreted 'forthwith' to mean 'as soon as practicable, when we have at our disposal the time and the money which is necessary. (Opposition laughter)'.[1]

Yet eighteen years later another Liberal government, one indeed which was now partly dependent on the vote of a small Labour Party, found it possible to introduce payment of members by House of Commons resolution only, without any fear of intervention by the Lords. It is difficult to see that the change of attitude was in any way due to the Parliament Act of 1911.

The fact is that working men – with the exception of the miners' officials – could only force their way into Parliament by fighting elections against the Liberal associations. Hence, by the turn of the century, there was a good deal of pressure on the part of trade-union leaders, particularly the younger ones who were already general secretaries of unions, to found a new political party based on union funds, which would be able to carry them into the Commons. (At this time, we must remember, the work both of a general secretary and of a Member of Parliament was less heavy than it is now.) The legal judgments against picketing and making union funds liable for damages were therefore a great convenience for them: it made the case for spending union money on parliamentary politics, temporarily at least, unanswerable. Even so, personal jealousy or conservatism could hinder the enthusiasm of union executives. The unions which joined the Labour Representation Committee first therefore tended to be unions of the unskilled, because their secretaries had most power over the members, and because their officials were mostly younger

[1] *H.C.Deb.*, ser. 4, x, 1121 (24 Mar 1893).

and so more ambitious; because they were most seriously affected by the restrictions on picketing, which were the result of judicial decisions of the 1890s; and finally because their members stood to gain most by legislation about conditions, hours and so on. We should remember, however, that there were really two Labour Parties founded at the beginning of the century: one was the Labour Representation Committee, theoretically independent of the Liberal Party for the reasons that I have suggested; the other was Ben Pickard's representation scheme adopted by the Miners Federation of Great Britain, whereby each of the district miners' unions was to pay money into a central fund for the financing of miners' candidates. With the exception of the Lancashire and Cheshire Miners who joined the Labour Party in 1903, the miners' candidates were in practice always members of the Liberal Party. But in 1908, after some years' experience of running candidates and seeing them in Parliament side by side with a national Labour Party, the miners decided to require their M.P.s to join the Labour Party. This was an important event in the growth of the Labour Party, and the reasons for it need further exploration. After all, the reverse might have happened and the existing Labour M.P.s might have been drawn into the Liberal Party.

But first, some points must be made about the long-term factors that were at work. The leaders of the Liberal Party were remiss in not realising the need to give more influence to the trade unions and more opportunity for working-class candidates in Liberal seats. Rapid economic change was taking place in the country at the time, and it was altering the social balance of many constituencies. It is true that the trade unions were still weak or non-existent in rural areas and that there at least the Nonconformist interest remained the backbone of the Liberal vote. In urban or industrial areas, however, this was ceasing to be the case. The larger the town, the smaller the proportion of the working class who came under the influence of organised religion, at any rate once they had left school. The proportion of ministers to the total population of the country was steadily dropping; and the annual conferences of the sects echoed to the complaints of the leading ministers about their loss of contact with the workers.[1]

[1] See, e.g., K. S. Inglis, *Churches and the Working Classes in Victorian England* (1963), pp. 115 ff.

Trade unionism, on the other hand, went from strength to strength. In 1880 the membership of the T.U.C. was less than half a million – admittedly a bad year. After 1893 it never again fell below a million, and after 1912 it was never below two million. In 1919 it was over six and a half million; and although this was a peak not reached again until the Second World War, the figure was always well above three million in the inter-war years. Meanwhile the urbanisation of the country went on and the number of genuinely rural constituencies declined still further.

The character of Labour Party organisation reflected the nature of its origin and main support. It was the creation of the national trade unions; and the trade unions, sectional though they often were, in most cases recognised no geographical boundaries within the United Kingdom. There had been a time when unions had been merely local clubs, associated only loosely, if at all, with similar local clubs in other towns. Economic forces – in particular the development of communications and the growth in the size of the market for labour and for manufactures that this caused – had seen to it that even the national borders within the United Kingdom had set no barrier to the expansion of the unions. Consequently, although an attempt was made to organise a separate Labour Party for Scotland, it proved a failure, and already in 1906 the Labour Representation Committee was sponsoring and winning elections in Scotland.[1] Even the miners, who still had their separate local or district unions, had come together nationally in the Miners Federation of Great Britain, both for industrial and political purposes. Only in Ireland did the Labour Party fail to make any progress, at any rate in the agricultural districts. But then, it made no progress in the agricultural districts of Britain either. The contrast between the Labour and Liberal Parties in their approach to the problem of nationality within the United Kingdom is well illustrated by the outcry at the T.U.C. against Lloyd George's decision to set up separate administrations for National Health Insurance, not only in Ireland, but also in Scotland and Wales.[2]

Finally, we come to the Labour Party's commitment to

[1] On Scottish Labour politics see the brief account in F. Bealey and H. Pelling, *Labour and Politics, 1900–6* (1958), pp. 293–7.

[2] T.U.C. *Report, 1912*, p. 298.

Socialism. This was almost certainly less significant than has generally been supposed. The working class as a whole was not Socialist; and the proportion of Socialists in the electorate at any time before 1930 cannot have been more than small. Labour candidates were forbidden to designate themselves officially as anything but 'Labour' candidates; few of them appear to have wished to alter this state of affairs or to rename the party. Of course, the Socialists believed that they would be able to 'capture' the Labour Party from within; when they discovered that, on the contrary, the Labour Party had 'captured' them, their disappointment was acute. It found expression in the periodic explosions that took place in the Independent Labour Party, which was more and more taken over by the Socialists as their distinctive organisation, until finally it led to separation from the Labour Party in 1932. But those Socialists who wanted to take an active part in government found it necessary to work through the Labour Party, and so they dribbled back as individual members. For if one thing was clear, it was that candidates who set up as independent Socialists could not get elected to Parliament. Nevertheless, in the period that we are examining, the spread of Socialist ideas among key sections of the working class, such as the miners' leaders in South Wales, was an important factor in the disintegration of the Liberal Party and the growth of Labour.

It is sometimes suggested that the Liberal Party failed because it would not take up the social reforms which the popular electorate demanded. It has been argued above that the new electorate was in no sense demanding social reform;[1] but even if it did, it can hardly be maintained that the Liberal Party was slower than Labour to satisfy such a demand. We may accept Dr Trevor Wilson's view that the Liberal Party was making the running in social reform before 1914, and we may add that before 1945 the Labour Party was curiously slow to develop plans of its own for improved social welfare. In the 1920s Keynes's fiscal ideas influenced the Liberal Party more than the Labour Party; and the conception of the National Health scheme is not to be found in any of Labour's inter-war election programmes. The distant goal of Socialism absorbed much of the thinking and even more of the talking of the Socialists themselves.

[1] See Ch. 1.

Let us look again at the events of 1906–14, and in particular at the Labour Party in that period. Was the Labour Party really on the defensive throughout this period? Was its electoral performance in 1910 and in by-elections thereafter 'abysmal', as Dr Wilson maintains? Or was it building up strength which could be used, sooner or later, for a struggle with the Liberals?

It is clear that the Labour Party would not have done anything like as well as it did in 1906 if it had not been in alliance with the Liberals. Of course, the Liberals would not have done so well either: it was from self-interest, not from generosity, that they made the agreement in the first place. But of Labour's twenty-nine successes, only five were won against Liberal opposition, whether official or unofficial. That does not mean that if Liberal candidates had stood in the other twenty-four constituencies, the Labour candidates would necessarily have been defeated. But the Labour Party might have numbered no more than a dozen members if its candidates had had to fight the Liberals all along the line. Liberal leaders who recognised this fact may have attached all the more significance to the Labour victory in the Jarrow by-election of July 1907, and to the success of an 'independent Socialist' at the Colne Valley by-election a few weeks later.[1] In both cases the seat had previously been held by a Liberal. After this, by-election gains for Labour came more rarely: but there was one further success during the existing Parliament, at Attercliffe, Sheffield, in 1909, when once again a Labour candidate replaced a Liberal. The record was encouraging because in each case it meant a victory in a contest against both Liberal and Conservative candidates. But the Labour Party was lucky in this period in not having to defend any of its own seats. No Labour M.P. died or retired and thus there were no Labour seats placed at risk. There were, however, four other by-elections, apart from those which the party won, where it contested seats which had also been fought by the Liberals in 1906. Compared with the Liberals, it gained ground in two (Huddersfield 1906, Dewsbury 1908) and lost ground in two (Leeds South 1908 and Croydon 1909).

But much more important than these skirmishes was the fact, already mentioned, that in 1908 the Miners Federation of Great Britain voted, by ballot of all the members, that the M.P.s

[1] For a study of these by-elections, see Ch. 8.

elected under its representation scheme should henceforth belong
to the Labour Party. To understand why the Miners Federation
chose independence of Liberalism, after so many years of loyalty
to it, we have to look at the way in which things had been
changing within the mining industry, and particularly within the
South Wales mining industry, for this is where change was most
rapid and, as it turned out, decisive.

The Miners Federation was founded in 1889 to unite the miners
of the country in support of the eight-hour day and a minimum
wage, whereby they might escape the insecurity of the old sliding
scale. The sliding scale was all very well for the miners as long as
it slid upwards, but this it failed consistently to do. In South
Wales the demand for coal was very great, and the expansion of
the mines particularly rapid in the late nineteenth century.
Organisation was for a long time poor and localised. The miners
accepted the sliding scale until 1898, when after serious fluctua-
tions in the scale they fought a long strike against the employers.
Although defeated in the strike and forced to retain the system,
they established a new union for the entire coalfield, and this
body, the South Wales Miners Federation, at once joined the
Miners Federation of Great Britain, promising to get rid of the
sliding scale as soon as possible. Already in 1900 the South Wales
Miners Federation could claim 127,894 members, which was over
a third of the total membership of the Miners Federation of Great
Britain.

Observers of the South Wales miners noticed how in these years
there was a growing estrangement between the men and their
employers, even though the latter were likely to be quite as Welsh
and quite as keen chapel-goers. It was perhaps the men themselves
who were becoming more heterogeneous, for many Englishmen
migrated into the valleys, attracted by the expansion of the
industry. The miners were aroused to hostility towards their
employers not just by their dislike of the sliding scale but also by
their concern at the growing unwillingness of the pit management
to make allowances for those who were working in 'abnormal
working places' – that is to say, places where the coal was poor or
the seam awkward, so that a man could not achieve piece rates
with the same ease as those in normal conditions.[1] The greater
difficulty of achieving output is shown by the fact that output per

[1] H. S. Jevons, *British Coal Trade* (1915), pp. 520 ff.

man declined from 309 tons per annum in 1883 to 260 early in the twentieth century.[1]

The South Wales Miners stepped up their hostility to the employers early in the new century, having secured a high membership and tightened their organisation. At first they could not eliminate the sliding scale which they had agreed to maintain until 1902. But they did break a point of agreement with the employers by taking one of the monthly holidays which they had been used to having before the 1898 strike – an institution known as 'Mabon's day' after the old miners' leader who had secured it. This happened shortly after the Taff Vale case, which made unions liable for damages in such an event. In a case which went to the House of Lords, damages amounting to £57,562 were awarded against the South Wales Miners Federation – a sum considerably larger than that involved in the Taff Vale case.[2] Meanwhile, early in 1903 the Federation secured a new contract with the employers in which the sliding scale was at last abandoned. On the subject of 'abnormal places', however, hostilities continued; and in 1907, in a case known as *Walters* v. *Ocean Coal Company*, a Glamorgan County Court judge decided that 'abnormal places' payments were *ex gratia* payments and hence not recoverable by law. Thus the legal system seemed to the miners to be stacked against their prospects of obtaining a livelihood.

It was against such a background that we find the growth of feeling among the South Wales Miners that it was time to sever their links with the Liberal Party. Their employers were nearly all Liberals, and Nonconformists as well. The younger generation of miners both ceased to support Liberalism, and also deserted the chapels which their fathers had frequented, at least as 'adherents'.[3] They were aware that the chairman of the Ocean Coal Company, David Davies, was a Liberal M.P.; and that the Glamorgan County Court judge who had decided the 'abnormal places' case, Bryn Roberts, had just retired from Parliament after twenty-one years as a Liberal member. To the old pattern of Welsh solidarity, expressed in the Liberal Party and closely allied

[1] E. W. Evans, *Miners of South Wales* (Cardiff, 1961), p. 241.

[2] Bealey and Pelling, *Labour and Politics*, p. 229.

[3] E. T. Davies, *Religion and the Industrial Revolution in South Wales* (Cardiff, 1965), pp. 148 ff.

to Nonconformity, they opposed a new philosophy – one of secular Socialism, British rather than Welsh in context. Whereas the old leaders of the miners were men with Welsh names – Abraham, Evans, Morgan – the new leaders tended to be of English origin, and had such names as Cook, Hartshorn, Hodges.

The impact of these new forces rapidly made itself felt in the Miners Federation of Great Britain. 1900 was the high peak for the selling price of coal, and, sliding scale or no sliding scale, the miners were forced to accept wage reductions in the ensuing years. Between 1903 and 1906 wage reductions that totalled $18\frac{3}{4}\%$ were accepted by the South Wales miners.[1] In 1907 their representatives at a conference of the M.F.G.B. proposed and carried a resolution in favour of the nationalisation of the mines – the first time that the organisation had committed itself to this.[2] In the early years of the century there had been some pressure on the M.F.G.B. to join the Labour Representation Committee, the initiative coming from the Scottish miners. In 1905 it was agreed that a ballot of the entire membership should be held on the subject of affiliation to the L.R.C., and this took place in 1906. The result was negative, only the Scottish, Welsh, Lancashire and Yorkshire districts favouring affiliation, and of these the Welsh being the most divided in their sympathies.[3] In 1907 a further initiative was made by the Welsh and Scottish leaders, and it was agreed to hold another ballot. The new vote, which took place in 1908, showed that some of the smaller districts favoured affiliation also, but the big change was that Wales was heavily in favour. Furthermore, whereas the Lancashire miners supported affiliation for the most conservative of reasons (the Orangemen in their ranks objected to backing a Home Rule party),[4] the Welsh were apparently motivated by a rising class-consciousness and hostility to their employers. The result was that the Federation M.P.s were told that they must join the Labour Party if they secured re-election at the next general election. This did not come until January 1910; but in the meantime, from early in 1909, the Miners Federation began payments to the Labour

[1] Evans, *Miners of South Wales*, p. 179.

[2] Miners Federation, *Annual Conference Report, 1907*, p. 28.

[3] Figures of the 1906 and 1908 ballots will be found in R. Page Arnot, *South Wales Miners* (1967), i, 149.

[4] Miners Federation, *Report, 1907*, pp. 52, 54.

Party funds.[1] Thus it was that although the Labour Party made no net gains in the election of January 1910, it nevertheless returned to Parliament with a membership of 40, as against only 29 immediately after the 1906 election.

We may proceed to examine in more detail the Labour Party's performance in both 1910 general elections, and also in the subsequent by-elections. This will help us to decide whether the party was advancing or declining in relation to the Liberals. Since all the official candidates of the M.F.G.B. accepted the demand that they should be prepared to join the Labour Party, in effect the Labour Party was in January 1910 defending a total of 45 seats. Eight seats were lost and three were gained, making a net loss of five compared with the situation at the Dissolution. But as five seats had been won at by-elections since 1906 – two by the Labour Party and three by the M.F.G.B. – there was in fact no net loss of seats compared with 1906. One would have supposed that the Labour Party would inevitably lose some ground, compared with 1906, owing to its identification with the Liberal stand on such important issues as the Lords' veto, Free Trade and Home Rule. Certainly the Liberals as a party lost a lot of ground: even after subtracting the M.F.G.B. members from their 1906 total, they returned in 1910 shorn of well over a quarter of their strength. And whereas in the 1906 Parliament they had a clear overall majority over the other parties, they were now dependent on the support of Labour and the Irish Nationalists.

The election of December 1910 was very much a repeat of that eleven months earlier. For the Labour Party, however, the number of candidates was much reduced. The Osborne Judgment of 1909 was threatening to cut its funds, and it was a natural economy to drop those contests which, on the basis of the January result, appeared to be unlikely to succeed. This had its incidental advantages. It proved possible to negotiate some further agreements with the Liberals for the mutual elimination of conflicting candidatures; and from this agreement emerged fresh victories for Labour in Bow and Bromley and Whitehaven. For the rest, the party suffered three losses in Lancashire, which swung somewhat

[1] Miners Federation, *Executive Committee Minutes*, Feb 1909, p. 35.

to the Conservatives as a result of Balfour's undertaking to make Tariff Reform the subject of a referendum; and to offset this it won three seats elsewhere – one of them, West Fife, being in a straight fight with a Liberal. Thus the party's membership now rose to its highest pre-war total of 42, a net gain of two.

This was no great success for Labour, but it is difficult to understand how Dr Wilson can say that the party fared 'abysmally' in contest with the Liberals in these two elections. Apart from the miners' seats, three of which had been taken over from representation by other types of Liberals since 1906, the Labour Party gained Derby, East Manchester and West Fife from the Liberals and lost to them no seats at all, except for Jarrow which had been won at a by-election. Of course it is true that in a few seats where Labour had run third in a three-cornered contest in 1906, the party did worse in 1910, no doubt because the electors thought that there at least Labour did not have a chance. There were also four instances of Labour receding from second place to third in three-cornered contests, either in January or in December 1910; but these cases (Chatham, Huddersfield, Leeds South and Portsmouth) may have been due to local or personal factors.[1]

It remains to look at the by-elections in the period 1911 to 1914. Four were fought in 1911, and in the only one which had previously been fought by a Labour candidate at a general election, North-East Lanarkshire, the Labour candidate considerably improved his proportion of the poll. At Keighley the Conservative was almost forced into third place, and the Labour Party's annual report justly remarked that the results showed 'how extensive is the grip of the Party on the constituencies'.[2] The following year, 1912, saw a substantial improvement in Labour polls in two seats which the party had previously fought in January 1910. But at Hanley, where a Labour M.P., Enoch Edwards, had died, the seat was lost to the Liberals, the Labour candidate securing a quite miserable poll. The trouble was that the miners of the Midlands, whose relations with their employers were still good compared with South Wales, and whose output apparently did

[1] Difficulties of this character at Leeds South are discussed in the Labour Party *Annual Report, 1909*, p. 5.
[2] Labour Party *Annual Report, 1912*, p. 5.

not suffer unduly from 'abnormal working places',[1] were as yet loyal Liberals and consequently made no effort to set up electoral machinery for the support of Labour candidates. Another Labour seat was lost at Bow and Bromley when the sitting M.P., George Lansbury, insisted on resigning and fighting a by-election on the Women's Suffrage question. He was denied official support from the Labour Party and was defeated.

In the nineteen months between the end of 1912 and the outbreak of war, the Labour Party fought six by-elections. In each case the Labour candidate was at the bottom of the poll in a three-cornered contest, but this should not make us ignore the fact that in most cases the party was really developing its strength. For instance, in two three-cornered contests in Durham never previously fought, it won in each case over a quarter of the total vote. Nevertheless it suffered two setbacks, similar in character to that at Hanley. When James Haslam, Labour and Miners' M.P. for Chesterfield in Derbyshire, died in 1913, the Derbyshire Miners Association insisted on nominating and supporting a 'Lib-Lab' candidate, Barnet Kenyon. The Labour Party therefore refused to recognise him, and the seat, though won by Kenyon, was lost to Labour. Then another Miners' M.P., W. E. Harvey, who sat for Derbyshire North-East, also died. Although this time the Derbyshire Miners put up a candidate who could secure official Labour endorsement, the Liberals put up a rival candidate, and in a three-cornered contest the seat was lost to a Unionist.

Thus the Labour Party lost four seats in by-elections between 1910 and 1914; and because the Miners' M.P.s for Nuneaton and for Mid-Derbyshire were expelled from the party early in 1914 for leanings towards Liberalism, the total of the parliamentary party had dwindled from 42 after the December 1910 election to a mere 36 in August 1914. Yet almost all the setbacks which had led to this decline were the result of a peculiar local situation in the Midlands mining districts. Other Miners' M.P.s were settling down within the new party, and the electorate as a whole showed an increasing willingness to vote for Labour candidates. Even in Derbyshire, moreover, as Dr J. E. Williams has pointed out, there were signs in 1914 of greater determination to take the line of

[1] In Derbyshire output per man fluctuated, but there was no trend of decline, in the period 1880–1913. J. E. Williams, *The Derbyshire Miners* (1962), p. 213.

independence from the Liberal Party. In the very month of the outbreak of war the Council of the Derbyshire Miners Association resolved to set up a Labour Party for the North-East constituency.[1]

It is easy to criticise the Labour Party of the 1910–14 period. Its M.P.s were divided in their views on a number of important issues – most notably National Insurance – and they could hardly impress the observer of the parliamentary scene. Mrs Webb's view though obviously that of a dissatisfied Socialist was not really untypical: 'The Labour M.P.s seem to me to be drifting into futility. . . . J. R. MacDonald has ceased to be a Socialist, the Trade Union M.P.s never were Socialists, Snowden is embittered and Lansbury is wild. At present there is no co-operation among the Labour Members themselves nor between them and the trade union leaders.'[2] Yet the difference between the Labour Party and other political parties was that its principal strength lay in its extra-parliamentary organisation, and in this period that organisation was constantly being strengthened. Between 1906 and 1914 the number of affiliated trade-union members rose from 904,496 to 1,572,391, with a consequent improvement in the party funds. If this very largely reflects the growth of trade unionism in the country, the actual expansion of political influence by the party is exemplified by the increase in the number of affiliated trades councils and local Labour Parties, which rose from 73 in 1905/6 to 177 in 1914. The number of persons elected as Labour members of local government authorities advanced from 56 in the year 1907 to 184 in 1913.[3]

These developments occurred in spite of the concurrent development of interest in the ideas of Syndicalism and direct action, rather than parliamentary methods. There is no real evidence that the 'labour unrest' of these years weakened the performance of the Labour Party in elections; and it is clear that the party's strength was increasing precisely among those workers

[1] Williams, *Derbyshire Miners*, p. 513.
[2] Entry of 11 Oct 1912, *Beatrice Webb's Diaries, 1912–1924*, ed. M. I. Cole (1952), pp. 6 f.
[3] Figures from Labour Party *Annual Reports*.

whose younger militants had taken up with Syndicalism – the South Wales miners and the railwaymen. Among the workers who were not Syndicalists nor even Socialists – and they were still by far the majority – a sort of undogmatic 'Labourism' was establishing itself, which consisted in little more than the opinion that the Labour Party, and not the Liberal, was the party for working men to belong to. This was of course particularly the case now with miners, whose political solidarity was unmatched by other occupational groups. Sooner or later – and there were indications that it would be sooner – the remnant of Liberalism among the Midland miners would be eliminated and they would be brought into line with their English, Welsh and Scottish fellows.

By 1914 the Labour Party was the party with the centralisation to take advantage of twentieth-century political conditions. Welsh nationalism had already begun to weaken in the face of South Wales's increasing links with English industry and the mining industry's growing class conflict; after the enactment of Welsh disestablishment, the political purpose of Welsh Nonconformity was achieved. Scottish nationalism was always somewhat weaker as a political force, and the demand for Scottish church disestablishment had already begun to fail in the 1890s.[1] By the turn of the century, it was apparent that the long-term solution of this problem lay in the reunion of the Presbyterian sects. Only Irish nationalism remained to provide a powerful ally and a major legislative purpose for the Liberal Party along traditional lines. But Irish nationalism was approaching a crisis which would take it beyond the stage of alliance with British Liberalism. It was about to burst the bonds of ordinary constitutional action. Here too the years of co-operation between English Liberalism and a Celtic nationalism were coming to an end.

The First World War was as much of a test for the unity of the Labour Party as it was for that of the Liberals. The I.L.P. Socialists in the parliamentary Labour Party opposed the war from the start, but the rest of the party supported it. For much of the wartime period MacDonald, the former chairman of the parliamentary party, was collaborating with a group of anti-war Liberals and had virtually cut himself off from his former Labour

[1] J. G. Kellas, 'The Liberal Party and the Scottish Church Disestablishment Crisis', *English Historical Review*, lxxix (1964), pp. 44 f.

colleagues. Yet at the end of the war it was possible for the Labour Party to reform its ranks and with a few exceptions to present a united front to the electorate. This was in large part because of wise leadership on the part of Arthur Henderson, but that leadership in itself reflected a sense of the solidarity of the working-class movement as expressed in Labour Party organisation. And the centralised character of the party, dependent as it was upon the financial support of the national trade unions, was the principal guarantee of unity.

The great gains made by the parliamentary Labour Party in the general elections of 1918 to 1924 were not simply the result of the divisions among the Liberals. They owed a great deal to factors which were independent even of the effects of the war – though, to be sure, the war may have hastened the operation of these factors. The coal industry's loss of overseas markets, clearly foreshadowed in the difficulties of South Wales before 1914, led to an increasing alienation of the miners from their employers and from the capitalist system. In 1918 no less than 25 of the 57 Labour M.P.s elected were members of the M.F.G.B.; and the number was to increase. Then with the termination of the old alliance between the Liberal Party and the Irish – an event which was not directly due to the war – the Irish voters in Britain, so many of whom were members of the working class, found themselves free to support the Labour Party: the result was, among other things, enormously to improve the party's position in Scotland, and to send a contingent of Labour M.P.s to Westminster from so-called 'Red Clydeside'. Finally, the completion of the progress towards full democracy by the enactment of a Franchise Act in 1918 considerably improved the position of the Labour Party in the constituencies. The likely effects of adult suffrage as it was enacted later had been carefully considered by the Liberal Whips and agents as early as 1911, and they had concluded that although it would benefit their party in its struggles against the Unionists, it would result in gains to Labour in such districts as Yorkshire, North England, and West Scotland.[1] These were in fact the districts in which Labour made its greatest gains in 1922.

We may conclude, therefore, that the decline of Liberalism was

[1] Memorandum by Master of Elibank, Chief Whip, Cabinet Papers, Nov 1911 : Public Record Office Cab. 37/108/148.

not due to a sordid intrigue between Lloyd George and a few Conservative leaders and press lords, as many widely-read historians of the present day would have us believe. Nor was it due solely or predominantly, as Dr Wilson has suggested, to the impact of the war upon Liberal values and upon the unity of the parliamentary Liberal Party. Rather it was the result of long-term social and economic changes which were simultaneously uniting Britain geographically and dividing her inhabitants in terms of class; enabling the population to achieve the full dimensions of political democracy but condemning it to years of bitter strife owing to the forced contraction of the staple industries which had prospered so remarkably in the later Victorian era – an era politically as well as socially distinct from that of the inter-war period.

7 The Story of the I.L.P.

THE Independent Labour Party played a crucial role in the development of British Socialism and in the formation of the Labour Party. It has long deserved a biography – and it ought to be one of the 'life and times' type, for the story of its evolution cannot be separated from that of the Labour and Socialist movements as a whole, nor indeed from the background of national and international events. The work would presumably start in the 1880s and gather momentum in the early 1890s when the party was actually founded. From there to 1932, at least, the party had a central position in the political development of the British Left, and a full treatment of its history is required. But where should the volume end? I remember hearing an old working-class Marxist, on learning that I was endeavouring to study the history of the I.L.P., say in tones of contempt 'The I.L.P.? A Socialist organisation should know when to die as well as when to be born'. But the I.L.P., which lives in a capitalist society, has probably been kept alive by the interest on the property that it has accumulated over the years. The same could be said, in part at least, of other Socialist organisations.

As a research student in the late 1940s I intended to write a history of the I.L.P. from its foundation in 1893 to the disaffiliation from the Labour Party in 1932. Somehow the subject on closer study seemed to be too big for a post-graduate thesis. In consultation with my supervisor[1] I cut the terminal date to 1918. Once again, the task overwhelmed me, and I altered the date to 1914. Then, after a few more months, I was down to 1906. Finally, I submitted a dissertation on 'The origins and early history of the I.L.P. 1893–1900'. Now more than fifteen years later Dr Dowse has written a study of the I.L.P., entitled *Left in the Centre*, and described by his publishers as 'the definitive work on the subject', which goes all the way to 1940 in hardly more than 200 pages.[2] This conciseness certainly attracts our initial good will.

[1] Professor (later Sir) Denis Brogan.
[2] R. E. Dowse, *Left in the Centre* (1966).

To understand how Dr Dowse has treated the story we may first turn to his preface. He is a good deal more modest than his publisher. This is not, he tells us, an 'exhaustive history', nor a 'detailed geographical analysis' of the party's sources of support. Rather the work is written by 'a social scientist intent on presenting an overall picture with emphasis on politics and activity at the national level'. For good measure, Dr Dowse tells us at once what his main conclusion is. 'My basic proposition is that the decline was a consequence of structural factors which left little room for manœuvre.' The emphasis, evidently, is on the later years of the party and not on its rise and early period of importance. The nature of the structural factors of decline is spelt out in rather more detail in the concluding chapter, and, if I interpret this section of the book correctly, they are in particular, first, the fact that the I.L.P. was strong in those parts of the country where the Labour Party was weak, for instance Scotland and Lancashire; and secondly, the fact that the party suffered from excessive decentralisation, which was 'a legacy from 1893'.

If these are the main points that Dr Dowse wishes to substantiate, it seems a great pity that he did not spend more time on geographical analysis, and also on a fuller treatment of the years close to the actual foundation of the party, which he passes over very cursorily. The strength of the I.L.P. in Scotland in the early years was largely a concomitant of the comparative weakness of trade unionism there; in later years, the weakness of trade unionism led to a corresponding weakness of the Labour Party and hence left the field open to the I.L.P. The situation in Lancashire would have to be explained along different lines, and it would be interesting to know Dr Dowse's views, which are not to be found in his book. Certainly, the Labour Party was not electorally very successful in Lancashire; and this may have enabled the I.L.P. to assume greater importance as a consequence. It was in the nature of things that the I.L.P., which was in a sense competitive with the Labour Party in the 1920s, should be successful in those parts of the country where the Labour Party was weak.

In tracing the decentralisation of the I.L.P. to its very foundation, Dr Dowse leaves the reader very unsatisfied because he says hardly anything new about the period before 1914, which he disposes of in a breathless nineteen pages. All the same, he tells us (p. 6) that the National Administrative Council, the executive of the party, always contained a majority of members chosen by regional divisions. This is an unfortunate error. In fact, the system of control of the party between 1894 and 1906 was a centralised one. There were no divisional representatives on the N.A.C., all of whose members were chosen by the annual conference of the party, voting by simple majority. Consequently it is not to 1893, but to 1905–6, that one should look for an explanation of the party's decentralisation.

It must be acknowledged that it is by no means easy to analyse the causes of decline in a party which lived through so many vicissitudes of national history, in which the labour movement and the Labour Party were both in a state of rapid evolution. It certainly requires an examination of the whole of the party's history, and not just part of it. We must be grateful to all those who have thrown fresh light on its development in the 1920s and 1930s, and particularly Dr Dowse and Mr Arthur Marwick. But, as Mr Marwick acknowledges in an important article summarising his research: 'The decline of the I.L.P. was a gradual thing. . . . To concentrate on the Labour Party constitution of 1918 would be similar in kind to attributing the waning influence of the Crown in the early nineteenth century entirely to the Reform Act of 1832.'[1]

It is essential to remember that the I.L.P. was founded with two different purposes in mind. One was, to make Socialists: and this purpose was embodied in the party's first constitution as its 'object', which was to secure the 'collective ownership of the means of production, distribution and exchange'. The other purpose, however, was more immediate – to secure a Labour Party in Parliament, whose members would hold the balance between the Liberal and Conservative Parties in the same way as the Irish did in 1885–6. For this purpose it was desirable to secure the sympathies of the workers in the West Riding and elsewhere, who were by no means Socialists, but who were critical of the Liberals because of their leaders' lack of concern with trade-union rights, the issue of free speech, the eight-hour day and certain other short-term questions. To attract this 'labour' but not 'Socialist' support,

[1] A. Marwick, 'The I.L.P. in the Nineteen-Twenties', *Bulletin of the Institute of Historical Research*, xxxv (1962), 64.

the party took the name which, against all proposals for change, it has maintained throughout its life.[1]

Unfortunately for the I.L.P. leaders, their more immediate purpose suffered a heavy setback at the 1895 election, when all their candidates were defeated. As a result they had to fall back on the more tortuous process of persuading the trade unions to join them in founding a party (the Labour Party) which did not even accept Socialism as its final object. This was bound to lead to trouble with that portion of the rank-and-file of the party who took the Socialist purpose seriously and who could not readily appreciate the political compromises that inevitably resulted from working with the trade unions.

It is time to look at the party structure. This was, in the foundation year 1893–4, highly decentralised, because the local parties had in fact been in existence, in many cases, before the national party was founded. But the experience of the first year's activity, and the attempts by such suspicious 'outsiders' as Champion and Aveling to use the organisation for their own purposes, led to the conviction that a party which sought national recognition would have to have a centralised constitution. It was the N.A.C. which decided that there should be no organisations loosely affiliated to the party, and that only bodies calling themselves I.L.P. branches should be recognised as belonging to the party. Then at the 1894 conference the size of the N.A.C. itself was cut down to a total of nine, including the officers, all of whom were to be elected nationally. Those who served on the N.A.C. in succeeding years tended to be re-elected regularly, and in time a very homogeneous group of leaders emerged. The group consisted principally of Keir Hardie, Ramsay MacDonald, Philip Snowden and Bruce Glasier. They combined lecturing with journalism and hence kept their personalities constantly before the local membership. Successfully dominating the party for twelve years, they maintained its independence from other more genuinely Socialist bodies, and carried through the policy of the 'labour alliance' – resulting in the formation of the Labour Representation Committee in 1900 and the Labour Party in 1906.

Nevertheless, even the architects of the 'labour alliance' found the immediate results at times disappointing. In 1903, for

[1] For a summary of the debate on this question at the foundation conference, see my *Origins of the Labour Party*, pp. 117 f.

instance, one of the trade-union leaders, John Hodge, contested a by-election at Preston, where Keir Hardie had fought an unsuccessful campaign in the general election of 1900. Though Hodge was an L.R.C. candidate, he preferred to do without Hardie's proffered assistance. Bruce Glasier wrote rather confusedly to Hardie at the time:

We are all – those of us who teach the faith – held to be a bit disqualified in these days. . . . But what does it matter if we sow and they reap! – the harvest is ours, or rather our cause's, just the same. (Yet, the wisdom of keeping Socialism and Socialists in the background at the last moment or at any time, is not true wisdom, neither is it successful electioneering policy.)[1]

Hardie replied, agreeing that Hodge's attitude was 'apt to raise strange rebellious thoughts'.[2]

With the very leaders who had forged the 'labour alliance' reacting in this way, it is not surprising that the Socialists who had not taken the primary responsibility were even more restless. Robert Blatchford of the *Clarion*, for instance, was fighting a circulation war against Hardie's *Labour Leader* and his proposals for 'Socialist Unity' instead of the 'labour alliance' secured support and readership within the I.L.P., and damaged the circulation of the *Labour Leader*. By 1905 there were already strong demands for new blood in the N.A.C., if not for the exclusion of existing leaders, and at the annual conference a resolution was carried demanding regional representation as a means of effecting this. The existing N.A.C. drew up a scheme which, after slight amendment by the 1906 conference, then came into operation.[3] It allowed for representation of each of nine regions or divisions, but there were still to be nationally elected representatives, and among these, the old 'caucus' continued to secure election.

The years after 1906, with a predominantly non-Socialist Labour Party in the Commons, put still greater strains upon the allegiance of a section of the rank-and-file. One cause of tension was the unwillingness of the leaders to favour contesting

[1] Glasier to Hardie, 15 May 1903, Glasier Correspondence.
[2] Hardie to Glasier, 18 May 1903, ibid.
[3] N.A.C. Minutes, 2 and 3 Oct 1905 and 8 Mar 1906; I.L.P. *Conference Report*, 1906.

parliamentary by-elections, because if successful the I.L.P. candidates would have to be supported from the Labour Party funds, and this would increase the disproportionate amount of money which the I.L.P. Members of Parliament already drew from what was a substantially trade-union treasury. The leaders of the I.L.P. 'caucus', moreover, were mostly too busy with work in Parliament to spend much time visiting the branches. MacDonald wrote to Glasier in 1908: 'I suppose the rank-and-filer does appear to see a junta and over-centralisation, and we had better try and devise some means of placing greater responsibility on the local federations. . . .'[1] He even considered resigning from the N.A.C., but dismissed the idea because he feared that it would then be too much dominated by Hardie, by now a slightly unreliable supporter of his own handiwork, the 'labour alliance'.

It is perhaps unnecessary to take the narrative much further, through the years which saw the culmination of the revolt of the rank-and-file, the resignation of the 'caucus' members from the N.A.C., their continued influence in the party and their temporary return to popularity during the First World War. Clearly, the forces that created the internal tension for the I.L.P. were, on the one hand, the trade-union element in the parliamentary party, which was hostile to the pretensions of the Socialists and unwilling to give the I.L.P. more weight in the 'labour alliance' than it already had; and on the other hand the rank-and-file of the I.L.P., subject as it was to propaganda from elements outside the party such as Blatchford and the S.D.F. The only solution lay in the conversion to Socialism of the entire working class, or at least a substantial section of it, which would in the end lead to the conversion of the trade-union leadership. Unfortunately for the I.L.P., this never took place. Furthermore, its own influence in the trade unions was hindered by the fact that many of its members were of the middle class. Frederick Rogers, for instance, who was the first chairman of the L.R.C., distrusted the I.L.P. for its 'large middle-class element';[2] and R. C. K. Ensor, in his important memorandum for the Fabian Society on the character of the I.L.P. (written in 1907) pointed to 'the presence and prominence of a middle-class element'. He noted also 'the presence of women –

[1] MacDonald to Glasier, 31 Dec 1908, Glasier Correspondence.

[2] F. Rogers, *Labour, Life and Literature* (1913), p. 210.

an element which has played a larger direct part in the I.L.P. than, probably, in any other English party or political society'.[1] To a large extent they were middle-class women, who had time to spare for politics.

The tendency of the I.L.P. to become increasingly middle-class was much accentuated during the First World War. Mrs Webb reckoned that by May 1915 the party had 'dropped about ten thousand of its working-class membership and added about as many hundreds of middle-class adherents'.[2] Brockway described the party during the war as 'isolated from the mass of the workers'. He drew a contrast between the U.D.C. group, 'bourgeois to the fingertips', and on the other hand the Glasgow leaders, though even the latter were 'not all working-class in the strict sense of the word'.[3] After the war was over, the reforms of Clifford Allen seemed only to strengthen the middle-class tendency of the party. It was Allen who brought to its leadership men such as Charles Roden Buxton and Charles Trevelyan, both of them sons of baronets.[4] The transformation of the *Labour Leader* into the *New Leader*; the appointment of H. N. Brailsford as its editor at a substantial salary; its new appeal as a journal at least half-way towards the *New Statesman* in character; the financing of the party largely by lavish subscriptions from Quakers; the interest in folk dancing and the Arts Guild – all these changes perpetuated the suspicion and even hostility that had arisen during the war and in some cases earlier between the trade unions and the I.L.P. And within the party, as John Paton put it, Allen had to face not so much genuine policy disagreements, but 'a rooted and probably largely instinctive distrust of the whole middle-class element'.[5]

The last great period of the I.L.P.'s history, between 1926 and 1931, was full of irony. Perhaps it was already too late to save the party as a working-class organisation; but little attempt was made. The overthrow of Allen was accomplished by an alliance of

[1] Fabian Society Executive Papers, Sep 1907.

[2] Entry of 3 May 1915, *Beatrice Webb's Diaries, 1912–1924*, ed. M. I. Cole (1952), p. 34.

[3] A. F. Brockway, *Inside the Left* (1942), p. 54.

[4] See Allen's letter to Buxton (n.d. ? Oct 1925) quoted M. Gilbert, *Plough My Own Furrow* (1965), p. 196.

[5] J. Paton, *Left Turn!* (1936), p. 194.

provincial left-wingers with the most traditional working class elements in the party. The result was the ascendancy of Maxton, whose policy of attacking the trade-union leadership (as embodied in the Cook-Maxton manifesto) could only alienate the I.L.P. still further from the bulk of the labour movement. In the final negotiations over I.L.P. acceptance of the Standing Orders of the Parliamentary Party, it was George Lansbury, a poacher turned gamekeeper if there ever was one, who obstinately demanded I.L.P. submission. And after the disaffiliation, it was the provincial working-class members, led by Dollan, Maxton's allies in the defeat of Allen, who headed the exodus into the Labour Party. We must not forget that the I.L.P.'s rapid membership decline only took place after disaffiliation: it sank from 16,773 in 1932 to 11,092 in 1933, 7,166 in 1934 and 4,392 in 1935.[1]

The value of Dr Dowse's study is primarily for these final years. He discusses usefully the class tensions within the party and the hostility of Dollan and of Sandham of Lancashire, the other main provincial 'chieftain', for the *New Leader* and the 'bohemianism' of Ernest Hunter. He shows interestingly how the former Conscientious Objectors who played such a big part in the formulation of the party's policy after the First World War found Guild Socialism attractive because of its anti-state implications – just at the time when there was a real need for state intervention in the economy. He describes how the working-class provincials were anxious to discuss unemployment rather than foreign policy, while the middle-class Londoners felt that the cause of the depression in trade lay in reparations from Germany. He recounts the frosty reception given by the T.U.C. to the 'Living Wage' proposals and particularly to the plan for family allowances. But it seems to me a pity that he has not worked out a consistent interpretation of the story. At one moment it looks as if he regards intelligent leadership as the key to political success, for he speaks of the Liberal Party having 'shrunk into the margins of British political history' because in 1917–20 it was 'robbed of its brains' who joined the I.L.P. and the Labour Party. But at another moment he speaks of the 'dismal intellectual record of the Labour Party', and elsewhere tells us that its story would hardly have been different if MacDonald, Maxton and all the

[1] These figures were kindly supplied to me by Mr Francis Johnson, then the Financial Secretary of the party.

rest had been 'men of greater intellectual stature and historical insight'.

The bibliography is useful, at least for the 1920s, but any student wishing to trace the location of I.L.P. primary sources would do better to consult Mr Marwick's article.

8 Two By-Elections: Jarrow
and Colne Valley, 1907

WHEN the Liberal Government secured its massive majority in 1906, it did so on an essentially negative programme – a programme of halting the Unionist trend towards fiscal reform, of reversing the Taff Vale judgment of 1901, and of repealing as much as possible of the Education Act of 1902. In their election addresses, with only one or two exceptions the members of the new Cabinet who were Commoners eschewed mention of particular measures of social reform, and only one of them, John Burns, went so far as to speak of Old Age Pensions as a desirable object for the new Parliament.[1]

Nevertheless both in the new ministry and among the rank-and-file of the Liberal Party there was a good deal of interest in social reform, and the more conservative Liberals were mostly of the older generation. Many of the Scottish M.P.s seemed to regard the Labour Party as the Socialist enemy of individualist Liberalism: but this view was much less common in England, except among genuine Conservatives. It is true that there was some excuse for confusion in Scotland, because both the Scottish T.U.C. and the Scottish Workers Representation Committee (the equivalent of the London-based Labour Representation Committee) were dominated by Socialists. This was because of the weakness of trade unionism in Scotland more than for any other reason.[2] The Scottish Liberal Association, confident of its strength, had refused to enter into negotiations with the Scottish Workers Representation Committee for the mutual avoidance of rival candidatures, and there was consequently no agreement in Scotland along the lines of the understanding made in 1903 for England and Wales. In the upshot, only two Labour M.P.s were elected for Scottish constituencies, and they had had to defeat Liberal as well as Unionist opponents.

[1] See election addresses in the National Liberal Club Collection.

[2] For a sketch of the history of the S.W.R.C., see F. Bealey and H. Pelling, *Labour and Politics, 1900–6* (1958), pp. 293–7.

It was therefore not very surprising that in the new Parliament the Scottish Liberals, who owed nothing to Labour support, were prepared to lead the way in denouncing the new Labour Party and in emphasising the differences between its creed and their own. An early by-election at Cockermouth in Cumberland in August 1906 provided them with their opportunity, for it appeared that this Liberal seat was lost to a Unionist owing to the intervention of a Labour candidate, who had not fought at the general election. The Labour candidate, Robert Smillie, was in fact a Scot – a leader of the Scottish Miners who was also a prominent associate of Keir Hardie in the I.L.P. Immediately after the result the Scottish Liberal Whip, the Master of Elibank, urged a Liberal 'crusade against Socialism',[1] and two months later the Scottish Liberal Association, meeting at Peebles, passed a resolution demanding opposition at elections to all candidates who would not dissociate themselves from Socialism.[2]

Responsible Liberal opinion in England could not take this line. For one thing, many of the Liberal M.P.s owed their seats to the tacit alliance with Labour at the general election. Moreover, it had always been the calculation of those who made this alliance that it would have the effect of making the Labour Party less intransigent. As Herbert Gladstone, the Liberal Chief Whip, put it to Campbell-Bannerman after the general election, 'The L.R.C. men know quite well how much support was given them by the Liberals, & this should be a steadying influence upon them.'[3] The advocates of this policy in the years before the general election naturally did not abandon it at the very first test afterwards. The *Manchester Guardian*, whose editor, C. P. Scott, had played an important part in the application of the alliance in Lancashire and Cheshire, refused even to allocate blame for the loss of the Cockermouth seat. Its solution for the electoral differences that were likely to occur between the Labour and Liberal Parties was the introduction of the Second Ballot.[4] The fullest answer to Elibank's speech was to be found in that journal of 'advanced' Liberalism the *Speaker*, which at once described his anti-Socialist 'crusade' as 'a will-o'-the-wisp'.[5] H. W. Massingham, the journal's

---

[1] *The Times*, 27 Aug 1906.   [2] Ibid., 6 Oct 1906.

[3] Gladstone to Campbell-Bannerman, 21 Jan 1906, B.M. Add. Mss. 41217.

[4] *Manchester Guardian*, 6 Aug 1906.   [5] *The Speaker*, 1 Sep 1906.

leading contributor, went on to attack Elibank for a 'breach of etiquette and good policy'. He pointed out that in point of fact the Labour Party was far more loyal to the government than many of the Liberal M.P.s themselves. Keir Hardie, it was true, was hostile to Liberalism, but 'It is notorious that he does not necessarily get his way in his own party, and that he is not so sedulous a Parliamentarian as Mr Shackleton or Mr MacDonald, whose general view of tactics seems to me to prevail.'[1]

Ministers, too, felt obliged to take up the issue. Lloyd George, speaking at Cardiff, declared that the Liberal Party need only worry about its relationship with Labour if at the end of its present term of office it had 'done nothing to cope seriously with the social condition of the people, to remove the national degradation of slums, widespread poverty and destitution in a land glittering with wealth. . . .' and he specifically instanced Old Age Pensions as a reform that was awaiting implementation.[2] So too, Churchill, speaking in Scotland, tactfully endorsed the Scottish Liberal Association's resolution but at once went on to advocate the *Manchester Guardian*'s policy – the Second Ballot. He also implicitly condemned the idea of an anti-Socialist campaign: 'No man could be either collectivist or individualist; everyone must be both. . . . They were all agreed that the State must concern itself with the care of the sick, of the aged and above all, of the children.'[3]

As time went on, the 'advanced' Liberals became more and more convinced that they were outpacing the Labour Party in their advocacy of social reform. One of them, C. F. G. Masterman, wrote at the end of the second session of the new Parliament that 'the realisation of the mildness of the Labour Party' was now an important factor in Liberal confidence. The party was, he said, 'a mixture of old-fashioned Trades Unionists, with a sprinkling of well-behaved and pleasant Socialists; more punctilious about the forms of the House than the oldest members; more eager in making a bargain with the Government and proving themselves agreeable supporters than the most truculent of the Radicals opposite'.[4] Masterman had in fact caught up with what the Socialists had been saying to themselves for some time. The Social-Democratic Federation had never expected much of the

[1] Ibid., 13 Oct 1906.
[3] Ibid.
[2] *The Times*, 12 Oct 1906.
[4] *Nation*, 24 Aug 1907.

Labour Party, and H. M. Hyndman, the leader of the group, pointed out sadly but without surprise at the end of 1906 that 'not a single Socialist speech has been delivered in the English Popular Assembly'.[1] Within the Independent Labour Party a rank-and-file revolt began to arise as the established leadership (now mostly in Parliament) accepted policies of compromise with the non-Socialist trade-union M.P.s and with the Liberal Government; and early in 1907 Bernard Shaw, who had long been a left-wing critic of the Labour Party, wrote in the *Clarion*: 'Socialism must achieve its independence of the Labor Party as the Labor Party has at last achieved its independence of the Liberal Party.'[2]

After Cockermouth, there were no by-elections which seriously disturbed the relations of the Liberal and Labour Parties until July 1907, when contests took place at Jarrow in Durham and at Colne Valley in Yorkshire. Both these seats were Liberal at the 1906 general election; but both now fell, Jarrow to a Labour candidate who was also a Socialist, and Colne Valley to a Socialist who fought without the endorsement of the Labour Party. It is necessary to examine these two elections in turn, for Jarrow was fought on 4 July and its repercussions had largely spent themselves before Colne Valley polled on the eighteenth.

The election at Jarrow was caused by the death of the sitting member, Sir Charles Mark Palmer. Palmer, now aged eighty-five, was one of the great pioneers of shipbuilding, and the firm that he built up was largely responsible for the growth of the town of Jarrow.[3] He was M.P. for North Durham from 1874, and when the boundaries were readjusted in 1885 he became M.P. for the Jarrow division of the county, which also included a stretch of Tyneside in the Hebburn direction, and some mining districts.[4]

[1] *Justice*, 15 Dec 1906, quoted C. Tsuzuki, *H. M. Hyndman and British Socialism* (Oxford, 1961), p. 163.

[2] *Clarion*, 5 Apr 1907.

[3] For Palmer's career, see *D.N.B.*; obituary in *Jarrow Guardian*, 7 Jun 1907.

[4] For a description of the constituency when it was first formed, see *Newcastle Daily Chronicle*, 9 Nov 1885.

Palmer was a Liberal, but he probably owed his almost undis-
turbed tenure of the constituency to his unique role in the
creation of the town of Jarrow. In 1906 he was opposed for the
first time in twenty-four years: his challenger was Pete Curran,
an official of the Gasworkers Union who, although of Irish origin,
came from the south of England. Curran was a member of the
I.L.P. and was really as prominent in the political as in the
industrial wing of the 'labour alliance'. He stood as an official
L.R.C. candidate and secured a substantial vote among the
miners, who may perhaps have felt that their interests were
somewhat neglected by Palmer. But the industrial vote of Jarrow
seems to have gone mostly to Palmer, who had the advantage of
an endorsement from the Irish Nationalist Party – an important
factor in a town with an Irish vote estimated as some three
thousand, or almost a fifth of the total electorate. The 1906
general election result thus turned out as follows:

Palmer (Liberal)	8,047
Curran (Labour)	5,093

Curran's performance was not unsatisfactory, under the
circumstances; and in view of Palmer's age he continued to nurse
the constituency. An I.L.P. organiser, M. T. Simm, also worked
for some time in the colliery district and helped to form several
new branches.[1] The result was that by the middle of 1907, when
Palmer died, Curran had, as a local paper put it, 'acquired some
sort of right to call himself a local man'.[2] This was just as well, for
he found himself confronted by a local working-man candidate as
well as two 'carpet-baggers'. The local man was J. O'Hanlon, a
Jarrow shipbuilding worker who was put forward by the Irish
Nationalists, who were no longer happy about their alliance with
the Liberals. The others were a London journalist, S. Leigh
Hughes, who stood as the official Liberal, and a barrister, P.
Rose-Innes, K.C., who stood as a Unionist and who talked of the
need to revive the 'ruined industries' of Tyneside by the introduction of Tariff Reform.[3]

The extra candidates were really an advantage to Curran.
Although an Irishman himself, he could not expect to gain much

---

[1] *Labour Leader*, 12 Jul 1907.

[2] *Newcastle Daily Chronicle*, 6 Jul 1907.

[3] S. Leigh Hughes, *Press, Platform and Parliament* (1918), p. 49.

of the Irish vote, which would go to the Liberal if not to an independent Irish candidate. As for the Unionist candidate, his potential vote was an uncertain factor, but if he had not stood, his supporters would probably have backed the official Liberal rather than a Labour challenger. In fact, Palmer's 1906 supporters were now likely to divide into three roughly equal sections, and all that Curran had to do was to retain his 1906 vote. He decided to play down his Socialist affiliation and to emphasise his trade-union connections, believing that this would appeal to the miners and to some at least of the Jarrow men.[1] He had the advantage of having started his campaign earlier than the other candidates; and his election address was on the walls for several days before the others appeared.[2] The by-election result was:

Curran (Labour)	4,698
Rose-Innes (Unionist)	3,930
Hughes (Liberal)	3,474
O'Hanlon (Irish Nat.)	2,122

Curran had in fact lost a few votes since 1906; but O'Hanlon had not polled the full Irish total. In spite of the comparative prosperity of local industry, Rose-Innes had done unexpectedly well – no doubt principally among the tradesmen of Jarrow and the freeholders of South Shields, who had votes in the division. The miners had once again been the backbone of Curran's support; and during the polling, his colours were particularly conspicuous at West Boldon and at Boldon Colliery. They were hardly to be seen at all at South Shields.[3]

Comment on the result suggested that political observers simply used it to confirm their own opinions. The Unionist press, which was already even keener than Elibank to denounce the threat of Socialism, found fresh evidence at Jarrow. *The Times* regarded the result as indicating that the real issue of politics lay between Socialism and Tariff Reform:

It is between the two positive schools, represented on the one hand by Labour-Socialism, with its appeals to class jealousy and

[1] For his election address see *Jarrow Guardian*, 14 Jun 1907. He did not mention that he was a Socialist.

[2] *Clarion*, 21 Jun 1907.

[3] *Newcastle Daily Chronicle*, 5 Jul 1907; *Jarrow Guardian*, 12 and 19 Jul 1907.

its impracticable panaceas, and on the other by constructive Unionism, with its appeal to the instinct of national and Imperial cohesion, and its programme of practical material progress, that the real political conflict of the future will mainly lie.[1]

The *Standard* and the *Pall Mall Gazette* took a similar line.[2] The Liberal press, on the other hand, saw nothing to be alarmed about. The *Newcastle Daily Chronicle*, with its local knowledge, pointed out that 'though Mr Curran subscribes to most of the tenets of the Collectivists, he has certainly not obtruded his faith in their aims'. The paper pointed out that Curran's poll had actually dropped, and concluded that the result was 'not a victory for any party, nor a defeat for any other'.[3] The *Manchester Guardian* took the same line: 'There is nothing in the result of the election to put Liberals about. . . . The falling off in the Liberal vote is only apparent, not real.'[4] And the *Tribune*, a short-lived Liberal daily, saw the result as primarily a rebuff to Tariff Reform. The Liberal vote in 1906 had been 'clearly a Palmer vote'. The moral of the election was the need for the Second Ballot.[5] The *Nation* (which was the new name of the *Speaker*) also argued, but at much greater length, the case for the Second Ballot, or for some other electoral reform, in order to accommodate the different standpoints of the Left without running the risk of allowing a minority Unionist candidate to win.[6]

Thus in mid-July it hardly seemed that the political scene had been much disturbed by Jarrow's change of allegiance. But the Colne Valley election was still to come. It may be that the electors of that other Northern industrial community were those most affected by the Jarrow result.

There were similarities between the two constituencies involved in the July by-elections, but the differences were also considerable. Colne Valley was, like Jarrow, an industrial division of a county,

---

[1] *The Times*, 6 Jul 1907.
[2] *Standard*, 6 Jul 1907; *Pall Mall Gazette*, 6 Jul 1907.
[3] *Newcastle Daily Chronicle*, 6 Jul 1907.
[4] *Manchester Guardian*, 6 Jul 1907.   [5] *Tribune*, 6 Jul 1907.
[6] *Nation*, 13 Jul 1907.

with a small proportion of freehold electors, in this case those who held property in the borough of Huddersfield. Like Jarrow, too, Colne Valley had long been held by a Liberal industrialist. But Sir James Kitson, the Leeds ironmaster who had held the seat since 1892, and who was now creating the vacancy by his acceptance of a peerage, had not possessed the same degree of personal influence that Palmer had at Jarrow. The seat was more genuinely Liberal in character, consisting of a number of small textile manufacturing towns and villages in the valley of the River Colne. On the east side, the constituency touched on the outskirts of Huddersfield; but on the west side it included some of the western slope of the Pennines and approached closely to Oldham. Most of the mills were manufacturing woollen goods, but on the west side, notably at Saddleworth, some cotton workers were to be found. The general political complexion of the division was Liberal, but Conservatism found some support in the Saddleworth area, and consequently Kitson had had to face Conservative opposition at every election except that of 1906, though it never came within reach of defeating him.[1]

In 1895 Kitson had also had to face a Labour candidate, the well-known industrial agitator Tom Mann, but he got less than one-eighth of the votes polled, and the challenge was not renewed at later elections. All the same, there was a tenacious I.L.P. organisation known as the Colne Valley Labour League, which had been founded in 1891 – that is to say, before the national I.L.P. had been formed;[2] and its leaders looked forward to the time when they could fight the constituency again. With the general boom experienced by all the I.L.P. branches after the successes of January 1906, the League flourished and a monthly Labour newspaper, the *Worker*, already established at Huddersfield in 1905, was turned into a weekly. At a general meeting of the League held in January 1907, a parliamentary candidate was chosen. His name was Victor Grayson, a young man of twenty-five who had studied at Owen's College, Manchester – a fiery speaker and altogether a different type of man from the middle-aged trade-

[1] *Yorkshire Post,* 14 Jul 1892; *Leeds Mercury,* 24 Jul 1895; *Oldham Standard,* 13 Oct 1900.

[2] S. Eastwood, *History of the Colne Valley Labour Party, 1891–1941* (Huddersfield, 1941); D. F. E. Sykes, *History of the Colne Valley* (Slaithwaite, 1906), pp. 366 ff.

K

union secretaries who now formed the bulk of the Labour Party at Westminster.[1]

Naturally the Colne Valley Labour League expected to secure the endorsement of their choice by the national I.L.P. and by the Labour Party itself. But there were difficulties. In the first place, the Labour Party did not recognise candidates who had not been approved by a joint conference of representatives of trade-union as well as of Socialist organisations in the constituency concerned. No such conference had been held in the Colne Valley, the adoption meeting having been one for members of the Labour League only. But in any case, the Labour Party executive might well have been unwilling to approve the selection. Its trade-union members felt that the I.L.P. was securing too many representatives in Parliament, where they had to be paid for by the funds contributed almost exclusively by the unions. The I.L.P. contribution was in 1906–7 only £83 6s. 8d., while its members who had been elected to Parliament, seven in number, drew a total of £1,400.[2] To make matters worse, Grayson was not even on the list of suitable parliamentary candidates which the I.L.P. had submitted to the Labour Party; and the I.L.P. leaders did not wish, as Keir Hardie later said, to put this young man ahead of 'men who had grown grey in the movement'.[3]

No solution had been found to the deadlock when the vacancy caused by Kitson's elevation was announced in June. No meeting of the Labour Party executive was to be held until after the date fixed for the by-election, and so the decision whether to make an exception for Grayson in view of the impending contest had to be dealt with by a small emergency committee which met on 28 June. The members of this body who were able to attend were four in number – David Shackleton, the leading non-Socialist who had almost beaten Keir Hardie for the chairmanship of the parliamentary party in 1906; Walter Hudson, also a trade-union M.P. but in addition a member of the I.L.P.; Edward Pease, the secretary of the Fabian Society; and Ramsay MacDonald, at this time both secretary of the Labour Party executive and chairman of the I.L.P. It may well be that Shackleton's was the decisive voice at this meeting. MacDonald had in the past been so insistent on non-Socialist candidates complying with all the formalities of the

---

[1] Wilfred Thompson, *Victor Grayson, His Life and Work* (Sheffield, 1910).
[2] I.L.P. *Report, 1907*, p. 16.   [3] Ibid., *1908*, p. 51.

party constitution that he found it difficult to press for an exception to be made in this instance. But in any case a clear departure from customary procedure could hardly be decided on by a little group of four men if they were not themselves united on such a course. It was therefore resolved: 'That as Mr Grayson's candidature has not been presented in accordance with our constitution and practice, we can take no action.' It was also decided, at Shackleton's insistence and apparently with Mac-Donald silently disagreeing, to advise officials of the national party and of the parliamentary party to take no part in the election.[1]

This decision naturally put the I.L.P. Council in 'a difficult and unpleasant position', as it reported to its next annual conference.[2] Hardie was annoyed by the Emergency Committee's inflexibility, and felt as he wrote to Bruce Glasier, the editor of the *Labour Leader*, that there was a danger of the I.L.P. itself 'underestimating the strength of local feeling'.[3] A long discussion took place at a meeting of the I.L.P. Council on 5 July – the day of the Jarrow result – and it was reported that the Colne Valley Labour League was making a virtue of necessity and 'under the special circumstances . . . did not wish for the endorsement of the Labour Party'. But the two I.L.P. leaders most closely in touch with rank-and-file opinion, Hardie and Snowden, both felt that the Council itself was partly at fault 'for not taking drastic action earlier' – presumably by insisting on a new adoption conference – and the upshot was that the Council agreed that while it could not officially endorse the candidature, it would not object to the Colne Valley Labour League doing so. Snowden was to go down and help Grayson in the contest, Glasier was to open a campaign fund in the *Labour Leader*, and MacDonald was to shut the stable door after the horse had bolted by sending a circular to all the branches warning them not to adopt parliamentary candidates without the Council's sanction.[4] As for Hardie, he was already committed to

[1] Labour Party Executive Minutes, Emergency Committee, 28 Jun 1907, Transport House Library. For MacDonald's account of the meeting, see his letter to Glasier, n.d. ? 20 or 21 Jul 1907, Glasier Papers, by courtesy of Mr Francis Johnson.

[2] I.L.P. *Report, 1908*, p. 17.

[3] Hardie to Glasier, n.d. ? 1 Jul 1907, Glasier Papers.

[4] I.L.P. Council Minutes, 5 Jul 1907, by courtesy of Mr Francis Johnson.

leaving England almost immediately on a long sea cruise, as he was in poor health. This saved him from the embarrassment of having to decide between his loyalty to the Labour Party's decision and his instinct to help in a fight against the Liberals.[1]

In the *Labour Leader* on July 12th, Glasier put the best construction possible on the whole business. The mix-up over endorsement, he said, was 'regrettable', but he did not blame anyone in particular. All the same, the local branches had a strong moral case:

The I.L.P. has made the political pace in the valley, and but for the work of its members in the division, as in most divisions in the country, there would be no resolute Labour representation movement at all. This the local Trade Unionists themselves recognise, and there is every indication that they will join with might and main in securing a victory for Mr Grayson.

Meanwhile Grayson proceeded with his campaign. He certainly made no attempt to conceal the fact that he was a Socialist, but from the outset he had made it clear to the electors that he wished to associate himself with the Labour Party. This is shown by his election address, the first paragraphs of which ran as follows:

Gentlemen,

In consequence of the promotion of your Parliamentary member to the House of Lords, I am enabled to offer myself as Socialist and Labour candidate for your support. This I do at the unanimous request of the Colne Valley Labour League, which is affiliated to the Independent Labour Party. The last General Election revealed a significant change in public opinion, and organised Labour was permitted to get its foot into the House of Commons. The result is before your eyes. The thirty Labour members have been able to wield an influence far out of proportion to their number. They have dragged from an evasive Liberal Government the little industrial reform that has been placed on the Statute Book in the last eighteen months. Without the Labour Party the Trades Disputes Act would have been colourless and ineffective, and it is highly questionable whether there would have been a Workmen's Compensation Act at all.

The era of industrial reform began with the advent of the

[1] Even so, some members of the Labour Party Executive took exception to his sending a message of support to Grayson. See Labour Party Executive Minutes, 25 Jul 1907.

Labour party in the House of Commons, and if questions affecting our lives and welfare as workers are to be considered in the House of Commons, it is absolutely necessary to strengthen the hands of the workers' representatives.

After this, it is true, Grayson made a brief avowal of his Socialist beliefs; but he then passed to a list of immediate political issues which suggested that he was very closely in line with Labour Party attitudes. He concluded, in a curious mixture of old-fashioned courtesy and revolutionary fervour:

For the next few years there lies a tremendous task in front of the Labour Party. Now is the time to strike a blow at Capitalism and Landlordism, and for the down-trodden and oppressed. Workers, Unite! You have a world to win and only your chains to lose.

> Trusting to receive your support,
> I am, your obedient servant
> Albert Victor Grayson.[1]

In the speeches that he made during the campaign, Grayson placed greater emphasis on Socialism, and spoke much less about the Labour Party. This may have been because he was embarrassed by the Labour Party's failure to endorse his candidature, and was afraid of hostile questioning on this point. Certainly the other candidates, and in particular the Liberal, did not fail to draw attention to the matter. But it may also have been the case that those who were sufficiently interested in politics to attend his meetings were those who were most likely to be susceptible to a crusading Socialist appeal.

By all accounts, the by-election was a stirring experience for those who took part. The contest was fought in very good summer weather, and the Pennine villages and dales were at their most attractive. Unlike most industrial workers, the inhabitants of the Colne Valley were for the most part well-housed. The solid stone cottages often had large living rooms which had originally been used for hand weaving. Wages were not particularly high, even by the standards of the day, but they were regular, for the textile industry was unusually prosperous and had been so for several years; and the villages offered few temptations to encourage a

---

[1] *Worker* (Huddersfield), 13 Jul 1907. Reg Groves in his *Mystery of Victor Grayson* (1946), p. 22 incorrectly quotes a shorter document – presumably a leaflet – as the election address.

waste of money. The women and girls with their crimson shawls, the men with their blue smocks, and the background of wild moorland provided a striking contrast to the drab scenery of most industrial districts, and, heartened by the good weather, it seems that the journalists following the campaign enjoyed their assignment. 'As I write', ran a report in the *Leeds Mercury*, 'the sun is sinking in golden glory behind the moors, and already the valleys are filled with those purple shadows which cast a veil of mystery and beauty even over mill chimneys.'[1]

But for many of the electors, the most exciting feature of the campaign must have been the magnetic oratory of the young Grayson, and the enthusiasm of his band of voluntary workers, who came from far and wide to give him their assistance. None of the candidates was a local man; but Grayson had the advantage of having been before the constituency for some months. The *Standard*, which was by no means favourable to his cause, noted how 'admiring crowds follow him, women wear his party colours'.[2] There were suffragettes working on his behalf; and in addition, his supporting speakers included a Congregational minister and an Anglican curate. Meanwhile the Huddersfield *Worker* supplied him with paper ammunition and the *Labour Leader* and *Clarion* also issued special by-election editions and appealed for funds on his behalf.

The other candidates were on the defensive in the face of the Socialist campaign. The Liberal candidate was Philip Bright, a son of John Bright, but himself a resident of London. After the campaign was over, he complained of the aspersions thrown on his father's attitude to the Factory Acts and on his own conduct as an employer.[3] The Unionist candidate, Granville Wheler, was a landowner in the Castleford area of East Yorkshire. He was saddled with the disadvantage of having to advocate Tariff Reform, which was not popular in the textile districts. Some 'Conservative Labour' spokesmen appeared to work on his behalf, but they attracted little attention.

On election day, it was as usual apparent that the Unionist strength lay at the Lancashire end of the division. 'At Greenfield, Upper Hill and Mossley', one report ran, 'the Tory blue is the predominating colour.'[4] At the opposite end, Milnsbridge, the

---

[1] *Leeds Mercury*, 19 Jul 1907.   [2] *Standard*, 18 Jul 1907.
[3] *Huddersfield Examiner*, 20 Jul 1907.   [4] *Leeds Mercury*, 19 Jul 1907.

suburb of Huddersfield, was an I.L.P. stronghold; so too was Honley. There it was the red that was predominant. The Liberal yellow was 'almost a monopoly' at Diggle, just inside Yorkshire, and yellow and red were 'equally matched' at Marsden.[1] Slaith-waite and Golcar showed the colours of all three candidates. The result showed how closely balanced the voting of all three candidates was:

Grayson (Socialist)	3,648
Bright (Liberal)	3,495
Wheler (Unionist)	3,227

It was a narrow enough victory, but it was victory – and according to Grayson, a victory for Socialism: 'The Liberals said Curran got in for Jarrow because he hid his Socialism. Will they say Grayson did the same when he got in for the Colne Valley ?'[2]

Certainly the Unionist papers gave Grayson his due, and perhaps a little more. The *Daily Telegraph* said that 'organised Socialism has risen up in the night', and the *Standard* spoke of the 'ominous growth of Socialism'.[3] The *Pall Mall Gazette* found the result 'epoch-making', and said that it gave 'a crushing blow to the self-complacency of the old political groupings'. Whereas Jarrow had been won by a candidate under the guise of Labour, in the Colne Valley 'Socialism stalked to victory naked and unashamed'.[4]

Nor did the Liberal press try to deny that it was a Socialist victory, though the advanced Radical journals were remarkably unmoved. The *Manchester Guardian* said that: 'The salient fact about the election is that the cause of political progress is immensely stronger in the division now than it has ever been before.'[5] The *Tribune* conceded that the result was 'surprising' but asserted that 'For all immediate practical purposes of the first order Mr Grayson's vote will be given with that of the Liberal majority at Westminster.'[6] And the *Nation* declared: 'We

---

[1] Ibid. Cf. *Oldham Standard*, 18 Jul 1907.

[2] *Huddersfield Examiner*, 20 Jul 1907.

[3] *Daily Telegraph*, 24 Jul 1907 ; *Standard*, 20 Jul 1907.

[4] *Pall Mall Gazette*, 20 Jul 1907.

[5] *Manchester Guardian*, 20 Jul 1907.   [6] *Tribune*, 20 Jul 1907.

profess ourselves unable to understand the alarm which the election ... has awakened in the breasts of the British people, or perhaps we should say in the minds of British journalists. ... For us it [Socialism] occupies about the same relation to Liberal politics as the Salvation Army to the regular churches.'[1]

It was left to the I.L.P. to argue that Grayson's success was a victory for Labour, at least as much as for Socialism. Ramsay MacDonald said: 'Whilst it is true that Mr Grayson was not put forward officially by us as our candidate, he undoubtedly used the influence of the Labour Party with good effect. ... The result of the election is highly encouraging and satisfactory to us.'[2] And the *Labour Leader* argued still more strongly:

We must not overstrain the Colne Valley victory as a Socialist victory. No one who knows the constituency and the general tide of feeling among the working class there will be disposed to say that Mr Grayson's success, so far as the intention of the electorate is concerned, stands out distinctively from the success of Jarrow and the general success of the Labour Party cause.[3]

Obviously the Labour Party and I.L.P. leaders had an axe to grind. If Socialism could win elections unaided, then there was little point in the 'labour alliance' policy to which they had been committed ever since 1900. Yet taking everything into account – including Grayson's election address – it is difficult not to feel that their interpretation of the election was the most sensible one.

How far can we conclude, as historians have suggested, that the Colne Valley election, or the two by-elections together, were responsible for prodding the Liberal Government into its subsequent policy of social reform?[4] Asquith introduced a definite plan for non-contributory Old Age Pensions in the 1908 Budget, but his intention to do this was already clear a full year earlier, when he announced that he intended to put aside £2¼ million in the ensuing year (1907–8) for this purpose. Thus he had evidently made up his mind in favour of Old Age Pensions before these by-elections. Lloyd George and Churchill were the initiators and the executants of the later programme of social reforms, and their

[1] *Nation*, 27 Jul 1907.   [2] *Leeds Mercury*, 20 Jul 1907.

[3] *Labour Leader*, 26 Jul 1907.

[4] E.g. B. B. Gilbert, *Evolution of National Insurance in Great Britain* (1966), p. 210.

favourable attitude to policies of this type was also evident well before the by-elections, for instance, as we have seen, in their speeches of the autumn of 1906. Then again, even if the government had wished to ignore the problems connected with the Poor Law, it is obvious that the Report of the Royal Commission on the subject, which reported in 1909, would have forced them to do something. Finally, it is by no means clear that those who were keenest on social reform thought even after the Colne Valley election that it would secure popular support. Thus Churchill wrote to J. A. Spender in the winter of 1907/8: 'The people are not satisfied, but neither are they offended against the government. . . . They may not be able, they may be willing to recognise themselves unable, to devise a new system. I think them very ready to be guided, and patient beyond conception.'[1] And late the following year, when he was urging Asquith to take action, he wrote to him: 'The Minister who will apply to this country the successful experiments of Germany in social organisation may or may not be supported at the polls, but he will at least have left a memorial which time will not deface of his Administration.'[2]

If the Liberal leaders were sceptical of the significance of these by-elections, events were to justify their attitude. In the 1910 general election, both seats reverted to Liberalism. At Jarrow, a member of the Palmer family was nominated as the Liberal candidate, and he won in January in a three-cornered fight. In the December election the Labour candidate was pushed down to third place. At Colne Valley Grayson, who had refused to accept the Labour whip at Westminster, but whose upkeep in Parliament had been provided by the I.L.P., was also defeated by a Liberal in the election of January 1910; in fact he was pushed into third place, and did not even contest the division in the December election. The personal factors which had told in his favour in 1907 – his youth and oratorical skill – were now more than counterbalanced by a growing reputation for instability and intemperance. But in any case, it seems to be a rule of politics that by-elections tend to produce much stronger protest votes than are recorded at general elections, when the electors are more concerned with the major parties which can form governments.

[1] Quoted H. W. Harris, *J. A. Spender* (1946), p. 80.
[2] Churchill to Asquith, 29 Dec 1908, Asquith Papers, Bodleian Library Mss., by courtesy of Mr Mark Bonham Carter.

Perhaps the principal results of the Jarrow and Colne Valley elections, therefore, are to be found in their impact on the two extremes in British politics at the time. Among the Unionists there developed an anti-Socialist campaign, which led to some twenty travelling vans being sent round the country, with lecturers, gramophones, magic lanterns and leaflets, to convert people back from Socialism. It would be difficult to gauge the campaign's success; but it is doubtful if in the long run it was of any major importance. Meanwhile, on the Left a formidable revolt against the 'labour alliance', headed by Grayson and encouraged by Hyndman of the S.D.F. and Blatchford of the *Clarion*, led in 1911 to a split in the I.L.P. and to the secession of many of its branches to join a new organisation known as the British Socialist Party.[1] The upshot of this was more to weaken the I.L.P. than to provide an alternative Socialist organisation, for within a couple of years the B.S.P. was little stronger than the S.D.F. which it absorbed had previously been. As for Victor Grayson, his personal unreliability increased and he emigrated from Britain a few months before the First World War. Whether he ever returned to Britain, and if not, where he spent the remainder of his life, is not known.[2] But Socialists long recalled the episode of the Colne Valley by-election with particular nostalgia, for they believed, probably incorrectly, that it was one of those rare occasions when a working-class electorate voted positively for Socialism – and, by doing so, helped to bring about social change.

[1] For an account of this see Tsuzuki, *Hyndman and British Socialism*, pp. 168–78.

[2] See Groves, *Mystery of Victor Grayson*, pp. 101 ff.

9 The Labour Unrest, 1911–14

THE years 1911–14 are marked in British history not only by the deepening crisis over the question of Irish Home Rule and by the increasing violence of the militant suffragettes, but also by the period of 'labour unrest', which involved bitter strikes, several of them national in character and requiring intervention by Cabinet ministers. In the course of the period a new philosophy of industrial action for political ends came into prominence; and at the same time a remarkable extension of the frontiers of trade unionism took place. Contemporaries cast around for explanations of these phenomena. Sir George Askwith, the government's chief industrial adviser, reported to the Cabinet in 1911 that the probable main causes were the rise in the cost of living, and the failure of wages to keep pace; the conspicuous display of luxury by the rich, particularly exemplified in the use they made of motorcars; and the growth of the press and the improvement of communications, which made for greater national co-ordination of news and activity.[1] Other, less well-informed observers added to this list of causes, without however producing any that seem more plausible.[2]

Historians who have so far turned their attention to this period have for the most part assumed that there was some sort of connection between the militancy of labour and that of the Unionists and the Nationalists over the Irish question, and even that of the suffragettes. Élie Halévy, writing in the early 1930s, was already convinced that the 'era of tyrannies' was at hand, and that the British belief in a 'moderate liberty' as 'the secret of moral and political stability' was now no more than a Victorian relic, a 'splendid illusion' soon to disappear.[3] For him, therefore, the events of 1910 to 1914 were a domestic curtain-raiser to the

[1] Report on Industrial Unrest, Cabinet Papers, Sep 1911: Public Record Office, Cab. 37/107/107.

[2] For a convenient summary, see R. V. Sires, 'Labour Unrest in England, 1910–1914', *Journal of Economic History*, xv (1955).

[3] É. Halévy, *History of the English People: Epilogue*, ii (1934), p. xiv.

violence of international war, which in turn seemed destined to be succeeded, after a brief Indian summer of parliamentarism, by even greater catastrophes. He saw it as a period of 'domestic anarchy', in which three parallel and associated developments took place: the 'Syndicalist Revolt', the 'Feminist Revolt', and the 'Irish Revolt'.[1] So too a British historian, George Dangerfield, who could surpass the distinguished Frenchman in rhetorical force if not in learning, wrote of the period under the title *The Strange Death of Liberal England*. For him, 'the assaults upon Parliament of the Tories, the women and the workers' had 'something profoundly in common'.[2] It is difficult to discover from his book, however, what this common element was, other than the spirit of revolt itself.

There was, of course, another historian of the period who wrote a good deal about the labour unrest, and who almost had a proprietary interest in the subject. This was G. D. H. Cole, the pioneer of Guild Socialism, the theory of which he helped to develop out of Syndicalism soon after Syndicalism first appeared. Cole, in his book *The World of Labour*, which was published in 1913, had nothing to say about Irish Home Rule or about Women's Suffrage: but he was convinced that the labour unrest indicated the emergence of 'a new and positive demand, . . . a nascent philosophy which needs formulation and interpretation'.[3] Cole was here thinking of the idea which his own Guild Socialism had in common with Syndicalism – namely, the idea of workers' control of industry. Some years later, however, after both the Syndicalist and Guild Socialist movements had waned, he saw the period in rather more negative terms, as being marked by 'a mass movement of sheer reaction against the failure of either orthodox trade unionism or modern parliamentarism to secure any improvement in the working-class standard of life'.[4] It was evidently the reaction against 'parliamentarism' which was common to the various tendencies of the period, in Cole's view, for we read in *The Common People*, a joint work by Cole and his brother-in-law, Raymond Postgate, 'Parliaments, everywhere where they had real power, were coming up against problems

[1] Ibid., p. xvi.   [2] Dangerfield, p. 226.
[3] G. D. H. Cole, *World of Labour*, p. 54.
[4] Cole, *Short History of the British Working Class Movement*, iii (1927), p. 70.

which could not be solved by traditional parliamentary methods.'[1] So far as British labour was concerned, Cole and Postgate summed up the pre-war situation as follows: 'The workers wanted their share [of increasing wealth], and they did not appear to be getting it, or the Labour Party to be helping them to get it. Hence the revulsion against Labour politics, and the resort to direct action by one body of trade unionists after another.'[2]

A study of the labour unrest should begin with the basic facts of the period, and move from these towards some assessment of the causes of change. We may examine, first of all, some of the main characteristics of the period 1911–14, so far as it affected labour, using for comparison the preceding four years 1907–10.

Year	Total union membership (000s)	No. of stoppages beginning in year	Total No. of working days lost by stoppages in progress (000s)	Average retail prices (1850= 100)	Average money wages (1850= 100)	Percentage unemployed
1907	2,513	585	2,150	95	182	3·7
1908	2,485	389	10,790	97	181	7·8
1909	2,477	422	2,690	97	179	7·7
1910	2,565	521	9,870	98	179½	4·7
1911	3,139	872	10,160	99	179	3·0
1912	3,416	834	40,890	103	184	3·2
1913	4,135	1,459	9,800	103	188½	2·1
1914	4,145	972	9,880	102	189½	3·3
	(1)	(2)	(3)	(4)	(5)	(6)

Sources: Columns (1), (2) and (3) – Committee on Industry and Trade, *Survey of Industrial Relations* (H.M.S.O., 1926); *Ministry of Labour Gazette*. Figures refer to Great Britain and Northern Ireland, or, in the case of Column (1), to trade unions with headquarters therein.

Columns (4) and (5) – W. T. Layton and G. Crowther, *Introduction to the Study of Prices* (1938), p. 274.

Column (6) – Percentage unemployed in certain trade unions, as listed in London and Cambridge Economic Service, *The British Economy: Key Statistics 1900–1966* (1967). The figures for 1913 and 1914 have been adjusted by J. Hilton.

---

[1] Cole and Postgate, *The Common People* (1938), p. 460. [2] Ibid., p. 463.

The figures in column (1) clearly indicate the substantial increase of trade-union membership which took place in the years 1911–14, after the preceding period of comparative stability of numbers. As is clear from columns (2) and (3), these were also years of a large number of stoppages and of working days lost. From columns (4) and (5) we may deduce that up to 1911 at least there was a gently-rising cost of living, side by side with an average wage level which was either falling or stable. Obviously Sir George Askwith and other contemporary observers were correct in saying that wages were failing to keep up with the rise in prices, at any rate up to 1912. There is some doubt, however, whether considerations of this character are more likely to stimulate labour unrest than, for instance, attempts to cut wages in a time of declining price-levels. According to K. G. J. C. Knowles, who has devoted a good deal of attention to the causation of strikes, 'Trade unions seem to have reacted to the need for resisting a money wage decrease much more strongly than to the need for achieving a money wage increase to keep up with the cost of living.'[1] Indeed, there was probably still much confusion in the minds of working men about the relationship between money wages and real wages.

A much more significant factor in the situation would appear to be provided by the pattern of the trade cycle. The unemployment figures in column (6) show that the years 1911–14 were exceptionally good years; and it may be added that the only parallel spells of low unemployment in the preceding twenty-five years were in 1888–91 and in 1896–1901. The years 1888–91 also form a period of labour unrest and of very rapid expansion of the frontiers of unionism, associated in particular with the foundation of the 'new unions'. The period 1896–1901 began as a period of increasing strikes, but this was muted from 1899 onwards, possibly owing to the South African War. Over these years, however, there was a marked expansion of trade-union membership, of the order of 25%. Since in the 1880s, at least, prices were still declining and real wages continuing a significant long-term improvement, the labour unrest of those years must be assumed to owe more to the conditions of low unemployment rates than to any acute dissatisfaction about the level of real wages. Men could more readily defy their employers when the supply of potential blacklegs was at its lowest.

[1] K. G. J. C. Knowles, *Strikes* (Oxford, 1954), p. 223.

If this argument is valid, it would seem that the labour unrest of 1911–14 would have taken place in much the same form even if real wages had been continuing the steady rise that had been characteristic of the 1880s. It is worth noticing that the highest annual total of strikes (1,459) occurred in 1913, when the percentage of unemployment was at its lowest (2·1). It is true that this does not coincide with the highest figure for working days lost, which occurs in 1912. But the figures of working days lost are heavily biassed by the impact of a single strike – the national coal strike, which accounted for about three-quarters of the exceptionally high annual figure.

The labour unrest of 1911–14, then, is to be compared, first and foremost, with earlier rapid expansions of union membership such as those of 1867–73 and 1888–91. Comparing 1914 with 1910, the total membership of all unions rose by over 60%. In particular, the membership of unions catering for seamen, dockers and general labourers – unions almost all of which had been founded in the late 1880s or even later – went up by over 300%. The immediate pre-war years in fact saw the fulfilment of the promise of New Unionism, a promise largely unfulfilled earlier, owing to the reaction that took place in the early 1890s.

There were indeed some remarkable parallels in the early development of the movement of 1911 with that of 1889. In both cases, the seamen's union had a role in triggering off the unrest among the dockers. In both cases, the success of a London dock strike stimulated activity in other centres and in other occupations. The Chief Registrar of Friendly Societies, in his report on Trade Unions in the year 1911, stated that the largest increases of membership during the year were in unions connected with transport.[1]

Later on, however, the labour unrest of 1911–14 asserted its own distinctive pattern. The following year, 1912, saw a distinct slackening in the tempo of union recruitment, but not on balance a reaction. Contemporaries hardly felt that there was any easing of the unrest, for this was the year of the national coal strike – a strike only settled by government intervention and the hasty

[1] *P.P.* 1912–13, lxxxi, 981.

enactment of a Minimum Wage Act. In London, the dockers came out on strike for a second time, but this time they met stiff resistance from the Port of London Authority, in the person of Lord Devonport. When they called for a sympathetic strike in other ports, through the newly-created National Transport Workers Federation, they secured a very poor response. Only the Bristol dockers came to their aid: and this was not sufficient to prevent the failure of the strike. The London dockers' union lost a considerable proportion of the new members that it had made in the preceding year.

As unemployment in 1912 remained at a low level, the slow growth of union membership in the course of the year (less than 9%) needs explanation, especially compared with the rapid growth of 1911 (over 22%). One suggestion which has been advanced is that the officials of unions were too busy with the problems raised by the National Insurance Act to spare the time for membership recruitment.[1] Certainly the Act presented a great challenge to the unions, as they were all invited to create 'approved societies' to administer health benefits. Most of the larger unions undertook to do so, and this involved special alterations in union rules and a great deal of extra administrative work for union officers.[2] Additional problems arose for unions which already offered unemployment benefits, for their schemes had to be dovetailed in with those of the government. It was agreed that employees in trades scheduled by the Act for the compulsory unemployment scheme (mainly in engineering or building) could have their benefits paid through the unions; and unions in other trades could obtain a subsidy towards the unemployment benefits they paid.

The unions hoped to be able to obtain some compensation for all this extra work by their officers, in the form of new members attracted to the approved societies or the union-administered unemployment benefits. In practice, however, few unions were able to increase their membership significantly by these means. In almost every trade it was found that the majority of eligible workers preferred to register with an industrial assurance society

[1] H. J. Fyrth and H. Collins, *The Foundry Workers* (Manchester, 1959), p. 134.

[2] See, e.g., Fox, *History of the National Union of Boot and Shoe Operatives*, pp. 324 f.

or with a friendly society as the agent for their health benefits. Out of over thirteen million employees registered with approved societies by 1914, less than a million and a half had chosen the bodies set up by the unions.[1] The unions' failure in the initial competition for members in 1912 was due in some cases to their officials' dislike of the contributory scheme, but usually it was the result of their lack of administrative skill and resources. Occasionally, too, they were faced by the active opposition of employers, who naturally feared that if workers joined a trade-union approved society, they might very well also join the union for industrial purposes.[2]

The only union which made spectacular gains in 1912, clearly attributable to the health provisions of the Act, was the Shop Assistants, which shot up from 22,148 members at the end of 1911 to 64,842 a year later.[3] A number of these new members did not at first realise that they could join the union's approved society without committing themselves to its industrial side; and in 1913 quite a few withdrew, though the industrial total remained above 50,000.[4] From the financial point of view, it was prudent for shop assistants to join an approved society consisting entirely of persons in the same occupation, for their accident rates were low and their occupational hazards much less than those of manual workers. This point was also apparent to the officers of the National Union of Clerks, but the annual conference of this body decided, most unwisely, to confine membership of their approved society to those who had already joined the union for all purposes.[5] For the rest, the unions which made steady if not sensational progress in 1912 were mostly those in the trades scheduled for compulsory unemployment insurance. The Amalgamated Society of Engineers reported an increase of 22,529 – a net gain of over 18%; and the Carpenters and Joiners added 12,600 – about 19%, although a third of this was due to a merger.

---

[1] Abstract of Labour Statistics, *P.P.* 1914–16, lxi, 483.

[2] T.U.C. *Report, 1912*, p. 200; National Amalgamated Union of Shop Assistants, &c., *Annual Report for 1912* (1913), p. 5.

[3] Chief Registrar of Friendly Societies, Report on Trade Unions, *P.P.* 1913, lvii, 767 f.

[4] Ibid., 1914, lxxvi, 629; Shop Assistants, &c., *Annual Report for 1913* (1914), p. 15.

[5] *The Clerk*, Aug 1912.

The following year, 1913, saw the largest increase of trade union membership that had yet taken place – no less than 719,000. As a proportion of the existing membership, however, this was slightly less than in 1911 – 21% as against 22%. All the same, it is obvious that recruitment had speeded up very much since the comparative quiescence of 1912. This time the increase was surprisingly uniform in all industries, though especially marked among railway workers and in general labour. Exceptionally full employment was evidently important. Union officials were also in many cases freer to go out and organise the unorganised workers than they had been in 1912, or even earlier. In the Agricultural Labourers' Union, for instance, the appointment of a clerk to run the approved society business enabled the general secretary to leave the office much more frequently.[1] The Chief Registrar of Friendly Societies, summing up his enquiries about the reasons for union growth in 1913, said that it was in large part due to 'better organisation and business methods'.[2] Of course, as he said, there was also unrest among the workers. It seems likely, although he did not add this point, that it was in no small degree caused by the deduction of fourpence a week from their wages for the health contributions. This was a heavy imposition for the poorer workers, and was much resented. The administration of the Act also had a number of shortcomings which caused widespread irritation in the first months of working: for instance, casual workers who had no continuous employer often had to pay the employer's contribution as well as their own.[3]

The most successful general union – and indeed, the most successful of all unions – in the years 1913 and 1914 was the Workers' Union. This had been founded in 1898 by Tom Mann, but its general secretary was now Charles Duncan, Labour M.P. for Barrow. In 1912 this union was already advertising its claims to protect any type of worker against the employer who would seek to 'transfer the whole cost of the New Insurance Act onto the backs of his unorganised workpeople'.[4] It also offered to represent the insured man who had a grievance about the operation of the

[1] G. Edwards, *From Crow-scaring to Westminster* (1922), p. 182.

[2] *P.P.* 1914–16, lix, 44.

[3] National Union of Dock Labourers, *Executive Report for 1912*, p. 6.

[4] Workers' Union, *A Dozen Spurs to Action* (1912). Copy in British Library of Political and Economic Science.

Act and wanted it remedied. This, it argued, was where trade unions had an advantage over other types of approved society: 'Trade unions have been proved to be right when they took political action'.[1] The rapid progress of the Workers' Union, from a membership of only 22,644 at the end of 1912 to 91,000 a year later, was partly due to vigorous agitation among the hollow-ware workers of the Black Country, who came under Trade Board jurisdiction in the course of the year; but it was also due to very enterprising advertising in the *Daily Citizen*, the new official Labour Party newspaper. The rapid growth of 1913 was continued the following year, and by the end of 1914 the union claimed a total of 159,600 members. The Gasworkers also advertised in the *Citizen*, but more soberly: it also made substantial gains, advancing in 1913 from 82,135 to 134,538.

The other sphere of very rapid growth in union membership in 1913 was the railway industry. Here the amalgamation of three of the five unions was a considerable spur to recruitment. The three unions joining in the amalgamation had a membership of 180,000 at the end of 1912, but the new organisation, the National Union of Railwaymen, reported a total of 267,611 at the end of the year – a net gain of almost 50%. In this industry, where the employers had so long resisted recognition of the unions, the mass of workers were at last plucking up their courage and entering the fold of unionism.

So far, the examination has suggested that the expansion of unionism in this period was very much what we would expect in view of the comparatively full employment of the period. But we have seen that the directions of advance were altered in 1912 by the coming into force of the National Insurance Act, and that they were again altered and probably speeded up in 1913 by the grievances and irritations involved in the initial working of the Act. The railway industry has been mentioned as a sphere of rapid expansion owing to amalgamation: and since amalgamation was one of the main aims of the Syndicalists it may be argued that Syndicalism was here of some importance. Yet the miners, whose militancy was particularly marked in the period, and among whose

[1] Ibid.

ranks also some Syndicalists were to be found, have not been mentioned at all in the narrative of union expansion – for the good reason that they made few gains until 1913, and even then seemed to do little more than keep up with the growth of employment in their industry.

Undoubtedly, Syndicalism was quite a novelty in 1911, at the beginning of the labour unrest. It had only just been imported from France, and needed some time to develop influence among the younger trade-union activists. Its essence was the belief that the workers could use their industrial, rather than their electoral, strength in order to win control of their industries, and to introduce a new system of society in which each industry would be controlled by the workers within that industry. This workers' control would be very different from State Socialism, which the Marxists, the Fabians and the I.L.P. all believed in, and which assumed that parliamentary means would be used to win power and then to nationalise industry. But State Socialism still had no great popularity among the working class, partly no doubt because it implied no more than the substitution of government-appointed managers for managers appointed by private employers. Syndicalism, on the other hand, offered the workers a direct control of their own production units, and an entire removal of the existing management. To those who had no love for bureaucrats or for the extension of the activities of the state, it had a definite appeal. To the French workers, who were not sufficiently numerous to dominate a predominantly agricultural electorate by the ordinary means of parliamentary democracy, it seemed to be the only way of achieving Socialism.

In Britain, Syndicalism found a fertile soil among a section of the younger generation of trade unionists who were already discussing ways of reorganising the unions industry by industry, and thus eliminating the old lines of demarcation along craft boundaries. They called themselves Industrial Unionists, and they had got their ideas mostly from the United States, where mass production was most advanced and craft unions, for xenophobic reasons, most exclusive.[1] Many of them soon fell under the sway of Syndicalism, particularly when there appeared as an advocate of the new doctrine one of the most vigorous leaders of

[1] For the American influence see my *America and the British Left* (1956), Ch. vi.

the New Unionism of the late 1880s – Tom Mann, who had been travelling widely in Australasia and South Africa, and who in 1910 visited France to acquaint himself with the latest developments in theory. Mann began to publish a series of monthly pamphlets under the title *Industrial Syndicalist*; and he had a part in the creation of the National Transport Workers Federation, which was designed to co-ordinate the largely local organisations of dockers and transport workers, other than railwaymen. In 1911 Mann was active in the strikes in the transport industry, and played a key role in the successful Liverpool Transport strike, serving as chairman of the Strike Committee.[1]

The most effective piece of Syndicalist propaganda was however the pamphlet produced by a group of South Wales miners, many of them former Industrial Unionists, which was called *The Miners' Next Step*. This work, published in 1912, envisaged a programme of reorganisation and centralisation of the miners' unions, leading to a national miners' union which could then make alliances with other unions in other industries with the intention of attaining the full Syndicalist goal. All that would be left of the state would be a Central Production Board, which,

... with a statistical department to ascertain the needs of the people, will issue its demands on the different departments of industry, leaving to the men themselves to determine under what conditions and how, the work should be done. This would mean real democracy in real life, making for real manhood and womanhood. Any other form of democracy is a delusion and a snare.[2]

The propaganda of Tom Mann, *The Miners' Next Step*, and the creation of the Transport Workers Federation all provided Syndicalism with a great deal of advertisement, and many observers attributed to it a greater responsibility for the labour unrest than it can properly bear.[3] The active Syndicalists were a tiny minority; and events in 1912 and thereafter showed that they had little influence on union policy. In the first place, the Transport Workers Federation proved quite ineffective when it called for a national sympathetic strike in support of the London

---

[1] Tom Mann, *Memoirs* (1923), pp. 254 ff.

[2] Unofficial Reform Committee, S.W.M.F., *The Miners' Next Step* (Tonypandy, 1912), p. 30.

[3] E.g. Lord Robert Cecil, *H.C.Deb.*, ser. 5, xxxv, 1766 (19 Mar 1912).

Dockers in 1912. The latter, as we have seen, were defeated in their new strike, and suffered a severe setback. Secondly, the Syndicalists were almost entirely unsuccessful in their attempts to reorganise the unions along industrial lines. A scheme to centralise the South Wales Miners Federation, as a first step to uniting the miners nationally, was voted down decisively by a ballot in 1912.[1] Any possibility of centralising the Miners Federation of Great Britain was of course even more remote; it was in fact only accomplished on the eve of the nationalisation of the mines in 1945. Even within the South Wales Miners Federation the strength of Syndicalism did not imply a general solidarity of the rank-and-file workers: so far as membership is concerned, the union had a poor record in the years 1908–12, steadily losing members at a time when the industry was still rapidly growing. There was a considerable increase once more in 1913, largely owing to the coercion of non-unionists; but even though this brought the membership total to its highest peak, as a proportion of the labour force in South Wales it was substantially below the figure of about 80% which was attained in the first year of the century.[2]

The other main industry in which Syndicalist strength appeared significant before the First World War was the railways; and as we have seen, the amalgamation of three of the five railway unions in 1913 may be ascribed in part to their influence. Yet it must be remembered that negotiations to this end had been going on for several years, indeed since long before Syndicalism appeared on the scene; and a merger between the Railway Servants and the General Railway Union – the main components of the 1913 amalgamation – had been agreed by both executives in 1910, only to be defeated at a ballot of the G.R.W.U. membership. The success of joint action between the unions in 1911, which was itself the result of rank-and-file discontent with the working of the 1907 Conciliation Scheme, was the decisive factor in bringing about the formation of the National Union of Railwaymen in 1913.[3] In spite of this, the locomen's union, A.S.L.E.F., remained independent, as did the Railway Clerks Association: so the success for amalgamation principles was only a partial one.

In other industries, the Syndicalists could hardly claim that

---

[1] Arnot, *South Wales Miners*, p. 324.   [2] Ibid., pp. 91, 335.
[3] P. S. Bagwell, *The Railwaymen* (1963), p. 325.

there were significant developments along the lines that they
favoured. In the Amalgamated Society of Engineers, the 1912
Delegate Meeting agreed to open the union to unskilled workers,
who were to be admitted to a special section called Section F. The
branches, however, failed to put this into operation and the result
was that the Section had to be abolished after a few years.[1] In the
building industry, an attempt was made to establish an industrial
union by the amalgamation of twenty-one existing societies. Only
eleven of them, however, agreed to hold ballots on the subject;
and when the ballots were held, in October 1912, only one
union – the Builders' Labourers, who had most to gain – showed
a majority in favour which would have been large enough to
satisfy the legal requirements of amalgamation. A second series
of ballots in 1913 was even more unsuccessful, there being an
absolute majority against one section of the proposals. The
supporters of reform, in despair, decided to set up a new union
of their own, and this was founded at a conference on 2 and 3
August 1914. The new body attracted little national support and
faded away during the war.[2]

One new development of the period, which certainly tied in with
Syndicalist theory, and which the Syndicalists had been advocating, was the so-called 'Triple Alliance', whereby the Miners
Federation, the Transport Workers Federation, and the Railwaymen agreed to terminate their contracts simultaneously, so as to
bring additional pressure to bear on their employers for their new
demands, whatever these might be. The proposal was initiated by
the South Wales Miners, accepted by the Miners Federation, and
put by their leaders to the other two bodies, who agreed to it in
1914. One major reason for the Alliance was the unions' discovery
that a national strike by the workers in one industry could inflict
severe damage on the members, and also on the funds, of unions
in other industries. Thus during the national miners' strike of
1912 the railway unions had to pay out over £100,000 in unemployment benefit for their members, who were not on strike.[3] It

[1] J. B. Jefferys, *The Engineers* (1945), p. 166.
[2] R. Postgate, *The Builders' History* (1923), pp. 400 ff. Postgate blames
the failure partly on the indifference of the new members who joined as
a result of the National Insurance Act.
[3] Chief Registrar of Friendly Societies, Report on Trade Unions,
1912, *P.P.* 1913, lvii, 764.

would clearly be more 'scientific', as Frank Hodges of South Wales put it in moving the proposal at the Miners Federation conference in 1913, if all industries were pressing their employers at the same moment. His seconder, a member of the Northumberland union, made the same point and also suggested that it was up to the unions to try to keep one move ahead of the employers in their degree of organisation.[1]

It is therefore not very likely that many of the supporters of the Triple Alliance saw it as a means to a social revolution. The Syndicalists, of course, hoped that it would be a step towards 'direct action'. Other trade unionists, however, simply looked upon it as a means of strengthening their respective bargaining positions, and perhaps even as a way of preventing strikes – just as, rightly or wrongly, foreign ministers look upon alliances between states as a deterrent to war. The Triple Alliance of the unions was not put into effect until after the First World War. Its record, and the whole series of events which culminated in the 1926 General Strike, were to show that the leaders of the unions, and the great bulk of the rank-and-file, had no ulterior purpose beyond that of securing better industrial conditions from their employers.

If, then, the doctrines of Syndicalism had little effect upon the course of the labour unrest of 1911–14, it may well be a mistake to maintain, as so many historians have done, that there was any working-class reaction in this period against the use of parliamentary methods, and in particular against the Labour Party. It is, of course, very difficult to estimate the degree of working-class interest in parliamentary politics, especially at a time when less than half the adult males of this class were in possession of the franchise. Nevertheless, there are some assertions about general elections which it is possible to test. One of them is R. Page Arnot's statement that people were already apathetic at the time of the general election of December 1910: 'The absence of public interest in these contrived electoral convulsions was shown by a very significant fact. . . . Although the electorate had increased

[1] Miners Federation, *Annual Conference Report*, 1913, pp. 139–42. Cf. F. Hodges, *My Adventures as a Labour Leader* (n.d.), pp. 67 f.

from 7·6 million to 7·7 million in ten months, the number who cast their votes fell from 6·6 million to 5·2 million.'[1] Mr Page Arnot seems to be unaware that in the later of the two elections many of the seats were uncontested, not because of popular apathy but because the majorities on one side or the other were so large in January that it seemed very unlikely that they would have faded away only a few months later. The proportion of voters who went to the poll in January was 86·6%, which is the highest figure that has been recorded in this century, and probably has never been exceeded. In December the proportion was 81·1%, a drop of 5·5%; but this drop is almost entirely accounted for by the fact that except in Scotland the election was fought on the same register as in January, and since then many electors had either died or emigrated. Even so, a figure of 81·1% is a larger proportion than has polled at most twentieth-century elections, and has only been exceeded in·1906, 1950, 1951, and of course January 1910.[2]

Nor is there any justification for the view that the workers began to despair of the Labour Party, either because of its failure to achieve social reforms, or because of the fact that it had received a severe setback in the form of the Osborne Judgment.[3] To be sure, there were disagreements within the Labour Party itself about policy, and the I.L.P. suffered a revolt of some of its branches in 1911, with the result that its total number of branches fell from 887 in 1910 to 713 in 1913.[4] But it was not unusual for the I.L.P. to suffer some loss of support in the interval between general elections; and in any case the body which the dissident branches joined, the British Socialist Party, was not hostile to parliamentary methods, and indeed by 1914 had decided to apply for affiliation to the Labour Party. So far as the Osborne Judgment is concerned, the reaction of the trade-union leadership was completely uniform: the *Railway Review*, the organ of the Railway Servants, who had had the misfortune to lose both cases, was quite justified in saying: 'There was more division, especially among the leaders, over the Taff Vale case than there

[1] Arnot, *South Wales Miners*, p. 232.

[2] Figures from D. E. Butler and J. Freeman, *British Political Facts, 1900–1960* (1963), pp. 122–4.

[3] For this view see Sires, 'Labour Unrest', p. 247; B. Pribicevic, *Shop Stewards' Movement and Workers' Control* (Oxford, 1959), pp. 161 f.

[4] R. E. Dowse, *Left in the Centre* (1966), p. 19.

is with regard to the Osborne decision, or than there has ever been.'[1]

When the Trade Union Act of 1913 was passed – not entirely in the form that the unions wished, but at least in a form that they could accept – the rank and file had a chance to show whether or not they supported political action through the Labour Party, for the Act laid down that the establishment of a political fund required prior approval by a ballot of the members. By the spring of 1914 sixty-three trade unions had held a ballot, and of these only three small societies had shown a majority against. Forty-nine other unions were in the process of instituting ballots.[2] In most cases, only a minority of the members of the unions concerned took part in the ballots: but the same had been true in the early years of the century, when payments for political representation were first authorised. This apathy of the majority was a constant feature of British working-class behaviour, not a novelty of the period of labour unrest. The steady growth of Labour Party organisation in the constituencies and of the number of unions which were prepared to affiliate in the immediate pre-war period has already been discussed.

What then was the relationship of the labour unrest to the bitter Irish conflict and to the violence of the suffragettes? It is certainly a mistake to suppose that the unrest was due to a belief that Parliament ought to have been passing more social reform, instead of concentrating on the Irish question. In the first place, it is not at all clear that the workers in general wanted to see the enactment of social reform; in the second place, some at least of the unrest was the direct result of whatever social reform was enacted – particularly the National Insurance Act, but also the Trade Boards Act of 1909, which, according to J. J. Mallon, a member of all the early trade boards, had 'brought a powerful stimulus to trade-union organisation'.[4] The stimulus was not due

[1] *Railway Review*, 23 Sep 1910.
[2] The figures up to 1914 are provided (oddly enough) in Chief Registrar of Friendly Societies, Report on Trade Unions, 1912, *P.P.* 1913, lvii, 763.
[3] See above, p. 117   [4] *New Statesman*, 21 Feb 1914, Supplement, p. ix.

in Mallon's opinion to any feeling on the part of the workers that
they were receiving a benefit from the legislation: 'the very
lowness of the rates fixed has been of service. . . . Administrative
friction helps too. . . .'¹ It was the impact of new social legislation,
rather than its absence, which caused the trouble. If the Irish
question slowed down social reform after 1911, we may assume
that this was more likely to ease the labour unrest than to
increase it. In fact, however, the government had no difficulty
even after 1911 in passing such social legislation as it felt to be
urgent, such as the Miners' Minimum Wage Act of 1912, which
passed through all its stages in eight days; or the National
Insurance Amendment Act of 1913, not to mention less important
legislation. The Trade Boards Act could be extended to additional
trades by ministerial order, and it was so extended in 1913.

On the other hand, Women's Suffrage was undoubtedly delayed
by the impasse over the Irish question, and the suffragettes were
goaded to their final and most desperate acts of militancy by the
knowledge that although a majority of the House of Commons
favoured their cause in principle, they would do nothing about it
in practice. The trouble arose because many Liberals and Labour
M.P.s were hostile to any enfranchisement of women on the
existing franchises, which they thought would only result in the
wealthier women getting votes, and hence in an access of strength
to the Conservatives. It was reported to the Cabinet that the local
Liberal Agents 'almost unanimously agreed' that the women to be
enfranchised by the Conciliation Bill 'being of the propertied
class, would by a large majority be against the Liberal Party'.²
If, however, Women's Suffrage were to be coupled with a measure
for the extension of the franchises, then these difficulties would no
longer apply. Franchise extension, however, could not expect to
avoid the Lords' veto, or at any rate their delaying power, unless
it were accompanied by a measure of redistribution such as the
Conservatives had been demanding for many years, knowing full
well that it would result in a drastic reduction of the number of
Irish seats. But the Irish Nationalists, of course, would accept no
reduction in their total representation at Westminster until Home
Rule was on the statute book.

¹ Ibid., p. xii.
² Memorandum by the Master of Elibank, Chief Whip, Cabinet
Papers, Nov 1911: Public Record Office, Cab. 37/108/148.

Between Home Rule and Women's Suffrage, then, there was a clear association. The Westminster legislative bottleneck in both cases encouraged a tendency towards violence, and the delay over the solution of the Irish question was responsible for the lack of progress on Women's Suffrage. In the case of labour unrest, however, there was no such direct link. Social legislation was not normally an issue of acute conflict between the political parties; the Conservatives supported the Miners' Minimum Wage Bill and also the National Insurance Bill, albeit with reservations. Historians seeking a link between the labour unrest and the Irish question have sometimes seen it in the Dublin Transport Strike of 1913–14, which was led by James Larkin. In reality, however, the strike demonstrated that the British labour leadership could readily be estranged by demands for sympathetic action from a left-wing militant across St George's Channel. Not even the spectacular despatch of supplies for the strikers and their families, paid for by British unionists and Socialists, could conceal the fact that the policy of the British T.U.C. was one of non-belligerence.[1]

Our conclusion must be, therefore, that the labour unrest was only coincidental with the acute phases of the Irish and Women's Suffrage questions. It had its own independent and sufficient causes; and in any case, it owed little to feelings of disappointment with parliamentary institutions or existing political parties. And the social and legislative changes of the period ran counter to the expectations of those who sought to direct the progress of the labour unrest – the Syndicalists – by strengthening the general unions much more than those with an industrial orientation, and by investing the unions with additional administrative functions and bringing them more fully into partnership with the state. The First World War was to continue these tendencies, and to deprive the Syndicalist movement of any fulfilment of its early promise.

[1] For an account of this see A. Wright, *Disturbed Dublin* (1914); E. Larkin, *James Larkin* (1965), chs v–viii.

10 Then and Now:
Popular Attitudes since 1945

IN the preceding essays an attempt has been made to determine the prevailing working-class attitudes in late Victorian and Edwardian times to such matters as education, the law, the political parties, the power of the State, and the importance of the Empire. For the great majority, the picture is on the whole one of political apathy and social conservatism, associated however with a profound class consciousness and quite commonly a marked sense of grievance. But the evidence is so fragmentary, and the conditions of life so diverse, that there are obvious dangers in generalisation. Perhaps the most that may be hoped for is that some doubts will have been raised in the reader's mind about the value of earlier generalisations, which have so often been based upon the assumption that politicians who claimed to voice working-class attitudes in fact did so. It may now be asked, is it possible today, in an age of social surveys, opinion polls, and quantified evidence, to find attitudes that resemble those that we have been discussing? Are people still as unconcerned and as tolerant about religious observance, as suspicious of the law, as ignorant of the outside world, as sceptical about the possibilities of education and the social services? Or have improvements in the educational and material well-being of the working class, and perhaps an increase of social mobility, transformed the climate of opinion in the course of half a century?

To be sure, there have been important changes in the relations between the social classes in the last fifty years. For one thing, manual workers and their families, with whom we are primarily concerned, are much less numerically predominant than they used to be. The expansion of white-collar occupations of all sorts, whether professional or clerical, has reduced the manual workers as a proportion of the occupied male population from about 75% before the First World War to about 65% in the 1950s.[1] Within the ranks of the manual workers themselves,

[1] The figures can only be approximate: but see A. L. Bowley, *Wages*

however, the long period has seen a partial erosion of differentials in pay.[1] The gradual improvement in educational standards, the prevalence of comparatively full employment since 1940, the spread of trade unionism among the less skilled, are all factors which have encouraged a greater homogeneity of conditions. There has also been a substantial rise in the general standard of living, which has helped to remove many of the more obvious indications of relative poverty. To all this we must add the influence of the welfare provisions made by successive governments since 1914. To be sure, there are still more than a few people who are very poor, not just relatively but also absolutely: many of the old, the disabled, the large families fall into this category. But the overall picture appears to be one of increasing social homogeneity within the manual working class in any particular locality. Probably, too, locality itself is of less significance than it used to be – but sociologists have not yet managed to compare working-class attitudes in different localities in any systematic way.[2]

It is perhaps not surprising that in the 1950s, when living standards rose rapidly and Conservative governments obtained increasing votes of confidence from the electorate, there was a tendency to assume that the most highly-paid sections of the working class were gradually adopting middle-class attitudes, rather like the old Marxist 'labour aristocracy'. Observers who took this view did not, as a rule, share the Marxist belief that this would be only temporary: on the contrary, they imagined that the change was permanent. Some even believed that it would

and Income in the United Kingdom since 1860 (Cambridge, 1937), p. 128; M. Abrams, quoted D. E. Butler and R. Rose, *British General Election of 1959* (1960), p. 10; G. Routh, *Occupation and Pay in Great Britain, 1906–60* (Cambridge, 1965), p. 144.

[1] K. G. J. C. Knowles and D. J. Robertson, 'Differences between the Wages of Skilled and Unskilled Workers, 1880–1950', *Bulletin of the Oxford Institute of Statistics*, xiii (1951); Routh, *Occupation and Pay*, p. 57.

[2] For a first attempt, see D. E. G. Plowman, W. E. Minchinton and M. Stacey, 'Local Social Status in England and Wales', *Sociological Review*, n.s., x (1962).

deprive the Labour Party of any chance of again winning a general election. This crude materialistic view of politics could not, of course, survive very long in the early 1960s, which saw a rapid decline in the fortunes of the Conservative Party.

Furthermore, sociologists who examined critically the concept of the *embourgeoisement* of the working class, or of a section of it, soon found that there was little statistical evidence for any sharp distinction between the social and political attitudes of workers on the basis of income.[1] Conservative sympathies in the early 1960s were no more common among the well-paid manual workers than they were among the poorly-paid.[2] To be sure, there has always been a substantial proportion of working-class people who are supporters of Conservatism. But they are to be distinguished from other working-class people by quite other criteria than income. In some parts of the country Conservatism is unusually strong among all classes, for reasons which are more closely related to the pattern of nineteenth-century politics than to that of today. Conservative voting is also well correlated with employment in small-scale industry or in agriculture or personal service, where it is difficult for any sense of the working-class community to emerge.[3]

If the more affluent sections of the working class could in fact rapidly merge into the middle class, there would of course be a stronger case for accepting the *embourgeoisement* thesis. In practice, however, this is not so. Investigations of social mobility suggest that the class barriers are not very much lower than they were half a century ago. In spite of all efforts to extend educational opportunities, the fact remains that the proportion of sons and daughters of manual workers who continue their schooling beyond the age of fifteen has been, until recently at any rate, very small; and those who reach universities are still only a

[1] J. H. Goldthorpe and D. Lockwood, 'Affluence and the British Class Structure', *Sociological Review*, n.s., xi (1963).

[2] R. T. McKenzie and A. Silver, 'Conservatism, Industrialism and the Working-class Tory in England', *Transactions of the World Congress of Sociology, 1962*, iii, 196; J. H. Goldthorpe, D. Lockwood, F. Bechhofer and J. Platt, 'The Affluent Worker and the Thesis of Embourgeoisement', *Sociology*, i (1967), 24.

[3] M. Stacey, *Tradition and Change* (Oxford, 1960), p. 46; E. A. Nordlinger, *Working-class Tories* (1967), p. 208.

tiny minority of the total entry. The 1944 Education Act, which abolished fee-paying in the grammar schools, has been shown to be largely ineffective in eliminating a class bias in selection procedures. As Jackson and Marsden put it in their study of Huddersfield, 'the fees are gone, but the grammar schools are still closed'.[1] This is largely because the home environment of the manual worker's child is not relatively conducive to academic success. For the working-class boys and girls who do enter the grammar school, the strain that is involved in the process of adapting to a middle-class environment is often enough to prevent perseverance and eventual university entry. Sometimes immigrants, already regarded as alien by the working-class community to which they belong, do better in this process of adaptation: Young and Willmott in their study of East London quote the evidence of a Jewish informant on this point.[2] But the general pattern remains clear. In 1953 only 9% of boys with parents of the unskilled manual working class in South-West Hertfordshire and in Middlesbrough were chosen for grammar-school education, as against 59% and 68% respectively of those from the professional and upper middle classes.[3] And the percentage of boys at these grammar schools who went on to university was markedly higher in the case of those of middle-class parentage than in the case of those from the working class. There are signs that working-class parents now attach more importance to the education of their children than they used to:[4] but up to the 1960s at least this can hardly have altered the general pattern of professional recruitment. The investigations of the Robbins Committee on Higher Education found that, among children born in 1940/1, the chance of attaining full-time degree-level higher education was eight times greater if the child's father was following a non-manual occupation than if the father was a manual worker.[5]

---

[1] B. Jackson and D. Marsden, *Education and the Working Class* (1962), p. 211.

[2] M. Young and P. Willmott, *Family and Kinship in East London* (Penguin ed., 1962), p. 177.

[3] J. E. Floud, A. H. Halsey and F. M. Martin, *Social Class and Educational Opportunity* (1956), p. 42.

[4] Ibid., p. 79.

[5] Cmnd 2154, *Report of the Committee on Higher Education* (1963), p. 50.

It is not surprising, then, if access to the professions seems almost as remote from the ordinary working-class family as it ever was. The law, for instance, continues to be administered by men drawn from the middle and upper classes. To be sure, juries are more democratic in their composition than they used to be. Special juries were abolished in 1949, and since the re-rating of 1963 nearly all, if not quite all, occupiers of dwelling-houses are now eligible for jury service: which means in practice almost a quarter of the registered electorate, though including comparatively few women.[1] But the professionals of the law – the judges, the barristers, and the solicitors – are still drawn almost exclusively from those who can afford to pay a considerable premium to acquire the necessary qualifications. To become a solicitor, several years' service in articles is necessary, from which the university graduate can obtain only partial exemption. Only in the later 1950s was the practice of demanding an actual financial premium for articles largely abandoned; but the articled clerk still receives only a nominal salary – in 1964 a Manchester study showed that it was only about £6 a week.[2] Barristers have to pay fees to their respective Inns, but the difficulty of becoming a barrister lies rather more after qualifying than before: it is necessary to have some means in order to survive while waiting for one's practice to build up. For the man who can afford the initial outlay, the reward comes, of course, in the eventual high rate of remuneration.

As for the working-class litigant, things are better than they were, but by no means satisfactory. The great change is that since the Legal Aid and Advice Act, 1949, divorce proceedings are available to the ordinary person, who is likely to be able to obtain legal aid if he needs it. Indeed, two-thirds of the net legal costs of all legal aid go on matrimonial proceedings.[3] But the tendency of government, faced by the conservatism of the professional organisations, has been to develop administrative tribunals to deal with many problems affecting the ordinary citizen; and although barristers are admitted to plead before these tribunals, and the arbitrator himself is often a barrister, the ordinary citizen cannot get legal aid to assist his case. The Citizens' Advice

[1] Cmnd 2627, *Report of the Departmental Committee on Jury Service* (1965), p. 15.

[2] B. Abel-Smith and R. Stevens, *Lawyers and the Courts* (1967), p. 356.

[3] *Legal Aid and Advice: Report of the Law Society, 1965–6*, p. 35.

Bureaux, the legal columns of newspapers, and one's Member of Parliament – increasingly resorted to in cases of this character – are no substitute for proper legal aid.[1]

One example of this development of the legal system, and of the difficulties to which it continues to give rise, is provided by the question of industrial injuries. In 1946 the Labour Government passed the Industrial Injuries Act, which created a system of insurance benefits to which the injured person, or if he had died, his next of kin, was entitled as of right. But disputes could of course arise as to the boundaries of the entitlement, and it was laid down that such disputes should no longer go to the ordinary courts, but should be decided by special tribunals. From these tribunals there was established a right of appeal to a Commissioner, who was to be a barrister of at least ten years' standing. As Professor Wedderburn has pointed out, the decisions of the Commissioners are often as 'legalistic' as any made by the judges under Workmen's Compensation.[2] But in any case, the workman may also have a claim for compensation for negligence; and this still requires action under the Common Law. Indeed, such actions have become much more numerous since the abolition of the doctrine of 'common employment' in 1948. As in the past, the ordinary worker will rely upon his union to act on his behalf. The General Secretary of the National Union of Railwaymen reported in 1966 that he still had to take legal action in a thousand accident cases every year. The decisions were often highly anomalous and led him to favour a system of compulsory insurance in order to remove the need for expensive actions in the High Court.[3]

It would be of interest to be able to quote evidence from opinion polls about the ordinary manual worker's attitude to the law: one may surmise that it has not changed very much over the last half century. But it does not appear that any social survey has yet been conducted in this particular field. So far as the trade unions are concerned, their industrial activities continue to be governed by the Trade Disputes Act of 1906; and while the legal profession remains in so traditional a mould, it is not to be expected that union leaders will show much enthusiasm for proposals to place

[1] For an interesting but brief discussion of this subject see M. Zander, 'Poverty and the Law', *Socialist Commentary*, Sep 1966.

[2] K. W. Wedderburn, *The Worker and the Law* (1965), p. 201.

[3] T.U.C. *Report, 1966*, pp. 422 f.

their activities more closely under judicial supervision. For a good many years after 1914 the climate of the courts became somewhat less frigid so far as the unions were concerned; but in recent years a certain hardening of public opinion against demarcation strikes and instances of the coercion of non-unionists appears also to be reflected in judicial decisions. The House of Lords decision in *Rookes* v. *Barnard*[1] raised doubts once more about the freedom of unionists from tort liability in a trade dispute, as it was understood to be established by the 1906 Act. Just as they would have done before the First World War, the unions agitated for the reversal of this decision, and secured it by the Trade Disputes Act of 1965. The irritation felt by the unions over this episode is recorded in the T.U.C.'s evidence to the recent Royal Commission on Trade Unions, where, with some historical explanation, it is emphasised that 'trade unionists have always been, and continue to be, very suspicious of the law and the judges who appear to make the law in their own image'.[2] Consequently, in spite of the pressure upon them to accept legal sanctions upon their activities, whether in demanding wage increases or in insisting upon the 'closed shop', union leaders remain bitterly hostile to any change which would place them more fully at the mercy of the courts. George Woodcock, the General Secretary of the T.U.C., summed up their attitude at the 1965 Congress:

In my view and the General Council's view, relations in industry, by their essence, are much more like a marriage between a man and a woman than any other contractual relationship within the law of this country. You cannot go rushing to the courts and preserve your marriage. You can go to the courts but when you start bringing the white-wigged judge into your marriage it is finished. . . .[3]

The sociologists have shown a good deal of interest in popular attitudes to religion, and here it is easy to find all the same reactions that were characteristic of the working class in the late

[1] [1964] 2.W.L.R. 269; [1964] All E.R. 367.
[2] T.U.C., *Trade Unionism* (1966), p. 125.
[3] T.U.C. *Report, 1965*, p. 470.

nineteenth century. We may take first the widespread absence of
interest in or commitment to definite religious doctrines. A
Mass-Observation survey of a London suburb in 1945 reported
that even among churchgoers at Anglican churches, 'less than a
third . . . give definite verbal assent to three basic affirmations of
the Apostle's creed. Over 40 per cent of them express doubts
about the possibility of an after life.'[1] Churchgoing itself seemed
to have little direct association with belief, as was shown by a
survey of two industrial towns, Rawmarsh and Scunthorpe,
where 'No one had abandoned religious practice because of an
inability to believe in the Trinity, the resurrection of Christ, or
even life after death: "You can still go to Church and not believe
these things!" Belief did not appear to motivate practice. Except
for faith in God dogmatic assertions were of little importance.'[2]

Consequently, people moved easily from one sect to another,
at any rate within the Protestant sects. No less than 34% of
worshippers at Rawmarsh, and 42% at Scunthorpe, had changed
from one denomination to another.[3] As usual, Catholics were an
exception on both counts: they were more regular attenders and
showed few gains or losses in proportion to their total attendance.

Churchgoing as a whole is no more common than it was in the
working class half a century ago; and the great difference today is
that the apathy has spread so widely in the middle class. If we
take regular attenders only, Catholics are now almost as numerous
throughout the United Kingdom as Anglicans are. A National
Opinion Poll of the early 1960s showed 16·9% of the adult
population having attended a church within the preceding seven
days, of whom 6·2% were Anglican, 5·4% Catholic, 2·7% Nonconformist and 1·6% Presbyterian. Occasional attendance, of
course, is far more widespread among non-Catholics.[4]

Among the population at large some observers have noticed a
tendency to anti-clericalism. This seems to be bound up with the
belief that the clergy have always been on the side of the higher
social classes. Ferdynand Zweig in his early post-war enquiries
found that: 'The first and capital grievance is that the Church

[1] Mass-Observation, *Puzzled People* (1947), pp. 156 f.
[2] W. S. F. Pickering, 'Religious Movement of Church Members',
Archives de Sociologie des Religions, xi (1961), 138 f.
[3] Ibid., p. 131.
[4] Cited by D. Martin, *Sociology of English Religion* (1967), p. 43.

sided against them in their struggle against their industrial masters.'[1] Rowntree and Lavers, in their study of York, felt that this hostility extended to the Nonconformist ministry also, but was of a more general character: 'they do not practise what they preach'.[2] Whatever truth might lie behind these views clearly had little or nothing to do with belief in religious doctrine.

If, then, the reasons for religious attendance and non-attendance are of a 'non-rational, non-theological kind',[3] we are likely to find that belief in God is almost as widely disseminated among the non-attenders as among the attenders at worship. The surveys bear out this assumption. Mass-Observation found in its London suburb that 'uncompromising disbelievers in a Deity amount to about one in twenty'.[4] At York, Rowntree and Lavers stressed the continuity of 'vestigial Christianity'.[5] And Zweig, exploring the attitudes of 'affluent' factory workers, found that: 'The overwhelming majority were believers in one way or another; only a small minority were non-believers or agnostics. However, the nature of their beliefs was, in many cases, very vague or groping.'[6] These impressions from comparatively small samples may be confirmed by a large-scale Gallup poll, which found that 78% of people believed in God, although less than one in six claimed to have been to Church or Chapel on the preceding Sunday.[7]

In spite of their abstention from religious observance, the great majority of parents still felt that their children should receive a religious education. In the Mass-Observation London survey, this was true of the majority 'even among those who openly doubt the existence of God'.[8] Zweig tells us that: 'The belief in the value of religion as an instrument of education for the children was accepted practically by everyone. The non-believers and agnostics subscribed to this view also, and most of them were sending their

---

[1] F. Zweig, *The British Worker* (1952), p. 234.

[2] B. S. Rowntree and G. R. Lavers, *English Life and Leisure* (1951), pp. 346–8.

[3] Pickering, 'Religious Movement of Church Members', 140.

[4] Mass-Observation, *Puzzled People*, p. 156.

[5] Rowntree and Lavers, *Life and Leisure*, p. 367.

[6] F. Zweig, *The Worker in an Affluent Society* (1961), p. 146.

[7] Cited T. Harrisson, *Britain Revisited* (1961), p. 257.

[8] Mass-Observation, *Puzzled People*, p 156.

children to Sunday schools.'[1] At Billingham-on-Tees, a survey in 1959 found that whereas nearly half of all children between 4 and 13 went to Sunday school, only a seventh of all adults (including over half of the Catholics) went to church or chapel even occasionally.[2]

Clearly, then, as in the late nineteenth century, the bulk of working-class people put off their direct religious associations when they leave school. As then, too, migration was a hindrance to the development of the habit of attendance among the small minority: 'removal from one town to another tends to damage churchgoing'.[3] But comparing the proportion of attenders in Britain with the much higher figure in the United States, a country of greater geographical mobility, it is difficult to believe that this factor is of great importance in determining the widespread religious apathy of modern Britain.

People do not appear to be as apathetic about politics as they are about religion: but this is partly because of the difference in the criteria generally used – in particular, attendance or otherwise at the polls for parliamentary elections, which often only occur once in five years. Certainly a turnout of 84% in 1950, the peak figure of post-war elections, suggests a satisfactory level of public interest.[4] The figure has been declining since then, partly because of the known existence of safe seats for one party or another, partly because of the reduction in the number of candidates (especially Liberals). In 1966 the turnout was 75·8%, the lowest figure since the war, but partly justified by proximity to the 1964 election – since when safe seats were unlikely to have become marginal.[5] These are of course the figures for the entire population. There is some evidence that working-class electors are less

[1] Zweig, *Worker in an Affluent Society*, p. 147.

[2] *Guardian*, 25 Jul 1962. I have not seen the published report of the survey, which is by Mr P. R. Kaim-Caudle.

[3] Pickering, *Religious Movement of Church Members*, pp. 135, 139.

[4] Turnout figures from D. E. Butler and J. Freeman, *British Political Facts, 1900–1960* (1963), p. 124.

[5] D. E. Butler and Anthony King, *British General Election of 1966* (1966), p. 262.

interested in voting than other electors, by a factor of about 10%.[1]

If, however, we examine the extent of active political commitment by the working-class adult, we obtain a rather different impression. The Labour Party is, so far as its membership is concerned, a party largely supported by the manual workers, of whom no less than 5½ million pay affiliation fees through their trade unions. A union member can, if he wishes, contract out from making this payment, under the Trade Union Act of 1946. This Act repealed the Act of 1927 whereby it was necessary to contract in if the payment was to be made. When the system was changed, the number of Labour Party members suddenly shot up by two million members, who apparently were indifferent as to whether or not their unions paid dues on their behalf to the party.[2] As the total membership of the party in 1947, including individual members, was only 5 million, it follows that some 40% of those 'actively' supporting the party were doing so, in fact, with complete indifference. Yet it has often been remarked by observers that trade unionists are in general much more loyal to the Labour Party at the polls than working-class people who are not trade unionists. Taking the working class as a whole to mean the manual workers, we find that in 1964, at a time when the two main political parties were evenly balanced, about 57% of those who voted at all, voted Labour. For trade unionists alone, it was 62·2%. Conservative voting was proportionately more widespread among the manual workers than Labour voting in the middle class.[3]

Nor can it be said that working-class supporters of the Labour Party have much enthusiasm for the main Socialist features of its policy. A 1964 survey of the attitudes of working-class Labour voters showed that slightly more (9%) disliked 'nationalisation

---

[1] R. S. Milne and H. C. Mackenzie, *Marginal Seat* (1955), p. 68; A. H. Birch, *Small-Town Politics* (Oxford, 1959), pp. 94, 106. Cf. J. Blondel, *Voters, Parties and Leaders* (1963), pp. 55 f.

[2] M. Harrison, *Trade Unions and the Labour Party since 1945* (1960), pp. 36 f. For an interesting study of rank-and-file apathy, but tolerance of a more 'committed' leadership, see A. J. M. Sykes, 'Political Affiliation in a Printing Trade Union', *Scottish Journal of Political Economy*, xii (1965).

[3] N.O.P. figures quoted D. E. Butler and Anthony King, *British General Election of 1964* (1965), p. 296.

and planning' than liked it (7%).[1] To be sure, most people had settled down to accept the main features of the Welfare State: a survey of about the same date found that 84% of respondents thought that the National Health Service was 'good', as against 8% who thought it 'bad'.[2] But trade-union leaders and Labour politicians appear to have exaggerated popular hostility to a means test for extensions of welfare. A. J. Willcocks found in the mid-1950s that people showed 'little bitterness or hatred of the phrase';[3] and in the early 1960s the majority of those who favoured state provision of family allowance for the first child, or subsidised rent, or free legal aid, thought that such a test should be applied.[4]

This of course is in no way incompatible with the retention of a decided sense of class consciousness and perhaps social injustice. As Zweig put it, 'Apart from a small minority, the working-class man is rarely politically minded, although he has a strong class consciousness.'[5] This even applies to many of those who vote Conservative, as is to be found in the fact that of a group of supposed 'Tory deference voters' in the working-class, which one survey had isolated from other respondents, no less than 58% believed that 'business groups had an inordinate amount of power which is used contrary to the majority's interests'.[6]

The social psychologist H. J. Eysenck, who investigated attitudes on a wide range of topics from child-rearing to the treatment of conscientious objectors, found that 'Working-class subjects were more conservative and more tough-minded compared with middle-class subjects having the same party allegiance.'[7] This might lead us to suppose that there would be bitter feelings in the working class about the gradual disappearance of the British Empire. No doubt such feelings do occur; but we must bear in mind George Orwell's remark that: 'The English are hypocritical about their Empire. In the working class this

---

[1] Nordlinger, *Working-Class Tories*, pp. 157 f.

[2] Institute of Economic Affairs, *Choice in Welfare* (1965), p. 77.

[3] A. J. Willcocks, 'The Means Test', *Sociological Review*, n.s., v (1957).

[4] W. G. Runciman, *Relative Deprivation and Social Justice* (1966), p. 225.

[5] F. Zweig, *Labour, Life and Poverty* (1948), p. 61.

[6] Nordlinger, *Working-Class Tories*, p. 109.

[7] H. J. Eysenck, 'Primary Social Attitudes as Related to Social Class and Political Party', *British Journal of Sociology*, ii (1951), p. 207.

hypocrisy takes the form of not knowing that the Empire exists.'[1] This is amply confirmed by a survey conducted for the Colonial Office in 1948, which found that less than half of the respondants could actually name at least one colony. Those who had travelled outside Europe were twice as good in their replies as those who had not; and middle-class people were much better than working men or women. But nearly half the subjects of the survey 'evinced little or no interest in the colonies'.[2]

No doubt ex-soldiers and sailors have a clearer idea of the extent of Britain's former imperial realms than those who have travelled less. During the Suez crisis it was maintained that ex-soldiers felt strongly that military action against Egypt was justified. Yet the opinion polls show no clear evidence of a general swing of working-class feeling in favour of Conservative policy at this juncture. The Gallup poll never showed a majority of voters in favour of military action; and the great majority of Labour voters were opposed to it. There was, however, a substantial body of undecided respondents – especially among those who had no party affiliation.[3]

So far as foreign and defence policy in general is concerned, the difficulty has been to find any large sections of the electorate, at any rate since 1951, who are prepared to regard it as a major criterion of their choice of parties.[4] In 1955 Labour candidates who discussed the horrors of atomic warfare with their constituencies obtained 'surprisingly little response'.[5] In 1959 a Gallup poll which asked people to name the issues with which they were 'especially concerned' found that whereas 73% mentioned the cost of living, prices, pensions or employment, only 20% referred to any matters in the field of foreign affairs and defence.[6] In 1964 Sir Alec Douglas-Home tried hard to focus attention on

[1] G. Orwell, *The Lion and the Unicorn* (1941), p. 20.

[2] Central Office of Information, *Social Survey: Public Opinion on Colonial Affairs* (1948).

[3] For the fullest treatment of this episode, see L. D. Epstein, *British Politics in the Suez Crisis* (Urbana, Ill, 1964), pp. 141–7.

[4] Foreign policy may have been of some importance in 1951, but the evidence is inconclusive: see R. S. Milne and H. C. Mackenzie, *Straight Fight* (1954), p. 102.

[5] D. E. Butler, *British General Election of 1955* (1955), p. 74.

[6] Butler and Rose, *General Election 1959*, p. 71.

defence policy, which he felt was an issue of principle between the parties. Yet whereas 72% of people thought the cost of living was a particularly important issue of the campaign, only 13% were prepared to rate the question of the independent deterrent as being of equal or greater importance.[1] These figures relate to the entire electorate and not just to the working class. But a special study of working-class voters in 1964 confirms that 'Only a small proportion of both Tory and Labour voters attach any importance to the parties' foreign and defence policies.'[2]

It is one thing, however, to ignore what goes on abroad, and another thing to approve of strangers from abroad who enter this country. Here we must bear in mind Eysenck's 'tough-minded-ness' and Orwell's remark that 'The famous "insularity" and "xenophobia" of the English is far stronger in the working class than in the bourgeoisie.'[3] All this has been indicated well enough in the reaction to coloured immigration, which has been surprisingly similar to the nineteenth-century reaction to the immigration of the Irish and the Jews. In July 1964 a Gallup poll on the continuance of immigration showed only 10% in favour of unrestricted entry.[4] Another sample survey during the same year revealed that 83% of North London employees 'would object' to working in an inferior capacity to a coloured immigrant.[5] During the 1964 election the issue had a significant influence upon the polling in several constituencies where there was a large immigrant population – the most obvious case being Smethwick, a working-class constituency where the sitting Labour member, Mr Patrick Gordon Walker, was unexpectedly defeated. It is a mistake to regard this hostility to the immigrant as necessarily 'racial' in character, any more than the nineteenth-century anti-Irish feeling was 'religious', as it was thought to be at the time. The fact is that heavy immigration is, in the most literal sense, a disturbing phenomenon: and if those who are disturbed are socially very conservative they are likely to react strongly against it.

[1] Butler and King, *General Election 1964*, p. 128. Cf. L. D. Epstein, 'The Nuclear Deterrent and the British General Election of 1964', *Journal of British Studies*, v (1966), p. 159.

[2] Nordlinger, *Working-Class Tories*, p. 159.

[3] Orwell, *Lion and the Unicorn*, p. 28.

[4] Butler and King, *General Election 1964*, p. 362.

[5] C. S. Hill, *How Colour Prejudiced is Britain?* (Panther ed., 1967), p. 137.

Thus in a changing world the British working class has maintained a continuity of social and political attitudes which had already become apparent in the later nineteenth century, but which no doubt have origins that go much further back in history. These attitudes go far to explain why the task of transforming society, taken in hand by successive generations of predominantly middle-class reformers, proves so arduous and slow. There may however be some who will find the situation to a certain extent reassuring, if only because it shows that human nature is not readily to be remoulded in accordance with an academic blueprint, and that only the fullest understanding of popular feelings can provide a firm basis for successful measures of social change.

Index